"At a time when many are disillusioned with Christianity's complicity in injustice, *Making It Plain* offers a vision of faith rooted in resistance, repair, and redemption. Rev. Dr. Drew G. I. Hart invites Christian activists to walk a new path, one shaped by the subversive teachings of Jesus, the radical witness of the Black Church, and the peace ethic of Anabaptism. This book doesn't just critique—it commissions. Please read it, wrestle with it, and let it sharpen your justice journey."
—**LATASHA MORRISON**, author of the *New York Times* bestseller *Be the Bridge*

"Both a love letter to the church and an indictment of mainstream Western Christianity, *Making It Plain* lifts the veil on Drew G. I. Hart's own faith journey, sharing what he discovered about the particular and necessary power of a spiritual formation that integrates both the Black Church and Anabaptist traditions, for such a time as this. With historical acumen and theological precision, Hart holds no punches, withholds no treasure, and comes with receipts."
—**LISA SHARON HARPER**, author of *The Very Good Gospel* and *Fortune: How Race Broke My Family and the World—and How to Repair It All*

"Anabaptism and the Black Church offer a much-needed cure to the malignant theology that is spreading quickly throughout the church in the United States and beyond. We need this book, now more than ever, to remember the past so that we can build a better future both for the church and for the world."
—**SHANE CLAIBORNE**, author, activist, and cofounder of Red Letter Christians

"I commend this passionate, creative, and invitational advocacy for how to 'salvage the Jesus Way' in our fraught moment of urgent white Christian nationalism...
—**CHED MYERS**, author of *Plutocracy: Luke's Jesus a*

"Wow! Drew Hart has given us a no-holes-barred unfiltered treatise that prompts readers to sit up straight, take a deep breath, and seriously consider who they are, what they believe, and what they should be doing at this critical moment in history. Hart educates and motivates us to pursue a better way—the radical way of Jesus which rebukes the perversion of civil religion, Christian nationalism, and all expressions of Christianity that privilege a few at the expense of others. This book makes plain where Christians have been, where we are, and where we need to go."
—**DENNIS R. EDWARDS**, dean and vice president of church relations at North Park Theological Seminary and author of *Humility Illuminated*

"Drew Hart's exploration of these two traditions is more than historical analysis—it's a reclamation of faith rooted in justice. In a time when 'Christian values' are too often distorted to uphold oppression, this work offers a necessary corrective and a deeply encouraging guide for those seeking a faithful path forward."
—**REGINA SHANDS STOLTZFUS**, professor and director of peace, justice, and conflict studies at Goshen College and coauthor of *Been in the Struggle*

"*Making It Plain* is a nonviolent-messianic-cocktail thrown into both the sanctuary and the academy, which have accommodated narcissistic self-congratulatory quietism while the crucified class in the streets cries out under the rise of white supremacy, plantation capitalism, and Christofascism. Rev. Dr. Drew Hart distills his scholarship and vocation in these pages to offer what I pray will be an incendiary invitation to Anablacktivism, the fire of radical discipleship that our Lord wishes were already ablaze!"
—**JARROD MCKENNA**, Australian peace award–winning pastor, social change trainer, and cohost of *InVerse Podcast* with Drew G. I. Hart and the *Good on Wood* podcast with Stephen Schallert

MAKING IT PLAIN

Why We NEED Anabaptism and the Black Church

DREW G. I. HART

HERALD
PRESS

Harrisonburg, Virginia

Herald Press
PO Box 866, Harrisonburg, Virginia 22803
www.HeraldPress.com

Library of Congress cataloging-in-publication data has been applied for.

Study guides are available for many Herald Press titles at www.HeraldPress.com.

MAKING IT PLAIN
© 2025 by Herald Press, Harrisonburg, Virginia 22803. 800-245-7894.
   All rights reserved.
Library of Congress Control Number: 2025010573
International Standard Book Number: 978-1-5138-1634-0 (paperback);
   978-1-5138-1636-4 (ebook); 978-1-5138-1638-8 (audiobook)
Printed in United States of America
Design by Merrill Miller

All rights reserved. This publication may not be reproduced, stored in a retrieval system, or transmitted in whole or in part, in any form, by any means, electronic, mechanical, photocopying, recording or otherwise without prior permission of the copyright owners.

Unless otherwise indicated, scripture quotations are taken from the New Revised Standard Version Updated Edition. Copyright © 2021 National Council of Churches of Christ in the United States of America. Used by permission. All rights reserved worldwide.
   Scripture quotations marked (NIV) are taken from the Holy Bible, New International Version®, NIV®. Copyright © 1973, 1978, 1984, 2011 by Biblica, Inc.® Used by permission of Zondervan. All rights reserved worldwide. www.zondervan.com The "NIV" and "New International Version" are trademarks registered in the United States Patent and Trademark Office by Biblica, Inc.®

29 28 27 26 25   10 9 8 7 6 5 4 3 2 1

For Renee

CONTENTS

Foreword 9
Introduction 13
1 My Journey to Anablacktivism 37
2 The Story of Christendom 55
3 Anabaptism, an Anti-Christendom Tradition 79
4 Has Anabaptism Failed in North America? 107
5 The Story of the Doctrine of Discovery and
   Antiblackness 127
6 The Black Church, an Antiracist Tradition 153
7 Is the Black Church Dead? .181
8 Seven Signposts for Anablacktivism 211
9 Salvaging the Way 233

Notes 261
The Author 277

FOREWORD

God wants us to experience peace. Not just you and me. God wants *all creation* to experience peace. But, where there is no justice, there can be no peace. The testimonies of both Scripture and human history affirm this truth. While the Bible has no shortage of calls to justice, the importance of justice is often understated by many Christians who have exhibited a tendency to view *justice* and *righteousness* as two distinct goals instead of two faces of the same coin. Failing to understand that justice and righteousness are inseparable and essential to peace (and therefore salvation), we have ended up with Christianities that are at least as fragmented and incoherent as our understandings of justice, righteousness, and peace.

Much of the injustice witnessed and experienced around the world today can be traced to seeds sown by those who claim to represent the name of Jesus. We are now reaping the fruit, and (far too often) it is a bitter harvest.

My faith has always been centered around the idea that God is a redeemer. Despite the messes that we tend to make of good creation, the Spirit is not only able but faithful to make all things new.

In *Making It Plain*, Rev. Dr. Drew G. I. Hart points us toward a path of renewal. I confess: at first glance, Anabaptism and the Black Church seem like strange bedfellows. A tradition that traces its roots to a group of stubbornly radical Europeans in the sixteenth century doesn't seem to have a ton of overlap with a witness that places its genesis on the underbelly of a racialized United States of America, but the common themes are difficult to miss once they're pointed out. Both the Anabaptist and Black Church traditions have held fast to Jesus as a deliverer—even when that hoped-for deliverance is from the dominion of other Christians. Anabaptists gifted us with the idea that discipleship is a serious, costly commitment. The Black Church provided us with a template for prophetic witness and critique. Both Anabaptists and the Black Church have illuminated a path that shows us that suffering need not dehumanize the persecuted, even as it reveals the truth about persecutors. In short: Anabaptists and the Black Church both provide snapshots of what the early church hoped to establish as its witness.

As academically qualified and gifted as he is, Rev. Dr. Hart doesn't approach this from a clinical distance. *Making It Plain* is the offering of one who is intimately familiar with the modern iterations of the Anabaptist and Black Church traditions. This book is the work of an *Anablacktivist*. It is through Hart's work that I first realized that I might have been a little Anabaptist before I knew what that meant. It is also because of his work that I now call myself an Anablacktivist.

In the pages that follow, you will encounter a guide whose desire to see the gospel proclaimed and embodied as unmistakably *good* news requires radical honesty about the journey we've traveled to the present moment. You will also be led to a road that points toward the peace that God is calling all creation to. The road will demand humility and commitment. It will require transparency and imagination. The road may be uncomfortable at times, but the road will lead you to peace if you stick with it.

> —Trey Ferguson
> Pastor of The Intention Church and author of *Theologizin' Bigger: Homilies on Living Freely and Loving Wholly*

Introduction

For centuries, mainstream Western Christianity spread across the planet while its followers oppressed people and plundered the earth for profits. And at the same time, right under the noses of authorities and political powers, followers of Jesus participated in God's deliverance, peacemaking, and healing of the nations. As long as Christians have had access to power, there have been those willing to grab it by the horns to control and dominate society. Simultaneously, there have been those who have fixed their eyes on Jesus, immersed themselves in his life and teachings, resolved to follow his way as a counter-witness to the logics of empire.

When someone asks me if Christianity is a liberating or an oppressive force in the world, I must ask, Which Christianity? I'm a deeply committed follower of Jesus, yet I cannot ignore that so much of what happens attached to the name of Christ represents religious beliefs and practices that appear diametrically opposed to most of what Jesus lived and taught. There are multiple Christianities.

On two separate occasions, I heard Rev. C. T. Vivian, the late Civil Rights leader and friend of Rev. Dr. Martin Luther King Jr., talk about how their struggle in the 1950s and '60s was a clash of two Christianities. And so we might ask, What was the nature of the character and convictions of each faith as it was lived out on the ground? What encouraged so many American Christians to either support racial segregation and antiblack oppression, or be politically quiet in response, allowing them to think that such social concerns had nothing to do with their faith in Christ? In contrast, what emboldened some Christians to resist the injustice and humiliating laws of the land, risking their livelihoods and even the threat of death? One expression of Christianity invited people to accept Jesus into their heart so they could go to heaven when they die—all while upholding the status quo here on earth. Yet the lived Christianity of others followed the teachings of Jesus by speaking truthfully, practicing nonviolent yet revolutionary love, and pursuing God's kingdom come on earth for the lowly, left out, and little ones.

People's understanding of what Christianity is about varies significantly, and how they live out their faith is just as conflicting. To this very day, the content and character of Christianity are conflicting in the public square.

I'll refer to the dominant and most popular expressions of Western Christianity as *mainstream Christianity*, meaning faith communities that have been more inclined to uphold the status quo of oppression, economic injustice, and violent systems that organize our society than to seek after and participate in God's shalom here on earth. I'm referring to the practice of Christianity that worships Jesus while simultaneously rejecting the narrow gate for the wide and comfortable one. The wide gate of mainstream Christianity claims Jesus, but it also serves mammon. It worships the God of creation, but it imposes human hierarchies and exclusion through nation-first ideology. It confesses that the cross has *spiritually* broken down all boundaries between people groups but upholds political and economic policies that advantage certain communities over others. The wide gate of mainstream Christianity claims God's grace for themselves but denies compassion and action for the most vulnerable domestically and abroad.

Right now, the greatest stumbling block for the Western church is mainstream Christianity. Yes, hostility toward Christianity is growing. It's not strange to hear people calling for new policies that include taxing churches, radical atheists making fun of people who believe in "a fairytale sky daddy," or to see a look of caution and concern when someone learns you are a Christian. However, much of the hostility that Christians experience in the public is initiated by *other* Christians. To this day, mainstream Christians frequently choose, again and again, to wage the culture wars. For many non-Christians, Christianity is about being anti–Black Lives Matter, pro-MAGA, anti-woke, anti-LGBTQ, and pro-birth but anti–policies that support vulnerable children and families from womb to tomb. The good news of Jesus and his reign is lost amid culture wars; nonbelievers' primary knowledge of Christianity is more often associated with mainstream Christians' hostility over who can use a public bathroom. When immoral leaders are baptized and proudly defended as God's chosen ones and churches protect or cover up abusers, it is hard to blame the rest of society for waging war back on the very terms that mainstream Christians have chosen.

In the United States, distrust of Christianity, churches, and clergy is at an all-time high. Weekly religious services attendance has dropped to 30 percent of Americans.[1] Trust in clergy, once a renowned profession, fell to 32 percent in 2023.[2] This is the first time that less than a third of Americans believed they could trust the ethical integrity of clergy. And especially following broad white American evangelical alignment with the MAGA movement in 2016, 2020, and 2024 elections, waves of young people have consistently described themselves as post-evangelical or as deconstructing their faith. Many people, young and old, have told me that they are struggling with the dissonance between being verbally taught by their worshiping communities to love their neighbors and treat everyone with mercy and kindness because everyone is made in the image of God, while watching these same communities embrace unethical political leaders in an effort to gain power regardless of the means and method, even if they directly counter the life of Jesus. They are seeing their faith communities put Jesus on the back burner for politics so people can "take back their country," ridicule their enemies, and exclude immigrants from American life. While some people who embrace these labels are leaving the faith altogether, many more are trying to figure out another way forward.

Throughout church history, Christianity has been a catalyst for justice, liberation, and peacemaking while also a destructive instrument of plunder, oppression, and violence across the globe. I imagine that most Christians think of their own beliefs, practices, and congregations as an overall inherent good in the world, yet past and present evidence usually troubles those judgments. Some Christians have indeed worked for the common good while prioritizing the least, the last, and the little ones along the way. Yet Christians have also bolstered social domination and the status quo, protecting the wealthy and powerful as they exploit vulnerable populations. The paradoxes of liberation and oppression, peace and violence, harm and healing, all intertwined in Christianity's legacy and witness in the world, raise the question of whether our faith is a net positive good for the world. Or is it time to end all religious projects as some radical secularists and atheists would suggest?

Cultivating faithfulness—or not

There are many examples of Christians cultivating and striving toward a more just, liberative, and peaceful world. In the early centuries of the church, followers of Jesus emphasized an equality that challenged the empire's social stratification: though some were dehumanized in the broader society (like enslaved people and many women), they were treated with much more dignity inside the church. In the fourth century, church leaders like Gregory of Nyssa, John Chrysostom, and Lactantius spoke or wrote against slavery and advocated for the inherent value of all people. Around that same time, Basil the Great, standing on the shoulders of earlier Christians, advocated for a radical redistribution of wealth as he scolded those who hoarded riches. He built a Christian complex named Basiliad organized around economic justice and provision for the poor and vulnerable, including hospitals, an orphanage, workhouses, and other facilities for the common good of the poor. The Benedictine monastic movements also continued a centuries-long tradition of caring for the poor beginning in the medieval period.

In the sixteenth century, radical reformers called for justice, rejected the sword of the state, or practiced radical economic sharing and a rejection of private property. Enslaved African

Christians resisted slavery through uprisings, slave narratives, rejecting mainstream white theology, and participating in the Underground Railroad. Most of the eighteenth- and nineteenth-century abolitionist movements were led by followers of Jesus. In the twentieth century, Christian women were vital in the suffrage movement and advocating for women's rights. During World War II, pastor André Trocmé and the village of Le Chambon-sur-Lignon courageously resisted the Nazi regime by providing refuge and aiding in the escape of thousands of Jews. When the Black freedom struggle in the United States exploded in the 1950s and 1960s, Black churches and their ministers, as well as other Christians, were central in mobilizing and organizing protests as well as leading voter registration drives. They shifted the American landscape and increased democratic values and practice.

In twentieth-century Latin America, Catholic priests like Gustavo Gutiérrez advocated for a Christian theology that once again held a preferential option for the poor while base ecclesial communities were rereading their Bibles for themselves and considering their experience of economic exploitation under oppressive regimes. Black ministers and theologians, especially in the United States, publicly articulated a theology highlighting God's solidarity, presence, identification with their struggles, and the divine commitment to liberate Black people from centuries of oppression. In the 1980s, some North American congregations provided sanctuary to undocumented immigrants to protect them from xenophobic policies and deportation. In the 1990s, South Africa's post-apartheid Truth and Reconciliation Commission, led by Archbishop Desmond Tutu, implemented Christian ethical frameworks like restorative justice and forgiveness in an effort to heal rather than seek retribution and revenge. Even though Western nations helped establish the secular nation-state of Israel after World War II by displacing Palestinians, for decades, dispossessed Palestinian Christians have sought liberation nonviolently under inhumane apartheid conditions and state violence. And even today, movements like the Poor People's Campaign, a multifaith movement with Christian leadership, is a witness for justice across the United States.

This list, though far from comprehensive, provides a beautiful glimpse into the embodied justice of God expressed through the historic and global church. However, there are just as many examples of Christians upholding unjust systems and imposing oppressive and violent policies and conditions on vulnerable people all around the world from very early in its history. Despite several centuries of living under persecution, when Christians gained power and prominence in the Roman Empire, some Christians began persecuting pagans and other Christians who didn't conform to imperial-backed doctrines designed to religiously homogenize the empire. Augustine, bishop of Hippo, argued that state coercion should be used to "compel" people back into true faith.[3] He also constructed the first Christian justification and criteria for war. Such state violence would be used against Donatist Christians in Africa. In other places, entire tribes underwent mass forced conversions.

The rise of Western Christendom in the eighth century significantly changed the character of Christianity in the West. Beginning in the eleventh century, the pope initiated "holy war" known as the Crusades, which led to the death of Muslims, Jews, and even some Eastern Christians. Then came the Inquisitions, witch hunts, and religious persecution of Protestants by Catholics, Catholics by Protestants, and Radical

Reformers by Catholics and Protestants. Starting in the fifteenth century, the Western church developed the Doctrine of Discovery, a series of papal edicts that were collectively used by Catholics and Protestants to justify colonial conquest, destruction of Indigenous cultures and religions, land theft, the transatlantic slave trade, and intergenerational enslavement across the Americas, Africa, and parts of Asia for five centuries. Racial apartheid, Jim Crow, and ongoing Native American displacement persisted well into the twentieth century under white Christian power and control. Atrocities like the Holocaust and the Rwandan genocide took place within purported "Christian nations." In the United States and beyond, the early twenty-first century has seen an ongoing reckoning with clergy sexual abuse and subsequent denominational coverups that seek to protect perpetrators while dismissing and gaslighting survivors. And mainstream American Christians continue to choose power over presence, law and order over love, and condemnation over curiosity.

Again, this list is not comprehensive, but it provides enough context for why the church has been a source of suffering for so many people.

Some Christians will quickly remind you that we are all sinners and that no one is perfect, offering a sort of strange dismissal to the reality that so many Christians have behaved so badly so often and all around the world. Rather than seeking to learn from Christian traditions with a legacy and witness of justice, peace, or liberation, some stick their heads in the sand. Too often, mainstream American Christians downplay, if not outright reject, Christian ethics that take seriously scriptural reasoning that calls for justice, peace, and liberation. Instead, their own unexamined and inherited reasoning pits liberating souls against liberating people. If people want to make the world a better place, some Christians rationalize, we need to focus on proselytizing and making Christian converts. When people become "saved," their heart change will lead to a life change that will eventually lead to social change. The highest priority is guiding people to accept Jesus as their Savior to avoid eternal torment in hell. The eventual byproduct will be a more loving society, because as more people convert to Christianity, there will be less mistreatment of others.

This sounds like a great plan—if it were accurate. Things have never worked this way in the real world within actual human history. Early Christians known for embodying a counter-witness to Roman society and for their ethic of nonviolence rigorously trained and received instruction sometimes for several years prior to baptism. Early Christians aren't above critique—many failed in social faithfulness. But they pursued consistency between a holistic conversion (not just of the soul) and intentional processes to socialize followers into a new life and new habits based on their understanding of the way of Jesus. This fully life-changing approach directly tied to the life and teachings of Jesus should not be ignored.

Throughout Christian history, communities of Jesus followers have approached the ethics and way of Jesus differently. The degree to which a congregation expects Christians to embody the way of Jesus is strongly related to the ethical lives of its adherents. Conversely, much of Western Christianity in general, and white American mainstream Christianity in particular, has had a terrible record of cultivating faithfulness during colonial conquest, slavery, Jim Crow, and our contemporary challenges because most mainstream, self-professed American Christians are not holistically discipled into the way of Jesus.

Not only is the logic that soul change leads to life change, which leads to social change, verifiably counter to history, but it is also counter to what the Bible teaches us about the ministry of Jesus. New Testament writers expected Christians to *embody* the way of Jesus, not only confess his name and register a heart change. It is possible to plunder out-of-context Bible verses to construct a theology that affirms mainstream American Christian beliefs about heart change. However, a full reading of the gospel accounts makes heart-change-alone reasoning illogical when the Jesus stories are the center of our lens for interpreting Scripture.

In fact, one must believe that Jesus' ministry missed the mark, that he prioritized the wrong things over and over again, to hold that a liberation-of-the-soul view is more important than the liberation-of-the-whole-human experience. Has Jesus come to preach good news to the poor, to liberate the oppressed and to set the captives free (Luke 4:18–19)? Are the poor blessed and the rich cursed (Luke 6:20–26)? Are the peacemakers blessed, and are we to love our enemies instead of killing them (Matthew 5–7), including those in ethnic or religious out-groups (Luke 10:25–37)? Is what we have done (commission) or not done (omission) to the vulnerable "least of these" really how we have treated Jesus, and does that action define divine judgment toward us (Matthew 25:31–46)? Does Jesus really want the rich to sell their possessions and redistribute them to the poor, and is Jesus correct that it is near impossible for the rich to enter the kingdom of God (Matthew 19:21–24)? Is the true meaning of Israel's scriptures calling us to practice justice, mercy, and faithfulness (Matthew 23:23)?

I could go on and on. My point is that Jesus does not reduce Christianity to accepting Christ into your heart, to Jesus being your substitute for God's wrath, or to belief becoming your ticket to escape this world and go to heaven. (Also observable in the rest of the New Testament, when not plundered out of context.) Jesus calls for a radical, holistic, and embodied repentance by fully participating in the right-now, upside-down reign of the Messiah. The scriptural expectations for how followers of Jesus ought to live are more radical than mainstream Christianity often presents. We are called to acknowledge and place our allegiance with the preeminence of Jesus Christ over the cosmos by rearranging our lives to the gospel of the Messiah and God's dream for creation. Jesus is Lord, which means Caesar (or the modern nation-state) is not. No substantive Christian transformation—that is, being conformed to the image of the Son—happens outside of discipleship to, participation in, abiding with, and making visible the birth, life and ministry, teachings, death, and resurrection of Jesus Christ. The moment our priorities contradict the witness of Jesus passed on by the church through the Scriptures, we are claiming Jesus with our mouths but denying him with our lives.

Mainstream Western Christianity has largely defined adherence to the faith in strange ways—following the life and teachings of Jesus is made optional for believers while centering and lifting up social and political commitments becomes the test of faithfulness. In that way, one can adhere to an abstract and spiritual Christology—maybe a creedal formulation or by reducing the meaning of Jesus to a penal substitutionary atonement transaction[4]—with true faithfulness tested by alignment with a political party's platform and one's commitment to a set of conservative or liberal social ideologies. It's no wonder mainstream Christians have demonstrated minimal resistance to (if not outright acceptance of) their society's embrace of conquest, slavery, and subsequent forms of racial segregation and oppression.

By devaluing the way of Jesus as revealed in Matthew, Mark, Luke, and John, domesticated mainstream Christianity requires very little repentance from national abuses of power while focusing on minor interior struggles of the flesh and moral religiosity about some people's sex lives. The inner battles on trivialities seamlessly coexist with anti-gospel views on wealth, poverty, abuse of power, and how we treat others. Whether being a Christian is tied solely to baptism, to doctrinal adherence, to saying the sinner's prayer, or to having an inner emotional experience, if spiritual conversion is severed from the way of Jesus, then it fundamentally detours the life of a believer from being an actual disciple of Jesus.

Something is terribly wrong with mainstream Western Christianity. Many Christians fervently call on the name of Jesus, yet it is rare to find faith communities that radically follow Jesus as a counter-witness to domination, complicity in social webs of oppression, and the death-dealing cycles of violence that destroy human thriving.

A snapshot of mainstream white American Christianity

For many oppressed and vulnerable people, the mainstream white American church is death-dealing. White American Christians have engaged in full-blown political and cultural war against us. The most politically and culturally influential form of Christianity in the United States is white evangelicalism, whose history is inextricably intertwined with centuries of white supremacy, from American evangelicalism's emergence in the nineteenth century onward, through legalized chattel slavery and Jim and Jane Crow,[5] to the Moral Majority movement, and all the way to massive politicized voting blocks in recent presidential elections. As scholar Anthea Bulter underscores in her concise history of the religious movement, upholding white supremacy has been characteristic at every stage.

Rather than focus on exceptions to the rule, Butler's *White Evangelical Racism* explores the heart of evangelicalism. Evangelical doctrine adapted to accommodate slavery, and large swaths of the evangelical movement coexisted with and often explicitly defended segregation. Emphasis on personal morality and personal salvation often resulted in opposition to Rev. Dr. Martin Luther King Jr. and the Civil Rights Movement. The Moral Majority political organization founded in the late 1970s used morality rhetoric to conceal racial politics, often coupling single-issue distractions with political partisanship efforts to avoid the desegregation of schools and neighborhoods across the country. Evangelicals shifted to language about "colorblindness" and moral values that cleverly masked racial motivations and consequences. In more recent years, white evangelicals have opposed the Black Lives Matter movement that decried police antiblack violence. And they overwhelmingly supported Donald Trump's presidential candidacies despite his long track record of explicitly racist, sexist, and xenophobic rhetoric, behavior, and policies. As Butler concludes, "Racism is a feature, not a bug, of American evangelicalism."[6]

It's too easy to point a finger solely at white evangelicals, scapegoating them for all national woes. But white supremacy runs deep. Compared to Christians of color and their non-Christian white counterparts, white American Christians (evangelical, mainline, and Catholic) are more likely to hold racist attitudes and racial resentments.[7] For white Christians, increased church attendance in white congregations seemingly reinforces and perpetuates rather than decreases white identity and racial prejudice. In other words, many white American congregations are cultivating or maintaining white racialization. As Robert P. Jones writes, "If you were recruiting for a white supremacist cause on a Sunday morning, you'd likely have more success handing out leaflets in the parking lot of an average white Christian church than approaching whites sitting out of service at the local coffee shop."[8] The average mainstream white American congregation has been part of the problem of racism, not its solution.

White conservative Christians have been politicized into partisan politics so that conservative Republican views are what binds people together more than shared Christian beliefs and practices. However, the argument in the opposite direction is also important. Race has been religionized into a "religion of whiteness" or "a unified system of beliefs and practices that venerates and sacralizes Whiteness while declaring profane all things not associated with Whiteness."[9] The beliefs and practices of many white Christians have entangled traditional Christian doctrines with another religion, the practice of whiteness. The religion of whiteness is not explicitly named or recognized by its adherents, but is expressed through beliefs and practices that venerate whiteness; white perspectives on race and racism are transcendent. White people and white culture are venerated above the bodies and culture of others.

Scholars Michael O. Emerson and Glenn E. Bracey II contend that we cannot fully understand racism without considering its religious dimensions. Sermons, congregations, publications, media, and so on cultivate the religion of whiteness and so uphold white dominance. In contrast, many Christians of color experience the religion of whiteness as traumatic betrayal, which has led to a mass exodus from many white and multicultural congregations that center, normalize, and prioritize white people's experiences, perspectives, and preferences above all others.

Drawing on surveys, interviews, and focus groups, Emerson and Bracey found that white Christians routinely claim to hold high authority of the Bible but then dismiss biblical passages and themes that don't conform to the religion of whiteness. Approximately two-thirds of white Christians, they conclude, adhere to the religion of whiteness. These adherents tend to fall into two categories: a "white might" group, which recognizes that we have a racist history but still actively defends white superiority over others. White people, they say, are the true victims of society. They believe white Americans deserve their disproportionate wealth and opportunities. Then there's the "white veil" group, which is oblivious to systemic racism and inequities but maintains white social and political advantages through pre-existing social arrangements and colorblind rhetoric. Consider when someone says that everyone has equal opportunity today but then uses their economic advantages to live in a white and wealthy neighborhood with the most resourced school districts yet would *never* live in Black neighborhoods that were redlined and exploited for decades or send their kids to underfunded majority-Black schools. Ironically, this second group is more likely to be situated in all-white neighborhoods and white social networks.[10]

Emerson and Bracey identified a third group of white Christians who were neither "white might" nor "white veil" that had very similar views on faith and race as the remaining diverse set of non-white Christians. Unfortunately, such Christians are not the majority of white Christians in the United States.

The Movement for Black Lives pulled back the curtain on antiblackness in our nation. When you step back and think about it, it is quite fanciful or magical to think that Black people could be deemed outside of humanity and considered property through antiblack frameworks, justifying the most horrendous torture of African ancestors for centuries, and not just in the United States, without this antiblackness lodging itself in our psyches, myths, ideology, laws, institutions, and embodied habits after so many generations had normalized it. We know that antiblackness didn't disappear after the Civil War. Neo-slavery, lynching, and other antiblack oppression and terror simply took new forms under Jim and Jane Crow. It would take incredible faith against all evidence to assume that the antiblackness baked into our minds and society for generations inexplicably evaporated because of Dr. King's "I Have a Dream" speech or because of his death.

All historical and social evidence reveals a highly racialized society after the Civil Rights Movement—significant racial segregation geographically and in many school districts, massive economic and health disparities, and most alarmingly, a sprawling prison industrial complex that incarcerates Black people at rates that rival enslavement numbers. The fact that so many people are hardhearted and apathetic toward Black poverty and suffering, but expect massive government intervention when white people suffer increased egg prices, exposes continued antiblackness in our society. After some of the most brutal and dehumanizing forms of racial oppression in the modern era took place for centuries in the United States, followed by Jim and Jane Crow laws, we live now in a more complex but severely racialized society that disproportionately harms Black people. That this has not led to discussions on reparations and healing for Black people so they can thrive demonstrates that most Americans do not love Black people concretely. Instead, many white Christians today support a politician who has called for reparations for white people who are supposedly harmed by DEI (diversity, equity, and inclusion) programs—the very few programs in the United States designed to create space for Black people and other marginalized people to participate in its institutions in the aftermath of slavery and subsequent oppression.[11]

Despite many people asserting that the past is unrelated to the present, a mutated cycle of racial oppression continues. Christianity is grounded in confession, lament, repentance, and amends, but that foundation has been nearly absent in relation to America's history of oppression and violence. There has never been a broad, soul-searching moment among mainstream white American Christians in response to the church's wretched Christian witness and history. White Christians have not sought intergenerational confession and truth-telling, lament and reckoning, repentance and healing in response to five (nearing six) centuries of colonial plunder, white supremacy, antiblack oppression, and settlerism.

Nonetheless, the doors of the church are open. It's never too late to come before the throne of grace at the feet of Jesus as one who seeks true holistic repentance and embodied transformation into a new way of life in the aftermath of Christendom and colonialism. One path to such deliverance is related to the faith journey I've been on, which I offer as a gift for others to consider: the practice of Anablacktivism. Mainstream Christianity often looks nothing like Jesus—which is why I believe all followers of Jesus could learn something from the Black Church and Anabaptism, since they are both traditions that learned to follow Jesus on the underside of Western Christian domination.

Join me at the river

I'm inviting you now to follow me to the river's edge. In this river we find the waters of Christianity beyond mainstream American traditions. This book is an attempt to show the engine that has been driving my work, offering more transparency around what has resonated with people from my writing and thinking on Christianity and racial oppression, Christian activism, and repair. It is my attempt to honor influences on my own life and faith by offering them as a gift to you. Come to these waters. We need these waters.

I want to introduce you to the communities and theologies of each stream within their historical context. But I want to start by sharing my own quirky journey to Anablacktivism—Black theology and Anabaptism and Jesus-shaped activism. My faith began in a Black evangelical stream of the Black Church, and I eventually journeyed into the prophetic stream of the Black Church and the radical discipleship wing of the Anabaptist tradition. The overlaps between radical Anabaptist discipleship and the prophetic witness of the Black Church led me into a more subversive Christian witness faithfully grounded in the way of Jesus. These traditions sprang up amid distinct experiences of persecution or oppression—Anabaptism in response to Western Christendom of the fifteenth century, and the Black Church and Black theology in the context of colonial conquest and antiblackness over the past five centuries. As we journey together, I invite you to notice mainstream Christianity's role in this harm and how Anabaptism and the Black Church emerged on its underside. Our journey will be messy, because neither Anabaptism nor the Black Church are perfect. We'll acknowledge that reality, while still learning how these two traditions combined can help each of us salvage our Christian witness in the aftermath of Christendom and colonial conquest and antiblackness.

Ultimately, I want to talk about salvaging the way of Jesus from its death-dealing habits. My emphasis on the "way of Jesus" language is intentionally infused with early Christian attempts to describe a holistic and comprehensive way. I'm interested in disciples who follow, participate in, abide in, and make visible the story of Jesus in their lives individually and collectively. Grounded in the combined wisdom of Black theology and Anabaptism, I invite readers to engage in a transformative discipleship that addresses the spiritual and societal crises of our time. Drawing from these rich traditions leads to a more compelling vision and a renewed Christian practice that is radical and prophetic, calling believers to embody the radical and life-giving way of Jesus in a post-Christendom, postcolonial, and explicitly antiblack society. As the church we catch, embody, and pursue God's dream of beloved community where everyone belongs, everyone matters, and everyone can thrive.

As we think about the way of Jesus for today, I invite you to step into the ancient world of Galatia, where the early followers of Jesus were wrestling with their newfound faith. They had heard the good news of Jesus Christ from Paul, a Jew grounded in the traditions of his people yet transformed by his encounter with the risen Christ. Yet not long after Paul's departure, the Galatians found themselves caught in a dilemma that Paul believed undermined the power of the gospel. Paul's letter, found in the book of Galatians, is an urgent plea to a community at risk of embracing a distorted gospel. These early Christ followers were insisting that those entering life in the Messiah needed to adopt Torah observances like circumcision to truly enter God's covenant. This was leading to hierarchy and division in the church. It wasn't just a debate about rituals or random cultural practices. At stake was what it meant to belong to the people of God in light of the resurrection of the Messiah.

I'm especially interested in Paul's opening words in the letter. He begins with a reminder of the gospel he preached that centers on Jesus Christ, "who gave himself for our sins to set us free from the present evil age, according to the will of our God and Father" (Galatians 1:4). Jesus' death and resurrection, says Paul, is not just about forgiving our individual sins, but about delivering us from the entire corrupt system of this world, "the present evil age." As a Jew, Paul was deeply concerned with the covenantal faithfulness of God. He understood Jesus to be the fulfillment of God's promises to Israel, bringing about a new creation, a new age, where God's people would no longer be defined by the boundaries of Torah observance but by their allegiance to, and union with, Jesus the Messiah. Therefore, Jews were to continue observing the Torah as the circumcised, and Gentiles were to remain as Gentiles, grafted into covenantal community through Jesus and the Holy Spirit.[12] In light of Paul's framing and his broader beliefs in other writings, we can perceive the clash between the old age dominated by sin, death, and the powers of this world, and the new age inaugurated by Jesus, where God's reign breaks into our reality. This will be a new age where everyone belongs, everyone matters, and everyone thrives, whether they are Jews or Gentiles, enslaved or free, and male or female (3:28).

Too many Western Christians have been presented with a domesticated, watered-down Christianity that is merely a ticket to heaven or insurance to secure an eternal future. But Paul says something different. He's telling us that Jesus died (and was resurrected) to set us free right now, from the very forces, cycles, and systems that oppress and dehumanize us in this life. Paul was concerned that Galatian Gentiles were being tempted to return to the old order. "Don't go back!" Paul urges. "Jesus has liberated you from that. Don't be captive to the old order ever again." Unfortunately, mainstream Christianity has reverted to the logics and values of this current evil age: "racism, materialism, and militarism," as Dr. King would say.

So what does God's salvation for a Christianity that is captive to the forces of white supremacy, plunder, antiblackness, and cycles of violence look like? It's not just freedom from sin in a personal sense, but freedom from the entire web of sin and death-dealing forces that pervade our society, our present evil age. This salvation renounces the imagination, ideology, habits, systems, and myths that define our age and are counter to God's dream for us. Jesus' death and resurrection were God's decisive action to liberate us from the forces of evil that hold this world captive.

The gospel is not primarily about eternal salvation (though it includes that); it is about God's reign and new social order coming to earth as it exists in heaven. Jesus sets us free so that we can live as citizens of God's reign on earth right now. Salvation is about being liberated to embody the new age in the midst of the old, to be a people who live out the practices of God's *kin*dom—healing justice and persevering love—in a world still dominated by injustice, apathy, and violence. Our salvation is about living the way of Jesus here and now. It's about standing in solidarity with the poor, the oppressed, and the most vulnerable among us, just as Jesus did. It's about resisting the evil and death-dealing forces of our society—white supremacy, economic plunder, environmental devastation, or any other manifestation of the present evil age.

We are called to be subversives in Christ, a counter-community reflecting the new age and society that Jesus has brought into being. We are called to be a visible and embodied witness to God's dream that is coming. We have been saved—not to return to the ways of this age, not to conform to the patterns of our death-dealing systems—but to live as citizens of God's anti-kingdom *kin*dom right here, right now. And when we live out our salvation with fear and trembling, when we resist the evil of this present age and stand in solidarity with those "whose backs are against the wall" and see the "faces at the bottom of the well," we make the reign of God visible on earth.[13]

Can you imagine the church unleashed in that way? Genuine followers of Jesus who have been set free. Free to do justice, free to show mercy to our vulnerable neighbors, free to walk humbly in the presence of our God. We've been liberated to live the way of Jesus—the old age is passing away, and the Messiah's age has begun a subversive insurrection. And one day, when Jesus returns again, when the fullness of the Messiah's reign is revealed, we will see "justice roll down like waters and righteousness like a mighty stream." We will see God's shalom and a new creation in all its glory. But until that day, we must keep on resisting, we must keep on loving others concretely, we must keep on healing the physical wounds and psychological traumas, we must keep on living out the salvation that Jesus has given us.

In the Black Church tradition, we say "make it plain" when we need the preacher to give us the word straight and accessible in a way everyone can understand. This phrase is also a reference to the Plain tradition of Anabaptism that resisted trendy consumerism and chose a countercultural way of life. Come with me to the river's edge, and I'll make plain the forces that have taken mainstream Christianity captive. I'll make plain the communities who dared to find and follow Jesus while purported Christians tortured them in Jesus' name. *Making It Plain* is an altar call for the church to meet and follow Jesus again through the vital witnesses of Anabaptism and the Black Church, both urgently needed right now.

– ONE –

My Journey to Anablacktivism

I was raised in a nondenominational and semi-independent Black church. I was a pastor's kid whose grandfather planted our church along with over ten other congregations in the Northeast. I can still remember the power and confidence in his preaching. Rev. Dr. B. Sam Hart made the preaching moment a living reality that commanded us to respond.[1]

I was just a little guy at the time, so those are my very earliest memories of my faith community. Many of the people there remained significant in my life even after I moved away as an adult. Countless people poured into my life, making me the person that I am today. Sunday school teachers, youth leaders, and unofficial "aunties." When I was a teen, some of the slightly older young Black men spent time with us on Sundays playing ball after church. In this community, I grew in my capacity as a leader. Participating in children's choir, Christmas skits, and youth group "teen president" leadership led to preaching and teaching in smaller then bigger opportunities, thus increasing my vocational comfort.

Theologically we were Black evangelicals—though that wasn't a label we would have used. We would have said we were "Bible-believing" Christians. My congregation and our sister churches mostly fit into the theological spectrum somewhere between Tony Evans and the late Tom Skinner. Skinner could be described as a "radical Black evangelical" for the ways that he put his Black male identity and social concerns arising from Black experience in conversation with his evangelical interpretation of the gospel of Jesus Christ. In 1970, Skinner preached on the US racial crisis and evangelism, prophetically challenging white evangelicals for their historic racism, reminding them of our history, and inviting them to participate in God's new order. Skinner embodied a hybrid of Black evangelicalism with Black theology and Black consciousness. Think of Stokely Carmichael mishmashed with Billy Graham.

For Tony Evans, race and social concerns were much more secondary, though not absent. He contextualized mainstream evangelicalism for Black people. He wrote multiple books tackling race, other social concerns, and a "kingdom agenda," but often with a dominant culture framework that confronted individual racial prejudice more than systemic oppression. Despite their differences, Evans and Skinner were both evangelical *theologically*. They assumed doctrines of biblical inerrancy and dispensationalism, and they (especially Evans) preached a reductionistic gospel focused on saving souls to go to heaven and avoid hell. Yet even Evans taught about God's kingdom here on earth and its relation to social concerns in his own way—this theology wasn't white evangelicalism (like pastor Voddie Baucham espouses), but it was still evangelicalism.

Skinner and Evans represent a big portion of the theological spectrum of my church growing up. In fact, Skinner and Evans were friends with my grandfather and dad, my first two senior pastors. My home congregation embraced some conversations about Black social concerns, but they were secondary to a spiritual, heaven-oriented gospel. The ultimate concern was for people to make the right, eternal decision to accept Jesus as Lord and Savior so they would not experience eternal torment in hell. Our Black faith, to different degrees, stretched and adapted evangelicalism in light of our own lived experience as Black people and our encounters with Jesus. For many of us, our faith formation had tensions with our lived experience and political intuitions.

Though my journey and studies have led to significant differences on important theological and ethical convictions from my first worshiping community, I have great appreciation for things I inherited. My church taught me to make Jesus the center of my joy, it provided me with a love for scripture, and it helped me internalize the radical idea that as a young Black boy, I was fearfully and wonderfully made by God. We held our heads high.

Faith and character were instilled in me through my community. My church had impressed upon us young people that our status as children of God was more important than any other group identity because of our mutual life in Christ, challenging dominant cultural efforts that sought to tell us who we were. Our lives were caught up in Christ. I came to love Jesus and to be attentive to the movement of the Spirit.

During high school, I felt a call on my life to serve God. I decided to apply to Christian colleges so that I could pursue biblical studies. I randomly applied to and chose to attend Messiah College, two hours away from home. Far enough to get outside of any circles that would know the last name Hart, yet close enough that I could return home if I needed to because I wasn't actually that adventurous.

My experience at Messiah was complex and challenging. While I had lots of great experiences there, living on campus among a majority of white evangelical students was one of the most prolonged explicitly racist experiences I have gone through. After two years, I had made many great friendships, and I also realized that I had held to a naïve understanding of what it meant to have a shared faith in Christ with white siblings. Many of my white peers had unconscious antiblack inclinations residing right below the surface. Even when smiling and being "nice," peers could say the most vile or hardhearted things yet interpret themselves as being pious and godly. My Black consciousness grew tremendously during those years.[2]

Thankfully, most of my time in the classroom, especially within the biblical and religious studies department, was a gift. This was where I first encountered the strange word "Anabaptism." At first I thought it was another way of saying "anti-Baptist" because I had no context for the word. When I learned that the Amish as well as Mennonites were Anabaptist, I concluded that it was a harmless, interesting tradition that was ultimately for white people in rural areas who rode horses and drove buggies. While many faculty in my major identified as Anabaptist, I didn't attend the school because of its Anabaptist heritage, and I never chose to take any Anabaptist courses.

Despite my disinterest, my four years at Messiah exposed me to general Anabaptist beliefs and convictions. By my final year, my curiosities from encountering Anabaptism led me to wrestle with how Christians should respond to violence in light of its historic peace position. Grappling with the ethics of peace and violence in the Bible and in my life was new for me. My studies also grounded my belief that justice for the vulnerable was central to the scriptural concerns, while providing a richer understanding of the historical and cultural backgrounds of our sacred texts. I interpreted how creation, covenant, exodus, empire, and exile became important themes in Israel's sacred texts. And my studies initiated my own journey of reflecting on how the gospel relates to the American church's history of racism and our call to respond to it. The Anabaptism I took in by osmosis as a student bolstered the challenge I felt about what it meant to follow Jesus' life and teachings through a life of discipleship to his way.

Meeting the Anabaptists

After college, I was hired as a youth pastor at a Brethren in Christ church in Harrisburg, Pennsylvania. The Brethren in Christ denomination broke from the Mennonites in the eighteenth century, combining Anabaptism with Wesleyanism and Pietism. I was drawn to the Harrisburg church because it was a multiracial congregation intentionally addressing race and racism. I was not drawn to it because it was Anabaptist, though I did have some bubbling Anabaptist convictions. The Brethren in Christ (BIC), compared to Mennonite Church USA and Church of the Brethren, is significantly more evangelical as a denomination. In fact, when I joined the pastoral team, I didn't know that many BIC congregations had been slowly assimilating into white evangelicalism throughout the twentieth century. My new congregation was more explicitly Anabaptist in convictions than many BIC congregations, but it had some evangelical impulses as well.

I didn't have to affirm Anabaptist leanings to be hired, I just needed to be "good" with their peace position. Ironically, during my four years at the church, I never identified as an Anabaptist. My convictions around discipleship in the way of Jesus, however, increasingly defined for me what a faithful Christian life was. And my ethics around peace and nonviolence developed as well.

During my time on pastoral staff at that congregation, I also took up the work of self-education. I wanted to learn about Rev. Dr. Martin Luther King Jr.'s life from the vantage point of his seeking justice as a Black follower of Jesus, which wasn't the emphasis from my formal education. I attended my first Civil Rights pilgrimage to the South; a year later I brought ten people along with me. I read vociferously from other Black authors and scholars on race, starting with Black evangelicals like John Perkins and Tom Skinner on justice and reconciliation, which encouraged my ongoing convictions. Then Black intellectuals like Michael Eric Dyson and Cornel West provided me with more nuanced and critical frameworks for understanding race and racism in society.

But when I read *God of the Oppressed* by James Cone, things changed. The book resonated instantly and deeply yet was distinct from the Black evangelical theology that had formed me. Cone's theological questions spoke to my lived experience in ways that I didn't yet have language to articulate myself. My time on a white Christian college campus had left me with so many questions about how so many of my white Christian peers could be so racist, and *God of the Oppressed* made more theological sense than any other God-talk I had encountered.

My sense of dissonance was also growing, and patience shrinking, with my white dominant cultured yet multiracial Anabaptist congregation. James Cone's Black liberation theology seemed more compelling than our congregation's racial reconciliation paradigm, which focused solely on interpersonal relationships across racial lines without challenging the power dynamics, systems, and norms that organized our relationships in the first place. In contrast, Cone aligned his theology with the scriptural reasoning that "God has chosen the weak to shame the strong" by demonstrating that God has always thoroughly identified with oppressed people and their struggle for liberation and justice. In contrast, white theologians always hid their particularity and contextual perspectives, claiming to be "universal people" speaking for all people at all times in all situations. They were oblivious to how their theology was deeply impacted by the context of racial oppression. Over the next decade, I read most of Cone's writings, and he continued to significantly influence my Christian convictions. Dr. King's life and James Cone's theology emerged with power and clarity as I came down to the riverside and began exploring the prophetic and liberationist streams of the Black Church.[3]

I sometimes describe the Brethren in Christ denomination as a whole as "Anabaptism lite" in comparison to other Anabaptist denominations like the Mennonites or the Church of the Brethren. This is partly because evangelicalism has significantly eclipsed Anabaptism in many BIC congregations. However, the Anabaptist convictions and practices of many folks in my worshiping community significantly shaped me. I might not have identified with Anabaptism explicitly, but I was being drawn in by the credible witness I encountered.

And then there was Yoder. I read John Howard Yoder's *The Politics of Jesus* after a Civil Rights pilgrimage in my last year at the Harrisburg church as I sought to make sense of Anabaptism in relation to Dr. King's nonviolent action. This was several years before Yoder's sexual abuse was broadly known.[4] Yoder was a Mennonite and the most influential Anabaptist theologian of the twentieth century. I found him lacking in comparison to Cone, but he significantly shaped my understanding of the sociopolitical dimensions and meaning of discipleship and the cross. He also influenced some of my reflections on power despite his gaps on the subject, like his inability to analyze his own tremendous power and the influence he wielded. With Cone already living rent free in my mind, I read Yoder critically and began to put them in conversation with each other's theological and ethical projects.

My life experience, my undergraduate learning, my ecclesial experience, Cone's Black theology of liberation, Yoder's Anabaptist politicizing of discipleship, and King's practice of nonviolent action combined initiated my early journey into Anablacktivist praxis. Praxis can be understood as an ongoing cycle of reflective action and active reflection. Reflecting on King's life, writings, and assassination while I was participating in Anabaptist community became a vital way for me to practice and internalize a contextualized, hybrid form of Anabaptism that was coherent with my Black experience and encounters with God.

Despite that cycle of reflection and action, I recognized the incoherence between Dr. King's life and the lived faith of most of the white Anabaptists I knew in BIC circles. I was reinterpreting Anabaptism in ways that were not embodied in my worshiping community. At the time, I probably was too grateful for the crumbs to name that incoherence.

One hypocrisy I did name while among white Anabaptists in my early twenties had to do with the language of "simple living." A common refrain was that we should "live simply, so others can simply live." It didn't take me long to realize that many white BIC folks I knew were fairly wealthy. I was amazed by the large churches with all the amenities throughout central Pennsylvania, the church members' expensive cars and homes (in de facto segregated neighborhoods), and their frequent overseas travel. As I joked at the time, if that was simple living, then sign me up! Though the stated conviction for simple living gestured at an important ethic of sustainability, it felt overly simplistic for grappling with our complex and inequal economic realities. The version of Anabaptism I was encountering didn't seem to take Black people's experiences seriously enough. I began to realize it was time to head back to Philly and to my Black church.

In 2008, I accepted a pastoral role at my home church. Returning to my Black evangelical church as an associate pastor quickly revealed how my interpretation of faith had shifted over my eight years away. I also enrolled at a local seminary, where my cohort was overwhelmingly Black, comprising many leaders from my home church's sister congregations. Many of my classmates knew my family well. It took coming home for me to realize how much I had changed. Living in Philadelphia in a majority Black neighborhood, attending a Black "Baptisty" (semi-independent) congregation, and pursuing my MDiv with an urban concentration at a seminary with a missional emphasis alongside Black peers, it suddenly hit me that those doggone Anabaptists had gotten me. Those pesky pacifists left an ongoing mark on who I was and how I saw my faith, despite some of my frustrations. Ironically, it wasn't until I left

Anabaptist spaces altogether and returned to an all-Black environment that I first used "Anabaptist" to describe part of my theological understanding.

Shortly after that I ran into a friend from Philly whom I first met while living in Harrisburg. He invited me to check out an urban Anabaptist network of leaders in Philadelphia that held monthly meetings. Gathering regularly with Black, Brown, Asian, and white Anabaptists from across Philadelphia, mostly from the Mennonite world, magnified my understanding of who Anabaptists were, what they cared about, how they lived, and what their congregations looked like. Meeting second- and third-generation Black Mennonites from longstanding Black or multiracial Mennonite congregations opened up a lot of curiosities. I thought my Harrisburg experience of engaging Black faith and Anabaptism was an exception. But as I discovered, there were broader, older communities with a tradition that combined Black Church cultural and spiritual orientations with Anabaptist beliefs and practices.

A cloud of witnesses

I began my PhD program in 2012. I planned for my dissertation, at its center, to have a critical and dialogical exploration of James Cone and John Howard Yoder's views on Jesus and what it meant to follow him. They were each the most influential theologian from their respective traditions. Like many others, I had not yet heard about Yoder's sexual abuse, though as time went on I began hearing vague stories to that effect. I didn't know specifics, but there certainly seemed to be a bigger story behind the concerns and rumors.

Early in my research, my work made clear that Yoder needed Cone more than Cone needed Yoder. For one, Yoder's theological reasoning was articulated as though he wrote as a person on the margins of society still persecuted alongside his sixteenth-century ancestors. In reality, he was a world-renowned white male ethicist with tremendous social advantage and influence. So my concern was that Yoder ignored and concealed his own power, his social location, and the lopsided influence he had over others because of his fame, while relentlessly exposing the power of others (especially those Christians with "Constantinian" inclinations). These contradictions would have benefited immensely from Black theology's concern with our social identification and solidarity with the oppressed generally, and womanist theologians' attentiveness to the interlocking of systems of oppression in particular. The incoherence of Yoder's missing self-awareness and self-examination needed a womanist intervention to unveil our multidimensional and complex experiences with social power. Even if Mennonite theology was not mainstream, Yoder was not writing from the margins of society.

When Yoder's history of sexual violence was more widely exposed in 2015 in a well-researched essay by historian Rachel Waltner Goossen,[5] I began saying to Mennonite friends that Yoder functioned a bit like a parable for the broader white Mennonite church in North America. Many white Mennonites, rooted in sixteenth-century stories of Anabaptist martyrdom and identity, often used smoke and mirrors to hide their ongoing assimilation into white dominant culture—how they benefitted from stolen Indigenous lands and accumulated wealth from an economy built on stolen labor. They failed to analyze their own social-power dynamics while critiquing other traditions that directly stole the land and enforced enslavement firsthand. Like Yoder, many white Anabaptists lacked self-awareness and a critical analysis of their social standing. Yoder, I argued, was a warning for the broader white Anabaptist community in North America.

For my emerging theology of radical discipleship and prophetic witness to have integrity, it needed to be lived and not just intellectualized. In 2011, the Occupy Wall Street movement had drawn me out into the public square, albeit in limited ways. I didn't camp out downtown (I left that to the mostly young white folks), but I attended some organized protests. I resonated with the movement's emphasis on economic disparities, and the attempt to shift the national conversation concerning the hoarding of wealth. Suddenly, many were talking about the 1 percent versus the 99 percent. Some Democrats who often preferred to center the middle class began to talk more frequently about poverty and the exploitation of everyday workers.[6]

In a broader sense, I was already an activist; I had been increasingly involved in antiracism and faith work since 2005. But when the social unrest of Occupy was quickly followed by the Ferguson uprisings in 2014, I could not sit back. Courageous Black people on the ground protested the killing of Michael Brown, ushering in the first big wave of the Movement for Black Lives. Despite my upcoming comprehensive exams, I knew I needed to hit the streets in between studying so I could stand in solidarity as we demanded an end to police brutality.

Joining mass protests is both powerful and limited in scope, but it reminds you, in bodily practice, that the state does not deserve our allegiance when injustice reigns, and we always can resist and begin to shift the narrative in the public square.[7] With my concerted intention toward public activism, I also joined a mass protest organized by multiple organizations that addressed police brutality, public education funding in Pennsylvania, increasing the minimum wage, and other important social concerns for Philadelphians. I had never seen such a massive protest before; it might have been one of the biggest in Philly's history. I didn't yet fully appreciate all the behind-the-scenes work that made possible such a public showing of people power.

Three significant friends aided my Anablacktivist journey. Rodney Thomas—a fellow Black Anabaptist rooted in a Black Baptist context—became my earliest and most consistent dialogue partner. His friendship and conversations helped push my reflections forward. In late 2012, Keven Sweeney, then wrapping up his MDiv, tweeted: "@DruHart Anabaptism/Black Theology/Theopolitical Practice = 'Anablacktivism'? Lol." What might have been playful wordplay became the perfect label for my work. I adopted it immediately, and Rodney embraced it too. I owe Kevin for encapsulating my journey so succinctly. Finally, my dear Australian friend Jarrod McKenna has been an ongoing partner in making good trouble through the *InVerse Podcast*. Jarrod's commitment to following Jesus and appreciation for Black theology, Anabaptism, and activism, among other influences, drew us together into overlapping projects, despite living on opposite sides of the globe.

As my studies continued, I researched the cloud of witnesses who lived at the intersections of Black faith and Anabaptism, or had written about it. I came across Hubert Brown's *Black and Mennonite*, a book written in 1976 exploring Black and Anabaptist intersections![8] I was particularly moved as I learned about Vincent Harding, a friend of Dr. King and veteran of the Civil Rights Movement who transgressed Black Church and Mennonite communities' boundaries.[9] The great cloud of witnesses past and present just kept enlarging. Elder Samuel Weir, James and Rowena Lark, Vincent Harding, Hubert Brown,

Tony Brown, Nekeisha Alexis, James Logan, Regina Shands Stoltzfus, Tobin Miller Shearer, Michelle Armster—the list could go on and on.

I also stumbled across the writings of J. Denny Weaver, starting with an essay comparing Cone and Yoder.[10] Then I read his atonement work that incorporated Black and womanist theology.[11] Over the years, he has continued to engage those streams as a Mennonite scholar.[12] When I began my PhD research, I felt like I was blazing a trail into something completely new, but by the end of my program I knew I was merely formalizing and academically recognizing what had been bubbling up at different moments for centuries. Though the term was new, *Anablacktivism* was an intergenerational river filled with important predecessors and contemporaries. I was grateful to grab the baton and run from there.

Toward the end of my PhD program, I stepped down from my associate pastor role and my family began worshiping at a more justice-oriented Black Baptist church in Philadelphia. This shift allowed me to focus on writing and public speaking, but it also coincided with the first wave of the Black Lives Matter movement. While I attended a few protests, my involvement felt limited, leaving me torn. As others fought for our communities' future, I wrestled with being confined to research and writing in the library. Was this the vocation God wanted for me? PhD programs often shape scholars who are great at theory but rarely engage directly with their subjects. I struggled to reconcile this reality with my call to radically follow Jesus into the world. James Cone wrestled with these struggles as well. *"My most difficult problem in graduate school was not learning how to write but rather learning how to stay in school during the peak of the civil rights movement,"* he wrote.

How could I write papers about the Barth-Brunner debates on natural theology while black people were being denied the right to vote? Many of my black classmates, including my brother, were deeply engaged in the civil rights struggle. Some blacks asked me how I could stay in the library, reading ancient documents about Nicaea and Chalcedon, while blacks were fighting for freedom in the streets. These were tough questions. While I am confident now that I made an appropriate decision for my vocational commitment, I was not certain at the time that I made the right decision. All I knew then was that I had an intellectual craving to do theology and to relate it to black people's struggle for justice.[13]

Nurtured into Anablacktivism

I didn't exactly follow Cone's path, but I needed this word. I also needed to carve a different path forward that was as much oriented toward practice as scholarship. So I transgressed the PhD process. Instead of working on my dissertation immediately following my comprehensive exams and getting my dissertation proposal approved, I decided to write a book. A mainstream trade book at that, not one for scholars. I did not tell my advisor or my committee that I would not immediately begin writing my dissertation. I knew what I would likely be told if I shared my plans, but I had to write. I was deeply disappointed in many Christian responses to the Black Lives Matter movement. And I'm not talking about the detractors. Even some Christians who wanted to support the movement were trapped in a reductionistic framework around race and faith shaped by decades of "bromance" reconciliation books that discussed race primarily in terms of relationships, personal bias, and proximity and were filled with stories of overcoming interpersonal challenges together. Drawing from a decade of antiracism work, I had gathered lots of stories, metaphors, and analogies that could help followers of Jesus understand racism through a focus on power dynamics, hierarchies, and the systemic character of white supremacy and antiblackness. While my book *Trouble I've Seen* didn't explicitly identify my theological influences, Black theology and Anabaptism were the waters I stood in as I wrote.

Ironically, I hadn't been part of an Anabaptist congregation since 2008, yet I was becoming known as an Anabaptist leader when my public speaking and antiracism work expanded beyond Pennsylvania. Initially, I was amused when invitations began pouring in. My first out-of-state talks at Anabaptist Mennonite Biblical Seminary in Indiana and Houghton College in New York were followed by opportunities across the country. About a third of these invitations came from my reputation in antiracism work, another third from my online presence during graduate school—particularly my responses to the killings of Trayvon Martin, Michael Brown, and others—and the final third from Mennonite and Anabaptist audiences aware of my focus on Black theology and Anabaptism. Though I had been introduced to Anabaptism through the Brethren in Christ, my deepest Anabaptist relationships were with Mennonites. I knew the Mennonite Church's history and complexities more intimately than any other Anabaptist stream, yet I had never been a member of a Mennonite congregation. Sometimes I was even introduced at speaking events as Mennonite, and I'd clarify that I was simply a "friend of the Mennonites." A Black Mennonite friend in Philadelphia would tease me, calling me a "closeted Mennonite."

In the spring of 2016, I defended my dissertation and earned my PhD. I also received and accepted an offer to return to Messiah as a professor of theology. The Biblical and Religious Studies department had also hired Emerson Powery, a well-respected Black scholar, and the department continued to have a robust Anabaptist influence. At Messiah, I could teach courses on African American theology and Anabaptist theology, along other courses within my expertise.

In our return to Harrisburg, my family initially planned to find another Black church to attend. However, after two years of visiting a few churches on and off, we eventually joined Harrisburg First Church of the Brethren, where Belita Mitchell, a Black Anabaptist, had been the lead pastor for about two decades. This church was small but emphasized peacemaking, justice, and service. It wasn't perfect, but we fit theologically in a way that would probably be nearly impossible to find otherwise in our small city. So after a decade of revisiting the Black church, I was worshiping once again with a different multiracial and socioeconomically diverse Anabaptist community in the city of Harrisburg.

I've been part of that congregation since 2018. Since then, the waters of Anabaptism and the Black Church have continued to nurture me as I seek to mutually learn from, contribute to, and participate in the prophetic stream of the Black Church as well as the radical discipleship wing of Anabaptism. Both shape my attempt at following, participating, abiding in, and making visible the Jesus story in my life.

While I was nurtured in the faith and learned to love Jesus in a Black congregation, since adulthood I have literally had a foot in both Black congregations and multiracial Anabaptist congregations. This experience, coupled with relationships in both communities, and scholarship rooted in both streams, has been a vital part of my own journey into Anablacktivism. It requires holding tensions between an ongoing praxis cycle of action and reflection. Holding tensions because I have found two distinct traditions that have their own complex conversations and histories that sometimes go together well and at other times cause friction. And praxis-oriented because it was the ongoing process of engaged reflection and reflective engagement as I sought to follow Jesus in our world that brought me to where I am today.

This holistic path has nurtured within me an anti-Christendom, decolonial, antiracist inclination that seems desperately needed for the present crisis in mainstream American Christianity. With the entrenchment of white Christian nationalism and many Christians co-signing neofascism in our society today, now is an important moment to share how Black theology and Anabaptism together can be a gift for those seeking to live out a faithful witness of Jesus and his Way. We need a more radical way, a prophetic witness to and worship of God that offers credible good news instead of the domesticated, violent, oppressive, whitened, status-quo, power-hungry, and savior-of-empires type of Christianity proclaimed by imperial puppets in the public square.

– TWO –

The Story of Christendom

The church in the West is in trouble. I was reminded of that in my own city when an Episcopal leader reached out to me and other leaders in the community. My reputation in Harrisburg as an explicitly Christian leader who loves partnering with ecumenical, multifaith, and nonreligious groups has provided a variety of opportunities to collaborate for the common good. This request, however, was different. They wanted to see if I would serve on a team of community leaders who would decide the fate of an empty building in our city—St. Andrews Episcopal Church. A building with sacred purpose now needed repurposing. What was once a building full of vibrancy, worship, and outreach now sat empty.

If this isn't a sign of the times, I don't know what is. Many other congregations in my city have shut down in recent years, and countless more across the country. Overall, Christianity in the West is in a decline. In the United States, for example, mainline Protestant denominations saw a 40 percent decline in membership between 2000 and 2015.[1] Nearly 40 percent more Americans attended church each week in 1983 than in 2020.[2] An estimated 3,850 to 7,700 churches close every year.[3] The evidence is everywhere.

Some Christians take note of this decline and get lost in nostalgia for a bygone era when the church stood at the center of society. From that perspective, secular people have lost a sense of what matters most, and society needs to return to the good old days when God and church were societal priorities. This line of reasoning usually correlates with arguments suggesting we need to reinstate prayer in schools and post the Ten Commandments in public spaces, and inevitably aligns with the agenda of Christian nationalism where people want to legislate their particular religion and morality and impose it on everyone else (the heart of the Make America Great Again or MAGA movement). People want to "take back their country," a desire that has always been grounded in white Christian nationalist nostalgia. It is too easy to romanticize the church's status and role in society in the early to mid-twentieth century, as though a return to that time would alleviate our contemporary challenges.

For the church to navigate the current climate well, it will first need to look in the mirror. People have departed the church in droves for a reason. Sure, there are some people who are wounded or not showing up as their best selves, and we know that hurt people hurt people and don't lean into healthy interdependence and mutuality in community. Yet, that can't explain it because in my experience those folks are just as present in the churches as they are outside of them. I believe people are leaving the church now because it is not a life-giving community where they have encountered good news. I don't mean they haven't heard some reductionistic sales pitch to escape hell and go to heaven. That watered down gospel message is still prevalent. I mean good news in the way Jesus did in his Luke 4 sermon drawing from Leviticus 25 and Isaiah 58 and 61. I'm talking about liberation from poverty, hunger, and incarceration. Healing and care for the body and mind. And the year of the Lord's favor, a Jubilee where we reboot our social system, canceling economic debts, returning land, and providing a fresh start for exploited laborers. More frequently, people have experienced or witnessed harm and cover-ups of abuse in the church rather than finding healing for those with trauma or provisions for those that lack health insurance. People have been disillusioned by clerical greed and how most churches' actual missions are summed up by the ABCs of institutional survival (attendance, buildings, and cash) rather than feeding the hungry, repairing social harms, and prioritizing the well-being of vulnerable people in our society. If people are well educated about church history, then they know the patterns of violence go back much further than just the last five hundred years. Terms like "Christendom" and the "Doctrine of Discovery" mean very little to most mainstream Christians, but the communities devastated in their wake frequently understand the church's role in these past and present forces.

We are in a moment where much of the mainstream church has betrayed its purpose for existing, to be a light to the world and the salt of the earth. The church has failed to participate in the delivering presence of God in felt ways. It should have lived the gospel so that it was actual good news for our neighbors. Too many churches practice bad news instead. If people were experiencing a life-giving community, even with all the challenges of being a community full of imperfect people (because we all can be difficult at times), then we would not be in this predicament. If death-dealing politics, apathy, selective historical memory, desires for domination and control, anti-intellectual religiosity, spiritualizing material conditions, and white grievances, to offer a few examples, weren't people's primary perception of what it means to be the church, then things would be much different. For us to break free and to be delivered from these patterns, we need to tell a more truthful story about ourselves.

The first task in understanding how so many Christians have claimed Jesus yet rejected his way that leads to life requires us to examine the root of the church's history, which is the Jesus story. And then we must follow the life of the church as it moves without power under empire, until it eventually merges with the state. We cannot look away from ecclesial unfaithfulness in history. We must remember how the mainstream church in the West transitioned from the margins to the center, morphed from the vulnerable to the imperially secure, aligned itself away from the poor in choosing solidarity with the wealthy, and ultimately switched from being the oppressed to those who dominate society. We must look at the story of Western Christendom, when Christianity and the social order became thoroughly entangled, each working on behalf of the other, coercively imposing a top-down vision that sought to forcibly synchronize every area of life within its geographic control because of a distorted and domesticated vision of the gospel of Jesus.

Jesus ushers in the kingdom

In 63 BCE, the Roman Empire occupied Judea and imposed oppressive policies and heavy and exploitative taxes and began destroying and eradicating local religious and cultural indigenous practices through military force. This is the historical and sociopolitical context for God's insurrection and revelation to take on flesh in the person of Jesus Christ. Jesus came preaching good news to the poor, declaring that a subversive counter-reign had arrived right underneath the noses of the Roman imperial powers. God was the ultimate authority and Jesus was God's Messiah who deserved our allegiance, not Caesar. The apostle Paul refers to this as the lordship of Jesus (Romans 10:9; 1 Corinthians 15:24–28; Philippians 2:9–11; Colossians 1:15–20).

Saying "Jesus is Lord" while in the Roman Empire defiantly declared that Caesar was not. In contrast to Jesus, Gentile rulers sought after greatness by "lording" over others (Matthew 20:20–28). Jesus subverted this social practice by demonstrating servanthood, kneeling in solidarity with those at the bottom of the social hierarchy, and ultimately giving his life for others. He taught his followers to practice this subversion and solidarity with the oppressed. Jesus' insurrection (God's kingdom) frequently flipped social norms on their head. In God's kingdom, the last are first and the first are last. When the kingdom comes, "every valley shall be filled, and every mountain and hill shall be made low, and the crooked shall be made straight, and the rough ways made smooth" (Luke 3:5).

Jesus taught that the poor and vulnerable were blessed and offered woes to the wealthy and self-sufficient. Jesus fed the hungry and told wealthy men to sell their possessions and give it to the poor. He himself was houseless (Matthew 8:20). He rejected many patriarchal gender customs of the day, allowing women to study or travel with him and choose the life of a disciple, which was otherwise exclusive to men at the time

(Luke 8:1–3; 10:38–42; John 4:7–30). He often highlighted the faith of vulnerable women in contrast to the powerful religious men in his circles (Mark 5:25–34; 12:41–44; Luke 7:36–50). Jesus transgressed ethnic, gender, and geographic boundaries in socially inappropriate ways, including with a woman publicly known as a sinner who intimately caressed Jesus' feet with her hair, with a despised Samaritan woman alone at a well, by telling parables that valorized the hated Samaritans by making one of them the embodiment of neighborly love across in-group/out-group boundaries. While Jesus' ministry characteristically went first to the Jews, it increasingly extended to the Gentiles. Jesus made people holistically well, whether they needed physical, spiritual, or mental healing. His way offered comprehensive transformation of the person, attending to inner and external well-being through his teachings (see especially Matthew 5–7).

Jesus preached that he came to liberate the oppressed. He taught his followers to hunger and thirst for the world to be set right, to be peacemakers and practice enemy love, and like the prophets of old, to prioritize the weightier matters of the Torah—justice, mercy, and faithfulness before God (Micah 6:8; Matthew 23:23). The Messiah came from Galilee to Jerusalem, spoke truth and disrupted the powerful, clashing with the religious and political establishment in the temple. This revolutionary yet nonviolent behavior eventually led to his arrest. He experienced brutality from the soldier-cops, condemnation in a broken justice system, and state-sanctioned death penalty through crucifixion. He joined the thousands of Jews crucified under the Roman Empire in the first century.

According to the testimony of the early church, on the third day, when hope that the Messiah would set the world right had shriveled into pessimism and despair, courageous women in Jesus' party went to the tomb and encountered the empty grave. They returned to the disciples, preaching the good news that God had resurrected Jesus from the dead. Jesus had not been defeated by the powers! He overcame the Roman authorities as well as the unseen forces of death.

The empty tomb expresses God's liberating and life-giving love. This is the blues and the spirituals coming through on the other side of suffering. Jesus went ahead of us into death, overcoming it and opening the way to resurrection so that death would lose its sting and power over us to live fully and faithfully before God right now (Romans 6:9–10; 1 Corinthians 15:55–57; Hebrews 2:14–15). Paul's response to the death and resurrection of Jesus was to vulnerably follow and participate in the Jesus story to the point of death: "I want to know Christ and the power of his resurrection and the sharing of his sufferings by becoming like him in his death, if somehow I may attain the resurrection from the dead" (Philippians 3:10–11). The crucifixion and resurrection of Jesus Christ unveils God's character and activity in the world among those whose backs are against the wall: God has indeed chosen the weak to shame the strong.

The early church bears witness

The encounters with the resurrected Jesus before he ascended and promised to return were paradigm- and reality-shifting experiences for his followers. According to Luke, the empowering of the Holy Spirit was so vital that many shared the good news of Jesus and his reign and established communities with Jews and Gentiles together where they were all invited and challenged to realign their entire lives according to the inbreaking insurrection and reign of Jesus rather than the status quo and cultural patterns of the Roman world. It was a revolution after the pattern of God's revelation in Jesus Christ. The Spirit of God led them to continue the radical, upside-down reign of God that Jesus began.

The Spirit leads them into increasingly decolonial, socially transgressive, and expansive community. We are told that on the day of Pentecost, the Holy Spirit descended on the disciples, and they began to speak in the languages of others rather than assimilating everyone into one supposedly respectable or civilized language. This decolonial moment broke down divisions between Hebraic and Hellenized Jews from different languages, cultures, and regions (Acts 2:1–13). Then the Holy Spirit pushed the boundaries even further, opening the disciples' heart for out-group Samaritans to join the Christian community. Philip went to Samaria and proclaimed the message of Jesus and taught about God's kingdom. Many came to know and follow Jesus Christ (Acts 8:4–25).

Even more surprising, the Spirit liberated Peter to mirror the heart of God even to the Gentiles through his encounter with Cornelius. Cornelius was a Roman centurion, and we are told he was a righteous Gentile who feared God. Through visions to Peter and Cornelius, God was preparing them to come together and cross a social boundary created by the Torah covenant. When Peter met Cornelius in his house, he experienced conversion along with Cornelius as he began to fully understand that the Messiah's revolution was not limited to Jewish people but extended fully to the Gentiles (Acts 10:1–48).

Paul, in contrast, felt called from the first moment of his conversion to be an apostle to the Gentiles. But this opened up a lot of questions and concerns. The Scriptures were Israel's stories, and Jesus was a Jew who said he came not to abolish but rather to fulfill the scriptures. If Gentiles were to be enfolded into covenant community, would they need to assimilate? A council in Jerusalem was convened to decide whether Gentile converts needed to follow all the Jewish covenant practices, including circumcision. Rather than merely quote the scriptures, the council considered what the Spirit had been up to. From a hybrid of scriptural reasoning and yielding to the work of the Spirit, they decided that Gentiles should not be coerced into all these religious and cultural requirements to be grafted into the body of Jesus. The work of the Spirit transcended ethnic boundaries, reconciling Jews and Gentiles into one body of Christ (Acts 15:1–35).

Paul's ministry to the Gentiles played a central role as a witness to the Jesus story to the Gentiles. He, too, crossed boundaries that were not supposed to be crossed. He communed at the table with those he was supposed to be separate from. His travels, led by the Holy Spirit, resulted in an expanded sense of shared belonging to those previously in the out-group to Jews.

Other apostles also established messianic communities near and far. Many of these early messianic communities were defined by economic justice. After the Day of Pentecost, the early believers in Jerusalem were characterized by sharing all their possessions and belongings and distributing what they had based on actual needs (Acts 2:44–45). Then came a deepening of this economic justice and mutuality and a radical embodiment of wealth redistribution akin to what Jesus called the rich young ruler to practice. Barnabas had wealth but sold his field and gave all the proceeds over to the church. The whole community shared all things in common, and economic need was abolished (Acts 4:32–37).

Soon after, as Hebraic and Hellenistic Jews were learning how to be one people gathered under the reign of Jesus, ethnic bias crept into their economic and food distribution practices. As faithful Jews, they already had a system in place to care for the widows in their community who were economically and socially vulnerable. Since Hellenized Jews from other nations were being overlooked in the distribution, they implemented an all-Greek deacon leadership (they all had Hellenized names) to overlook the process. Executing economic justice was discerned by the out-group, not the in-group (Acts 6:1–7).

Economic justice is an often overlooked distinctive of messianic communities. Wealthy people imagine that their money and status ought to provide communal and social advantages, even in the church. Such was the case with Simon the magician. He offered money to the apostles in exchange for spiritual power, which they renounced and rejected. The wealthy could not buy their way into the kingdom (Acts 8:9–24). Acts also tells of small and larger examples of economic mutual aid. A woman named Tabitha from Joppa made clothing for the widows and the poor. She cared for them practically while addressing their economic needs (Acts 9:36–43). In Acts 11:27–30, during a time of famine, the church in Antioch recognized the suffering in Jerusalem as their own. They redistributed their resources and sent the money to the church in Judea.

When these messianic communities were filled with the Holy Spirit, they were empowered to transcend ethnic boundaries, practice justice for the most vulnerable, and participate in God's dream for all creation. There is so much more we could say about these early Christian communities and their leaders, including about their inconsistent and sometimes conflicting teachings on slavery or women's roles in church and society. Even then, some people or communities were unfaithful or missed the point of the gospel. We could also focus on the subversive nature of many leaders who resisted governmental authorities and were incarcerated repeatedly. The recidivism rate in the New Testament is quite high! While some sought to assimilate into broader culture, others had the reputation that they were "turning the world upside down" wherever they went (Acts 17:6). Being a part of the people of Jesus meant a radical break and clash with the social order. Many radically transformed their lives, often secretively, to bear witness to the broader society that God's new society had begun. This faithful stance was contagious and led to unanticipated decades of growth from the margins and cracks of the empire.[4]

Christian tradition suggests that both Peter and Paul were executed in Rome, demonstrating that by the end of the era of the apostles, this primarily Jewish religious movement that was grounded in the East in the first century had already begun to take root beyond those boundaries, including in the West. Nonetheless, Christianity was most prominent in what we would call the Middle East and North Africa. In 64 CE, Christians in the city of Rome experienced severe persecution under Emperor Nero. Followers of Jesus were brutally burned alive, or ripped apart by wild animals, or tortured by authorities. This persecution was significant but also local to Rome rather than across the empire. Still, Christians were highly suspect because they refused to participate in Roman cultic worship and their largely underground movement typically met secretively in homes rather than in the public square.[5]

A glimpse into late first-century or early second-century church life is visible in the ancient text the *Didache*. We see how the church's way of life was passed on, the centrality and significance of baptism, the Lord's table, honoring the poor and not showing deference to those of high status in the worshiping community, and reconciliation processes to deal with conflict in the community were taken seriously very early in the life of the church.[6] Surprisingly, the church didn't engage in traditional "evangelistic outreach" but instead embodied a distinct way of life that was attractive to many watching eyes. This is how the church grew.

In the East, Christianity grew significantly among Gentiles and within more Hellenized cultural contexts, with a decreasing Jewish influence. In the second century, Christians were increasingly seen as a threat to the social order, and their refusal to participate in Roman customs sparked hostility from the authorities. Sometimes persecution followed. Leaders like Justin Martyr intellectually defended Christianity to Roman powers and Hellenized audiences. However, he also began pulling the threads of Christian identity away from Judaism, fostering anti-Judaism orientation, and making Greek philosophical thought rather than the Hebrew Scriptures the primary prism for understanding the meaning of Jesus Christ. Contextualization and inculturation were inevitable, but unfortunately parts of the church creeped toward supersessionism, or the troubling belief that the church replaced the Jews as God's people.

The first-century church attracted many from the margins of society, especially women and enslaved people. This continued into the second century; however, as more and more Gentiles entered the church, diversity increased across the social strata. Wealthier members stepped down the social ladder, finding relief from their affluence in a more egalitarian arrangement than the broader society. The leadership of the church crystalized into hierarchal structures with defined roles like bishops, elders, and deacons, which were more fluid terms when they originated. However, Jesus' teachings continued central to the formation of early Christians.

Christians navigated their relationship toward mainstream culture under the Roman Empire in different ways. Like Justin Martyr, Origen in the second and early third centuries immersed himself in Hellenized intellectual thought and drew on Platonic ideas that significantly shaped his preference for allegorical interpretations and deeper spiritual meanings beyond the surface of a text. (His method of biblical interpretation was common in the church at the time.) By contrast, Irenaeus took a middling position. Irenaeus selectively used Greek philosophical terminology and language, especially concerning the "logos," to defend Christianity. But he was also more grounded in the Hebrew Scriptures, which shaped his interpretation of Christianity, his "rule of faith," and his confession of the unity of the Old and New Testaments. Tertullian, meanwhile, took an oppositional posture to the Roman Empire and Greek thought and society. "What has Athens to do with Jerusalem?" he famously asked.[7] Tertullian believed Christians ought to separate from the problematic influences of Hellenized culture.

Tertullian, Irenaeus, and Origen reflect the diversity of Christianity as they emerged in different contexts in the early centuries of the church. Persecution through the second century remained limited to particular regions, but many famous persecutions at that time shaped early Christian identity, reflections around martyrdom, and the public narrative of how Christians responded to suffering courageously. Tertullian summarized it succinctly: "The blood of the martyrs is [the] seed [of the faith]."[8]

In the third century, Christianity continued to grow and become even more diverse. Ecclesial structures became more entrenched with deepening differentiations between clergy and laity. More wealthy, highly educated, and socially respected people were joining the church. The church's continued growth exacerbated the perception that Christianity was a threat to the stability of society and the empire. By the middle of the third century, Emperor Decius and, soon after, Emperor Valerian imposed broader policies targeting Christians or Christian leaders. When persecution was imposed under Decius, many Christians became martyrs, or "witnesses"—that is, they fully bore witness to the truth of the gospel even to the point of death. However, some became apostates as they renounced their faith and cursed Christ under threat of torture and death.

A third group intentionally fled or hid from the authorities to spare their lives. Cyprian was one leader who chose to flee and hide. After the persecution under Decius subsided, Christian communities had different approaches for responding to these different Christians. Some offered grace and forgiveness, and some believed that apostates should be permanently excommunicated from the church. Cyprian, however, believed that these disciples could eventually be restored through penance. When Valerian's persecutions followed only a few years later, they targeted Christian leaders. This time, Cyprian was captured, and he joined the cloud of martyrs along with many other leaders of his day. Through it all, Tertullian was proven right. The persecutions did not stop the church as intended. Underground, extensive, and vibrant networks of house churches continued worshiping Jesus and seeking to follow his way.[9]

Emperors pave the way for Christendom

The fourth century shook the foundations of the church and accelerated the growth of the church, its hierarchy, and its entangled relationship with state power, resulting in the rise of Christendom. Ironically, these shifts began with severe persecution. The emperor Diocletian believed he could unify the empire by eradicating Christianity, which undermined traditional pagan practice. In contrast to previous persecutions that often were quite limited in scope and geography, his edict of 303 (and subsequent edicts) included broad imperial orders to prohibit Christian worship, destroy Christian scriptures, arrest clergy, and demand public sacrifice to Roman gods or face torture and death. Some local leaders were more zealous than others, and Christians in the East (who were more populous at the time) experienced more severe persecution.

Despite the persecution and growing list of martyrs, Christianity persisted with underground worshiping communities. In 306, Constantine was controversially declared Caesar by soldiers under his control, and he began attacking the other Roman emperors (there was a brief four-member imperial reign), consolidating power. Constantine achieved a key victory at the Milvian Bridge outside of Rome in 312, where he claimed to receive a vision of a Christian symbol and the message "By this sign you will conquer."[10]

In 313, Constantine signed the Edict of Milan, adopting a policy of religious tolerance, permanently ending Christian persecution, and progressively instituting Christianity as the favored and advantaged religion within the Roman Empire. By 324, Constantine had become the sole ruler of the Roman Empire, and he was unashamedly aligned with the church. He poured massive wealth into the church, building large basilicas in Rome and Jerusalem. He exempted clergy from military service and taxes and supported them financially while significantly bolstering the imperial status of the bishops, who were on their way to exchanging social roles with the Roman senate.[11] Constantine made Sunday a day of rest across the empire, promoted Christians to top imperial positions, and adopted Christian symbols for official imperial usage, thereby visually tying Christianity to state power. Constantine did engage in some common good work, like ending gladiatorial games violence, providing better treatment to imprisoned people, and making it easier to emancipate enslaved people. Symbolically, Constantine's clearest identification with Christianity was in convening the Nicaean Council in 325 in an effort to unify and homogenize the diversity of Christian expressions that had always existed in various regions. He aimed to establish a single, official, and orthodox imperial religion.

Constantine presided over the deliberations of the Bishops as they debated Arianism, leading to the adoption of the Nicene Creed. Arius, whose views were longstanding among many diverse Christian expressions, was condemned and exiled, and his teaching was determined heresy by imperial and council decree. (Arianism persisted in the East nonetheless.) One thing was clear: Christianity had fully transitioned from an underground and secretive nonviolent revolution from the bottom up to a central and imperially backed religion. Paganism now found itself marginalized, discriminated against, and disadvantaged in the public square under the powerful influence of Christian authorities.[12]

While no single moment thoroughly changed Christianity, many ongoing decisive moments over many centuries put the faith on a trajectory toward entrenched Christendom. In 380, Emperor Theodosius made Nicene Christianity the official religion of the empire through the Edict of Thessalonica. In 410, Visigoths sacked Rome. Since the Visigoths were

(Arian) Christians themselves, they left the church intact even as the Roman Empire in the West fell away. In the empire's absence, Christianity and the church became the cultural glue that would help unify Europe. More and more regions were Christianized. In 496, King Clovis converted from paganism to Nicene Christianity because he believed the Christian God supported his military victory, which immediately led to a mass compulsory conversion of his soldiers and, later, his subjects.[13]

Sophisticated Christian theology blossomed after Constantine. In the fourth and fifth centuries, theologians provided nuanced philosophical articulations on Christian doctrine. In the East, where the Roman Empire had persisted, Athanasius and the Cappadocians (Gregory, Gregory, and Basil) articulated significant theological trajectories, and Augustine did the same for the West. Augustine was brilliant and innovative, navigating extra hurdles because he worked with Latin translations of Greek texts that led to significant departures from previous interpretations of Christian doctrine. For example, Augustine invented the idea of "original sin," describing how people inherited sin as well as guilt from Adam through sexual reproduction. He introduced brand-new interpretations and emphases on predestination based on his reading of Romans.

Augustine also shifted Western Christian teachings on war and coercive power. The official teachings of early Christian leaders consistently espoused a nonviolent ethic of peace. Augustine still saw that as the ideal, but he also developed the first arguments for just war theory and why, at times, it was necessary to compel (read: coerce) people toward faithfulness.

As Christianity shifted, emphases on social justice persisted, often with more comprehensive impact for the common good.

The Cappadocians in the East combined abstract, sophisticated philosophical nuance with concrete ethics informed by Christianity's previous concerns for the vulnerable. Gregory of Nyssa condemned the practice of slavery, Basil the Great was a juggernaut for economic justice and the redistribution of wealth to care for the poor, and Gregory of Nazianzus advocated for hospitality and care for the vulnerable and poor.[14] And the emerging monasticism movement provided opportunities for ordinary people to take their faith more seriously through asceticism and common life.

Charlemagne inaugurates the new Western Christendom

What began in the early 300s when Constantine aligned Christianity with the state took a decisive step toward Christendom in 800 CE. Charlemagne, the Frankish king, was coronated as the emperor of the (new) Roman Empire by the pope, who sought Charlemagne's powerful support. The church's role in recognizing and blessing the imperial powers helped birth Western Christendom, as it would become known in the coming centuries. With the launch of a new Holy Roman Empire, with church and state working on behalf of one another and coercively implementing Christianity from the top down, Western Europe was unified once again. This unification included campaigns of conquest and forced conversion to Nicene Christianity. Those who resisted suffered mass executions. Charlemagne had little patience for religious opposition, seeing it as his duty to use the sword to "compel" alignment. State-sponsored "missions" to advance Christianity also developed around this time, shaping Western Christian beliefs and practices (to this day) around instinctive approaches to world evangelization efforts. Sacred versus secular binaries increased, as did the polarization of the geographic boundaries of Western European Christendom, which were considered "civilized" in contrast to the world beyond.[15]

The rifts between Western and Eastern Christianity had been widening for some time. Western Christian doctrine changed significantly during the medieval period, and language and cultural barriers exacerbated the divide. In 1054, what was already a reality on the ground became official: the Western Catholic Church and Eastern Orthodox Church officially broke communion. Things came to a head over disagreements about the historic Nicene Creed and papal authority.

Where the earliest Christian leaders were anti-war, and Augustine believed war was evil but sometimes justified, the Western church during the height of the Middle Ages declared holy war campaigns. In 1095, the pope initiated a holy crusade to remove Muslim control of Jerusalem. Ongoing crusades continued into the thirteenth century.

Around the time of the first crusade, Anselm of Canterbury innovated Christian doctrines on atonement. For the first millennium of Christianity, various streams had emphasized participating in the life of Christ through his death and, more importantly, his resurrection. The resurrection was believed to be God's decisive victory over sin, death, and the forces of evil in the world. The goal was ever-increasing union with God through Christ Jesus, known as "divinization" by Eastern Christians. Jesus' victory over sin, death, and the forces of this world was not as compelling for Anselm because the church seemed to have triumphed over the world. So he contrived the satisfaction theory of atonement, which removed the resurrection from the equation and explained Jesus' death as satisfaction for our infinite dishonoring of God. Dishonoring God, rather than human captivity to sin and death and alienation from God, was the new problem to be solved. And only a God-man, through death, could provide infinite satisfaction to restore the relationship. Technically, it was a theology of reparations to God, not punishment, but in later centuries this satisfaction model would morph into the perceived need for salvation from punishment and God's wrath. In Protestant Christianity, this is now *the* mainstream way to understand Jesus' crucifixion. After Anselm, Western Christianity increasingly celebrated the death of Jesus rather than God's healing through the life of Jesus, his victory over crucifixion and death through the resurrection, and our deepening union with Christ forevermore.[16]

Western Christendom reached its zenith in the eleventh through fourteenth centuries. All of society within the geographic boundaries of Christendom was believed to be unified and synchronized from the top down, pointing to the lordship of Jesus Christ who reigned over, and had conquered, society. It felt like God had triumphed. The church and state were intertwined, each playing their role to sustain a Christian society, protect its people, create law and order, and engage in further conquest or missionary expansion in Jesus' name. Papal supremacy was at its height during the High Middle Ages, and doctrinal consensus was also top-down. This era also produced scholasticism and birthed our modern understanding of universities. Thomas Aquinas is the premier example. He synthesized Western Catholic teaching, developed new arguments, and helped solidify a powerful intellectual tradition. The eternal torment of nonbelievers and salvation as the means for escaping hell became unrivaled Christian doctrines in the West.

There were still teachings on social justice, but they lacked powerful prophetic critiques against the structures, institutions, and authorities of the day: feudal lords, landowners, powerful elites, and the church itself now perpetuated the economic inequities and exploitation. Poor peasants were vulnerable. They worked hard, and usually on the land of feudal lords. They had little protection and were severely exploited. Beginning in the eighth century, the church had enforced tithing, but it became more widespread during the Middle Ages.

For the earliest Christians, following Jesus concretely, as described in the gospel narratives, was essential to being Christian. Now it was increasingly defined by doctrinal belief, cultural norms, and participation in church ritual. Following Jesus became more complicated. It was mediated through complex scholasticism and traditions that frequently obscured the practical and subversive meaning of Jesus' life and teachings. The creeds and the sacraments as means of grace took higher priority. But Western Christendom was also complex. Both the Franciscan movement and the Waldensians, for example, embraced voluntary poverty and rejected the wealth and corruption of the church and broader society while not breaking from the church itself. From the early church to this very day, radically following Jesus has always been an option.[17]

Christendom mindsets, instincts, and desires

Most modern Christians admire the early church in some capacity. Of course, the lives of early Jesus followers were messier than we understand. Even when we can isolate admirable characteristics of the early church, it's difficult to discern how to draw on their lives for contemporary practice. It may be difficult to acknowledge, but the Christianity of the first several centuries is thoroughly alien to most of us today. Instead, Christendom is what most directly shapes our mindsets, instincts, and desires when reacting to the church's current place in society. As scholar Peter Brown notes, "Much as we may admire the Fathers of the Church as representatives of the last, spectacular flowering of ancient culture, it is the contemporaries of Gregory the Great, Columbanus, and Charlemagne who are 'directly ancestral' to the Christianity of the European Middle Ages and so of modern times. Whether we like it or not, it is their blood, and not the blood of the Early Church, which runs in our veins."[18]

My retelling of the story of Christendom—coercive, top-down Christianity aligned with the state imposing itself over the social order—briefly (and inevitably insufficiently) narrates how the church distorted its faith as it fused with Western imperial powers. While we no longer live within formal Christendom, we do live in its aftermath. Jesus' resistance of the devil in the wilderness was an explicit rejection of the lure to dominate political, religious, and material control over society, but the church still succumbed to that very temptation. And in doing so, it misconstrued what it meant to follow Jesus. Where Jesus rejects "lording it over" others like the Gentiles do, the contemporary mainstream American church has sought to grab hold of all the levers of concentrated power so it can turn back the clock on demographic shifts and impose its political inclinations. Of course, wanting power and control is not limited to any segment of the church. It is a very human instinct. But when we bless the ways of empire we curse the ways of Jesus. As Isaiah warned, "Woe to those who call evil good and good evil, who put darkness for light and light for darkness, who put bitter for sweet and sweet for bitter!" (Isaiah 5:20).

Today we don't have Christendom, but we do have Christendom mindsets, instincts, and desires. Most mainstream Christians are dissatisfied with the radical way of Jesus Christ for their lives. Life in God's reign is not enough. Christendom mindsets are reflected in our rejection of living well with our non-Christian neighbors. Christendom mindsets are revealed when Christians choose white Christian nationalist policies that seek to impose interpretations of Christian morality onto everyone else rather than living as faithful noncoercive witnesses to Jesus through our lives. Forcing everyone to live like Christians rejects Jesus' voluntary invitation to follow him. It smothers the grace of God and makes the Jesus way compulsory.

Rather than working within our pluralistic society, informed by our Christian convictions and ethics, toward the common good for all, many want to legislate Christianity in their preferred form. Still worse, many Christians don't want to legislate justice for the vulnerable, mercy for the suffering, and love of neighbor in the way early Christians leaders did even after Constantine assumed power. Instead, our modern Christendom mindset replaces God's dream of shalom for all creation with the American Dream. We have quite a stomach for unbridled power, greed, and wealth, asserting that might makes something right, that the ends justify the means, and that winning trumps everything (pun intended). Thus so many have vandalized the name of Jesus in the public square and have lost the way of Jesus in the church. Thankfully, some Christians within Western Christendom were not satisfied with betrayals to the life they were called to. Their witness points us toward radical discipleship in the way of Jesus that is explicitly anti-Christendom in character.

– THREE –

Anabaptism, an Anti-Christendom Tradition

Christendom couldn't hold forever. In the sixteenth century, reformers, revolutionaries, and radicals transformed the political and religious landscape of Western Europe. This included a spectrum of reformations—Protestant, Radical, and the Counter-Reformation in the Catholic Church. Some of these reformations were magisterial and in one way or another kept church and state alliances, but the radical expressions made a more decisive break with Christendom ecclesiology while seeking to ground their faith in the way of Jesus. The seeds of Anabaptism, a stigmatized movement that sprang up around Europe and inspired adherents from a range of traditions, were planted in the Radical Reformation and its critique of both Catholic and Protestant practice and doctrine.

Michael Sattler was a Benedictine monk in the Black Forest in Germany. Monastic communities began as early as the 300s, attracting people who were not interested in the often-domesticated faith and lives of mainstream Christians. Instead, monasticism offered ordinary people opportunities to take their faith seriously via shared communal life, common prayer, and asceticism. Even though it often meant some form of withdrawal from mainstream society or practice, monasticism ultimately worked with Christendom rather than resisted it.

In 1524, the Poor Peasants' uprisings reached Sattler's monastery in the Black Forest. Inspired by Protestant Reformation calls to reform corrupt church practices, the peasants had economic, political, and religious demands. This was a pivotal experience for Sattler; he left St. Peter's Monastery and not long after, he began associating with Anabaptists, an inherently risky endeavor. His leadership was immediately useful among the Swiss Brethren Anabaptists. He helped organize communities around baptism for repentant believers, the ban (excommunication), breaking of bread (communion), separation from the world, renouncing the sword, and refusing oaths. This subversive ecclesiology troubled authorities.[1] Like many Anabaptists, the Swiss Brethren centered the life and teachings of Jesus as the interpretive key for reading the rest of Scripture.[2] This led to a radical break with Catholics and the Magisterial Protestants (like Martin Luther and Huldrych Zwingli), who persisted with church and state top-down governance. When the Anabaptists rejected the civic mandate of infant baptism as legitimate for their own faith and practice, they immediately became enemies of the state. Sattler was eventually arrested for his leadership as part of an illegal ecclesial movement.

Sattler's story is just one among thousands of sixteenth-century Anabaptists who experienced persecution under Catholic and Protestant governments, exposing the abuse of "the Sword" that sixteenth-century Anabaptists endured. Sattler was charged with teaching against infant baptism, rejecting the state church, and opposing Christian state violence. He refused to recant and affirmed the need to live by scripture and the teachings of Jesus. His sentence was gruesome: "The executioner . . . shall take him to the square and there first cut out his tongue, then forge him fast to a wagon and there with glowing iron tongs twice tear pieces from his body, then on the way to the site of the execution five times more as above and then burn his body to powder as an arch-heretic."[3]

On May 20, 1527, the authorities did just that. Through the pain and torture, Sattler remained faithful, praying to God. Finally, after suffering greatly, he was burned at the stake as an "arch-heretic" who violated the law, order, and orthodoxy of Christendom. His wife Margaretha was drowned by the authorities a few days later.

Sattler was an influential Anabaptist leader and one of the movement's earliest martyrs. Western Christendom might have been fracturing during the Reformation, but Catholics and Protestants, though at war with one another, were united in their persecution of Anabaptists. Remembering Sattler's commitment to Scripture and the way of Jesus, even in the face of arrest at the hands of church-and-state-sanctioned execution, provides an opportunity for mainstream Christians today to reflect on what it means to follow Jesus in the aftermath of Christendom.[4]

Reformers, revolutionaries, and radicals

It is impossible to understand the early Anabaptists outside of the backdrop of the Reformation. The Protestant Reformation, ignited in 1517 by Martin Luther and his Ninety-Five Theses decrying abuses in the Catholic Church, challenged medieval Christendom corruption and doctrine and ultimately fragmented Christendom's power over Western Europe. Led by leaders like Luther, Zwingli, and John Calvin—known as Magisterial Reformers—the reformation challenged papal Catholic authority and denounced practices like the sale of indulgences, which allowed Christians to purchase reduced punishment in purgatory.

Protestant doctrine emphasized salvation through faith alone as well as the sole authority of Scripture (when interpreted through their tradition's confessional statements). Church leaders solidified doctrines that centered God's wrath as part of the emerging penal substitutionary atonement theory, the inevitable outcome of Anselm's satisfaction theory combined with medieval beliefs of eternal torment in the fires of hell. Fragmenting Western Christianity led to the birth of Protestant traditions like Lutheranism, Calvinism, and eventually Anglicanism, which were distinct from radical reform movements like the Anabaptists. The Magisterial Reformation impacted everyday religious belief and practice and led to massive social, political, and cultural upheavals, reshaping Western Europe. Still, these reforms retained some form of church and state Christendom to coercively impose religious and civic control over their geopolitical domain. And they all used their distinct, fractured Christendom powers to persecute Anabaptists.[5]

The early 1500s were also marked by socioeconomic unrest among the poor across Western Europe. The Poor Peasants' uprisings of 1524–1525 were ignited by economic exploitation and struggles, feudal oppression, and a hunger for justice. Some were inspired by the Reformation's push for reform, including Luther's Ninety-Five Theses. Many peasants saw themselves as participating in these Protestant reforms, and their Twelve Articles expressed a desire for ecclesial and socioeconomic liberation. However, Luther ended up not being their guy. When the violent uprisings began, Martin Luther—the most influential of the Magisterial Reformers—not only distanced himself from the rebellion but outright called for the rulers and authorities to "stab, smite, slay, whoever you can" to put down the uprisings.[6] Over a hundred thousand peasants were brutally killed.

In *Anabaptist History and Theology*, historian C. Arnold Snyder notes the complex relationship between the Poor Peasants' uprisings and early Anabaptists.[7] Just as we can't understand Anabaptism without understanding the fracturing of Western Christendom, the peasants' liberation-oriented uprisings are key to understanding Anabaptist origins. Many contemporary white Anabaptists have significantly marginalized, if not outright ignored, this important history. For sixteenth-century Anabaptists, their exploited situation and their material conditions were unavoidable. The economic and political unrest of the time significantly influenced the emerging movement. Some participated in the 1524–1525 uprisings and the 1534–35 Münster Rebellion as Anabaptists, and others did so before becoming Anabaptists; very early on, Anabaptism was not synonymous with nonviolence in all regions.

Of course, Snyder is right to note that *most* Anabaptists rejected violent revolutionary action. And most Anabaptists eventually coalesced around nonviolence, defenseless Christian witness, and a rejection of the sword. However, it's vital to not lose sight of the overlapping unrest and concerns of Anabaptists and the peasants. Compare, for example, the 1527 Swiss Anabaptist Schleitheim Articles with the peasants' Twelve Articles written two years earlier. The peasants' first two demands were about choosing their own pastor and ecclesial reform for modest pay for clergy while reserving the remainder for the poor. They also used the gospel to argue for their liberation from serfdom. Beyond that, their demands were economic and political: the end of serfdom, the right to use the lands and water, an end to exploitative and excessive labor demands, fair rents, protection from unjust laws, and fair trials as well as a fair justice system.[8] The Schleitheim Articles focused on ecclesial concerns, but the Swiss Anabaptist communities also practiced mutual aid, rejected material excess, and reaffirmed the old position of the church that usury (charging interest on loans) was sin. Poor peasants *and* Anabaptists were responsive to economic exploitation and the need for radical ecclesial reform.

The Poor Peasants' uprisings didn't succeed, but they exposed the pervasive discontent from below and the ongoing desire for radical reformation. While most early Anabaptists rejected the violent uprisings as an option for followers of Jesus, they also rejected the economic status quo by radically reorganizing communal life rather than the whole society. This turn to the radical reorganization of their communities increased as efforts to dialogue with Christian authorities resulted in their own persecution. It's fair to describe early Anabaptism as a *liberationist ecclesial witness*. In other words, Anabaptism expected Christian community to practice a preferential solidarity with and for the poor.

Early Anabaptist plurality

Despite what some might assume, there's always been significant plurality among Anabaptists. Anabaptism emerged as simultaneous movements bubbling up under the nose of Christendom from a variety of regions across Europe. Each group was grappling with the fusion of church and state (Christendom), infant baptism, the peace witness of Jesus, economic mutuality, and what it meant to follow Jesus, obey Scripture, and follow the leading of the Spirit—but sometimes in conflicting ways.

In early 1525, a group gathered for Bible study in Zurich. Based on their personal reading of Scripture, they believed that only adult believers baptism was genuine, and therefore they went against Huldrych Zwingli and the authorities by baptizing one another during their home meeting. As this Swiss Brethren movement grew in Switzerland and South Germany, they emphasized a literal and plain reading of Scripture, believers baptism, separation of church and state, rejecting the use of the sword because it was outside of the perfection of Christ, and the use of the ban. Very early on they had a community of goods, which later developed into emphasizing mutual sharing of resources. They emphasized discipleship in the way of Jesus as well as Christian community as a people called out and separated from society to be a distinct and visible witness to society. This was the group that Michael Sattler joined. Other famous early leaders included Conrad Grebel, Felix Manz, George Blaurock, and Balthasar Hubmaier, all of whom became martyrs.

Anabaptism is often thought of as a peace church tradition, but that isn't completely true today, and it wasn't the case back then either. In the Netherlands and North Germany, an Anabaptist movement emerged under the influence of Melchior Hoffman's apocalyptic and prophetic teachings. Hoffman, who emphasized the Old Testament prophets, believed that Christ would return to Strasburg in 1533 and establish his kingdom after his followers took up the sword and helped usher it in. His teachings and influence eventually led to violent rebellion in Münster, Germany, in 1534–35. As with the Poor Peasants' uprisings a decade earlier, economic conditions played an enormous role in drawing people into the revolt.

Many in Münster had embraced a militant eschatology, and they believed that there soon would be the imminent establishment of God's kingdom on earth. They just needed to act in faith to usher it into reality. So they took up arms and overthrew their exploiters and authorities of the city. When the Anabaptists were defeated after a lengthy siege, thousands of participants were slaughtered.

Many were disillusioned in the aftermath of the rebellion. In 1536, a priest named Menno Simons left the Catholic Church and became a significant leader redirecting the convictions and practices of the Dutch Anabaptist movement. Menno (from whom Mennonites draw their name) retained some of the doctrinal teachings of this Dutch and German expression of Anabaptism but rejected the use of violence, transforming the movement into a nonviolent tradition and adopting a two-kingdom theology that emphasized a break with Christendom. Genuine Christians, Menno reasoned, couldn't participate in the worldly kingdom, because they followed the spiritual and nonviolent teachings of Jesus. While a few marginal groups persisted in violent militancy, most took a more ecclesial response by embodying their distinctive ecclesial faithfulness as a community through obedience to Christ (with a very literal interpretation), church discipline, and the practice of economic mutual aid.

In South Germany and Austria, another Anabaptist movement emerged in 1526 shortly after the Swiss Anabaptists. It initially had a strong spiritualist and mystical emphasis and was also inclined toward violent revolutionary action for the poor and disinherited. Many early leaders and participants in this movement had been directly involved in the Poor Peasants' uprisings. However, they were violently put down by Catholic and Protestant Magistrates, including Luther's directive to "stab, smite, slay" the revolting peasants. These Anabaptists held to believers baptism, and early on were very apocalyptic. Under the leadership of people like Pilgram Marpeck, this movement shifted toward nonviolence. Marpeck practiced an ongoing desire for social transformation through a faithful Christian participatory witness in society without coercive force. He also held a sophisticated position that transgressed the literalism and spiritualism found in varying Anabaptist camps. He believed Scripture ought to provide guidelines for living but also rejected the legalism often seen among the literalists (like Sattler and Menno). While Marpeck's movement was short-lived, many scholars consider him a particularly compelling early Anabaptist leader who still has much to teach us today.

The Hutterite Anabaptists also originated from Austria and South Germany. They practiced believers baptism, breaking with the involuntary baptism that Western Christendom had practiced for centuries. A Hutterite distinctive was their ongoing practice of their community of goods. If Anabaptism could be understood as a proto-liberationist ecclesiology with a preferential solidarity for the poor lived out by the community, then the Hutterites had the most radical ongoing vision for the economic life of the church. In rejecting private ownership and adopting a strong collectivist approach, including a common purse, they rejected capitalism's growing inclination toward hyper-individuality, competition, and greed. Communal commitments were more than economic—daily life was organized around their common life. This included strict community discipline. The Hutterites, initially led by Jackob Hutter, held a creative tension between the literal words of Scripture and yielding to the Spirit's guidance. When it came to following the teachings of Jesus around peace or economics, they took Scripture literally. But they also emphasized an inner spiritual life and experience that was necessary for new life and following the Spirit's leading every day.

Another distinct Anabaptist stream sprang up in Germany in the early 1700s. The Brethren, or Dunkers (referring to their baptismal practices), wanted to restore "New Testament" Christianity by emphasizing adult baptism through the practice of triple immersion, nonviolence, community, and discipleship in the way of Jesus. They distinctively combined Anabaptism and radical pietism, fusing two separate renewal movements. They, too, faced persecution for rejecting state churches. Many Brethren fled to the United States in the eighteenth century, settling near many Mennonites who had already migrated there, looking for refuge from religious persecution and seizing economic opportunities. The Brethren have stood out for their very practical orientation to Christian faith and their rejection of creeds and dogmatic confessions. Alexander Mack, a key founder of the movement, was central in organizing this Anabaptist tradition, navigating them through persecution, and leading them to Pennsylvania in North America, where he pastored until his death.

Today, Anabaptism is a diverse global movement birthed by multiple streams and influences. Despite the stereotype of an Anabaptist as a white Old Order Amish person driving a horse and buggy, most contemporary Anabaptists are Black and Brown members of the majority world. Many of the shifting global demographics reflect ways that Anabaptists mimicked

Western Christian missions and the global expansion efforts of mainstream Western Christianity.

In North America today, there are a range of Anabaptist traditions, denominations, and groups. This includes Old Order Amish, Old Order Mennonites, and River Brethren; contemporary Anabaptist traditions like Mennonite Church USA and Canada and the Church of the Brethren; and Hutterites and the Bruderhof. More evangelical-oriented Anabaptist denominations include the Brethren in Christ, the Mennonite Brethren, Evana Network, and more conservative groups like the Covenant Brethren Church. Mennonite Church USA is the most ethnically diverse denomination in North America, with active Black, Latino, Asian, and Native American membership (many with congregations that go back multiple generations). Many of the Anabaptist groups who derive from the sixteenth-century movements share organizations or participate in Mennonite World Conference. Finally, there are also neo-Anabaptists, an ever-growing category of Christians from Christian traditions and denominations around the globe who have been influenced by Anabaptism and have infused their own belief and practices with a hybrid faith, seeking to follow Jesus through fresh expressions of discipleship in our post-Christendom world.

Anabaptist emphases today

Contemporary Anabaptists often highlight three emphases to describe Anabaptist belief and practice today.[9] First is the commitment to follow and be disciples of Jesus and to make him the center of our faith. Next, they emphasize the fundamental belief that the church is a voluntary community where we share our lives together. Finally, they typically articulate some kind of ethic of peace or reconciliation that we practice in the face of violence and conflict.

Attempts to broadly categorize all Anabaptists have value, but also limits. Such attempts can overly homogenize a more diverse community. Or, we might find some shared convictions, but they are so watered down in order to keep a big tent for all Anabaptists that many Christians who would not consider themselves Anabaptist could also cosign the tradition. There is also a danger of ripping abstract ideals out of their social, cultural, and historical fabric, making Anabaptism a site for shallow appropriation. Early Anabaptists faced complex lived experiences and obstacles that they navigated as faithfully as they understood how to in that moment. However, had they lived under different circumstances, they would have adapted their Anabaptism in fresh ways, but not necessarily as universal positions good for all time and all places.

To be fair, the simplifications of the movement are helpful entry points for those outside the tradition who have been inspired by disembodied and overly idealistic norms that aren't quite what any Anabaptist community has lived out. For some of the historic Anabaptist denominations, the emphases have also ignited a renewed sense of the significance of their ecclesial communities. With these considerations in mind, I want to take a closer look at common Anabaptist emphases and how we might reinterpret or redefine them for today.

Following Jesus is central to faith

In my own experience, Anabaptists have helped me redefine what it ought to mean to be a Christian. Anabaptism emphasizes the particularity of Jesus' life and teachings and its import for following the way of Jesus. In Black evangelicalism, we certainly talked about becoming more Christlike. And Jesus was definitely at the center of our faith. However, the death of Jesus and our tradition's understanding of how that provided salvation and eternal life were usually the focus. Jesus was a present help in times of trouble we could talk to and rely on along our pilgrim's journey. In that way, Jesus was associated with a Westernized view of salvation (Jesus died for you so you can go to heaven) and was also immanent and with us amid daily life and hardship. I'm still aligned with that later point, but I've realized, through engaging the Anabaptist community, that I hadn't really taken seriously the full story of Jesus in Scripture as the pivotal story to which all of Scripture points and is fulfilled. Nor had I fully considered how my life ought to follow after, participate in, and make visible (through the empowerment of the Spirit) the story of Jesus in my life.

Academic Anabaptist theologies have sometimes failed to take seriously the spiritual and contemplative life of a follower of Jesus. But Anabaptism more broadly has a lot to offer mainstream Christian traditions, which are frequently squeezed and restrained by the norms of Christendom. One of the ways that immediately resonated with me was through the vocabulary of *Gelassenheit*, a German term that means yieldedness or resignation. For many early Anabaptists, one of humanity's central problems was how we often willingly chose what God does not desire for us. Yieldedness to God invites us to respond by getting out of the way. The Anabaptist concept of yieldedness remains relevant today: By surrendering our false self—with its wounds, apathy, hubris, and selfishness—and by restoring the image of God in all of us, we yield to God's activity in the present and God's dream for all creation, breaking cycles of sin and participating with God in God's new creation.

Following Jesus requires community

Engaging the Anabaptist community also shifted my understanding of the church. Growing up, I was taught that the church is not a building, it is the body of Christ. And in my experience, we often tried to live that out. My worshiping community was family. In many ways, they will always be family, even though Black evangelicalism doesn't align with my own theo-ethical (that is, ethics informed by theology rather than Western philosophy) convictions and practices. The faith I learned as a child had many individualistic dimensions. Salvation was only individual. We were accountable to an individualistic pietism (inner response to the Spirit) that didn't need to be discerned in community with others. We hadn't envisioned the church as a visible and embodied counter-politic and counter-witness to the death-dealing patterns and norms of empire. Anabaptism, as a discourse and a way of life, highlights the importance of the church seeking to be such a community. It has pushed my understanding of the priesthood of all believers (something I was also taught growing up) to another level.

Communal discernment is another significant ecclesial practice anchored in the Anabaptist tradition. Many Anabaptists hold a deep conviction that the Holy Spirit can speak through any individual in the community, not just its more educated, learned, older, wiser, literate, or respectable members. The Holy Spirit blows where it wants. Authors Stuart Murray and Sian Murray-Williams call this *multivoiced church*: "No longer is the Christian community largely passive, dependent on a few authorized ministers to preach, conduct worship, provide pastoral care, engage in mission, and exercise leadership," they write. "Men and women, young and old, educated and illiterate, rich and poor find their voices and discover their vocations."[10]

Communal discernment also means that an individual's interpretation of scripture or the Spirit's leading must be affirmed and tested by the community. We discern together, not as lone rangers. We all can think of times when people have claimed that God told them to do something that made you suspicious. Even pastors can believe or practice problematic things. Still, the Anabaptist community trusts that the Holy Spirit is leading them collectively through the activity of the Holy Spirit. This practice requires a sense of interconnectedness as the body of Christ that challenges the strongly self-reliant, independent, hyper-individualistic orientation of Western civilization.

Discernment in community also builds the communal muscles to have conversations about hard things, where people may disagree. This is multivoiced church with open dialogue and mutual exchange rather than monovoiced structures where only the pastor's perspective is heard. Anabaptist congregations that practice communal discernment still believe in pastoral guidance, but that ecclesial role is not a singular authoritative voice. I've seen communal discernment embodied in church life through talk-backs and working through social concerns. Talk-backs happen after sermons where people discern, and sometimes even disagree with, aspects of the sermon as they work through their understanding of God's call on their lives together. Working through social concerns through communal discernment happens when the church must respond to an urgent or contemporary reality affecting their community or neighbors. Congregations might come to shift their views on women's roles in the church, how to respond faithfully to LGBTQ neighbors or members, or how to show up in a neighborhood racial justice uprising. The point is that the congregation, in both urgency and patience, dialogues vulnerably together, seeking God's desire for us. The end is consensus, where all members either agree or, if they disagree, are willing to support the direction of the body.

The Brethren, or Dunkers, offer a distinct contribution to conversations about the spiritual and religious life of followers of Jesus within Anabaptism. The Church of the Brethren officially describe themselves as Anabaptist and Radical Pietist. The Pietist tradition pushed believers away from thinking of faith as primarily intellectual assent and toward personal devotion to God, stressing the importance of internal religious experiences leading to holy life. Radical pietism called for a full break from Christendom churches. For these Anabaptists, internal change resulted in an external impulse to follow Jesus as the early church did.

Today, not all Anabaptists are pietists. However, for the Brethren, the common and communal life is held in tension with individual conscience, personal inner experience with God, and at times a yieldedness to follow God by acting out of step with the community when one believes God is leading otherwise. Together, communal discernment and radical pietism create a healthy paradox for being led by the Spirit. Many mainstream Christians practice a general form of pietism that leads to hyper-individualistic understandings of how to follow God. Yieldedness through communal discernment is swapped out for merely yielding to clergy.

Peace (or reconciliation) is how we participate in God's work

Anabaptism hosts an ever-evolving conversation on matters of peace and violence. There is no one way that Anabaptists have expressed or understood their conviction around peace and violence. Overall, the trajectory has moved from more passive to more active understandings of peace, but even today the lived peace theology of Anabaptists varies quite a bit. In the sixteenth century, some Anabaptists saw violent revolution as a viable option, though most had broadly rejected it by 1535. The overarching Anabaptist tradition has centered some form of peace ethic as essential for faithful Christian witness.

Early on, language like "defenselessness" and rejecting "the Sword" gave way to "enemy love" and "nonresistance." These terms were grounded in language from the Sermon on the Mount. Along with that came the language of "the way of the cross." In the eighteenth and nineteenth centuries, Anabaptists incorporated nonconformity and separation from the world, which had a lot to do with how they lived by a different ethic concerning violence, along with other concerns. In the early twentieth century, US Anabaptism was influenced by American social gospel pacifism. Terms like "pacifism," "nonresistance," and a "peace witness" became significant. Conscientious objection in response to military inscription was the primary focus. But overall, Anabaptist conceptions around peace and violence were still very passive.

The 1950s and '60s Civil Rights Movement shifted some paradigms. The visibility of Dr. King and many Black Christians, who were implementing nonviolent action and nonviolent resistance, provided a different lens for a peace ethic. "Peacemaking" and "peace and justice" became more prominent, and for some, language evolved further into "peacebuilding," "a just peace," "conflict transformation," "transformative peace," or sometimes simply "reconciliation." In all, the changing sociopolitical contexts, dialogue partners, biblical and theological interpretations, and lived experiences of Anabaptists themselves have provided a dynamic, improvisational, and evolving framework around its peace witness. Today some talk about peacemaking in robust ways that address the systemic violence embedded in society in ways that seem very similar to how some Black Christians might talk about justice and liberation as a Christian ethic, orienting how one is discipled to respond to systemic oppression and injustice.

Redefining Anabaptism

The third emphasis on peace is typically seen as one of if not *the* most distinctive elements of Anabaptism. But even with the shifting language and practice around peace, I believe, perhaps controversially, that Anabaptism should not be first and foremost understood as a "peace church" tradition but as an anti-Christendom tradition. The language of "peace church" doesn't work for all Anabaptists, especially Western European and white settler North American Anabaptists. In some ways the inaccuracy of the label is obvious, yet it has frequently been understated among many white Anabaptists in preference for fronting pacifism as its most defining feature. Anabaptists rejected Christendom's state-church fusion, opted out of the civic practice of infant baptism, argued for a needed distinction between church and the broader Christendom society, increasingly adopted nonviolence while denouncing the state's use of the sword, insisted on a free church model with ecclesial autonomy from the authorities (including voluntary rather than mandatory civic enrollment into the church), made Jesus' way their political priority against civil expectations, and understood enemy love and centering the poor as a new organizing principle for the church. Anabaptists centered their tradition's identity in martyrdom precisely because they so subversively rejected, renounced, and resisted the Christendom arrangements of their day as part of their discipleship to Jesus, and it led to thousands of executions as part of the inevitable consequences that come with following Jesus.

Today, Anabaptists remain mindful of the context and critique of Constantine and Christendom, as well as the Catholic and Protestant arrangements that practiced Christendom. Christendom is almost never thought to be a positive characteristic among Anabaptists (unless one has deeply assimilated into mainstream thought and is only loosely connected to the tradition's stories and conversations). Even the complex ways that various peace and violence positions among Anabaptists have been held can all be related to the various ways they have interpreted them in relation to Christendom norms.[11] Understanding the Anabaptist story requires us to take its anti-Christendom orientation seriously. Fronting Anabaptism's anti-Christendom orientation, and even understanding its convictions on peace and violence from within that disposition, is a more helpful way for white settler Anabaptists in North America to reckon with their past and anchor themselves as they confront today's white Christian nationalist, hyper-militarized, and neo-liberalist society.

I also want to emphasize one aspect of sixteenth-century Anabaptism that has been domesticated in many North American contexts but should have significant importance for today. Along with an anti-Christendom proclivity, early Anabaptists practiced a liberationist ecclesiology. Latin American liberation theology, especially as framed by Gustavo Gutiérrez in the twentieth century, reckons with the pervasive and persistent critique of economic stratification, exploitation, and hoarding wealth within the Jesus stories. Jesus' life and teachings demonstrate a commitment to the poor, and call us to join and live in solidarity with the poor and those who are suffering. Gutiérrez's theological framework may best be summed up as God's "preferential option for the poor."[12] The church is called to embody God's mission priority to the poor, for whom God prefers to bring divine intervention.

In varying ways, the early Anabaptists responded to the exploitation and poverty conditions many folks were struggling to survive. These material concerns led some Anabaptists to participate in the Poor Peasants' uprisings and others the Münster Rebellion. The communities that began with commitments to peace and nonviolence also took seriously the practice of economic sharing, while some convicted by the Acts model of common life renounced private ownership and lived from a common purse. Early Anabaptism embodied a sixteenth-century liberationist ecclesiology.

Today, it is very common for North American Anabaptists to talk about simple living as their economic practice. "We live simply so others can simply live" is a common saying. This, to me, appears to be a significant dilution of a much stronger economic critique early Anabaptists held to, and how they mutually shared resources in response. As I shared before, in my early years among the Anabaptists, I found out very quickly that many white "cradle" Anabaptists were quite wealthy, despite how simply some might dress. Folks drove expensive cars, took frequent vacations around the globe, and had significant property and investments, tallying up to a lot of wealth that was being passed from generation to generation. In rural central Pennsylvania, many of the BIC church buildings I encountered after college were small megachurches with fancy coffee shops, mall-like foyers, and all the conveniences one might hope for within their facilities. My point isn't to shame any individuals or congregations for their choices. But when I saw the fancy cars outside in the church parking lot, all I could think was, I wish I could have had some of this "simple living" growing up.

The greater concern, however, is that our society is built on stolen land and stolen labor. Millions of Black and Native American communities are still trying to survive. A robust recovery of a liberationist ecclesiology could orient Anabaptist and other worshiping communities to resist, provide mutual aid, and be a prophetic voice in response to the massive portion of our society who lives under or near the poverty line or are working-class folks living paycheck to paycheck under the constraints of a capitalist system whose policies favor the wealthy. Some Anabaptist congregations still allow this heritage to shape their collective practices. Hopefully, moving away from merely simple dress and other overly simplistic symbols of wealth and poverty can inspire all Anabaptists to practice solidarity with, and as, the poor in our congregations today.

The radical discipleship stream of Anabaptism

Anabaptist plurality continues. Many mainstream Anabaptists functionally practice a passive peace witness in contrast to the radical discipleship stream of Anabaptism. "Radical" has two useful meanings for us. First, there is the original meaning of the word: getting to the root of something. The radical discipleship Anabaptist stream invites the church to return to the root of our faith—the way of Jesus Christ—and be willing to follow him fully in every area of life, including cultural nonconformity, nonviolent resistance, and struggling for justice as a counter-witness within our society.

The word "radical" also suggests that as followers of Jesus, we are willing to make a radical or dramatic break with the norms and patterns of society, even to the point of suffering the consequences of faithfully and fully taking up the way of Jesus. In this way, the radical discipleship stream within mainstream Anabaptism itself is a renewal movement and witness to the complacent and too well-adjusted and assimilated lives within the comforts of North American life. Radical discipleship is engaged locally, through community, embodying the peacemaking of Jesus, and seeking the shalom of our world in concrete ways. It differentiates our present political and economic systems from the kingdom of God, but it also recognizes that the differences operate on a spectrum, with some societies being more unjust or just than others. This means that we have the opportunity to love our neighbors and world as peacemakers who must challenge our society to always take another step in the direction toward God's shalom. And sometimes the whirlwind of God allows for big transformative change to happen.

When I think about what that looks like, I think about communities of disciples who grapple with how to live faithfully in a world shaped by white supremacy and colonial conquest, such as by discerning how Jesus' teachings and way relate to our pervasive poverty and policies that facilitate the exploitation of laborers, by speaking truthfully about the evils of our military and prison industrial complexes, and by becoming a witness to our ecological crisis through sustainable communities while resisting corporations and governments that prioritize profits over people and our planet. The anti-Christendom sentiment in Anabaptism leads the radical discipleship tradition to resist white Christian nationalism's influence over church and society. I'm grateful for those I've met in these waters who challenge me to follow Jesus in ways that I might not be inclined to but that are aligned with God's dream for us and creation. Here, too, we need yieldedness to God.

The language of "third way" is common to modern Anabaptism, but it is used differently by mainstream Anabaptists and those in the radical discipleship stream. A "third way" implies taking another way forward than the two prevailing options. Many Anabaptists talk about following Jesus as their politics, but what that means often varies dramatically. In the United States, Anabaptists love to say, "We don't follow the donkey or an elephant, we follow the way of the Lamb." This is a healthy way of grounding our witness without becoming ideological puppets to political partisanship. We are called to a third way in response to the sociopolitical options available to us.

Often, mainstream Anabaptists frame this third way as being neither left nor right politically. This can look like distancing the life of the church from controversial political and social matters where people must take the risk of taking sides on urgent matters. That is, for mainstream Anabaptists, the third way is understood often as a middle or centrist way forward. They believe they are called to not take sides, thereby breaking the binary options presented to us.

However, if third way language is to be useful, it should be tied more intimately with the Jesus story. In his writings on the third way, theologian Walter Wink directs Christians to follow Jesus in ways that reject our fight-or-flight impulse.[13] In response to oppression, there are options other than violent uprisings or passively going along with the system. The way of Jesus shows us how to struggle against the powers, but doing so through nonviolent resistance, even to the point of death. This better reflects the story of Jesus, who didn't merely resist the way of the freedom fighters seeking God's liberation and that of the Sadducees or Herodians (the establishment) but entered into the conflicts of the day by standing in solidarity with the poor, the Samaritans, vulnerable women, the sick, and those on the margins of society. This was not centrism.

Jesus confronted many authorities and the establishment of his time that were perpetuating harm. Jesus was not a violent revolutionary, yet even his disciples, up until their encounter with the soldiers in the garden of Gethsemane, mistook his nonviolent messianic witness with that of the "Barabbas way." Jesus was interchangeable with his contemporary Barabbas, a violent revolutionary, because of his definitive solidarity and commitment to those at the bottom. The third way is not an invitation to adopt political partisanship coupled with pacifism. It is a call to discern the messiness of actually following Jesus, and the political priorities of God's upside-down reign, in ways that don't conflate Barabbas (a revolutionary) and Herod (an imperial puppet) as though they are just two sides of the same coin. The risk of faith is to follow, encounter, and make visible the life of Jesus in our lives, as best as we can discern in community with others, and as faithfully as we can comprehend our vocation, in ways that sometimes may get mistakenly identified as partisanship when it is in fact a counter-politic.

Why Anabaptism matters today

Over many centuries, and in different geographies, Anabaptism has repeatedly invited its own communities, and those beyond them, to take the life and teachings of Jesus seriously, to discern how we must seek after God's reign together as we grapple with how we live well in a society filled with violence, coercive religious power, and economic exploitation. Sometimes Anabaptist communities' responsiveness to the challenges they faced have reminded us of Jesus' story expressed through a mobilized community. Anabaptists have also at times turned their eyes away from the violation of others, primarily consumed in their own lives without attention to "those whose backs are against the wall." Yet those committed to the Anabaptist tradition in North America have largely held to their anti-Christendom legacy, which is no insignificant matter given the challenges the twenty-first-century church must confront.

Behind many of the United States' biggest social concerns stands white mainstream Christianity impeding justice and righteousness from rolling down like waters. When it comes to racism, anti-immigrant xenophobia, and Islamophobia, white mainstream Christianity too often stands for exclusion, supremacy, and pushing dangerous stereotypes. In response to the yearly death toll of forty thousand people—including little children in school classrooms—through gun violence, many white Christians still support unrestricted gun access, refusing even to ask their elected officials to implement universal background checks. I could say similar things about the death penalty, fiscal policies and tax rates that favor the wealthy, unjust distribution of funds for public education, lack of access to quality, preventative, and universal healthcare, or how we respond to our global ecological crisis. Or mass incarceration and unjust policing systems or our military industrial complex, which is funded by billions of tax dollars. Or the fascist elimination of truthfulness about our nation's history of genocide, displacement, slavery, and racialized oppression.

The problem is not merely that many mainstream American Christians have a mangled Christian witness. So many mainstream Christians in general, and white Christians in particular, have been formed to conceive of the settler geopolitical experiment called the United States as a property they are entitled to and ought to dominate. Mainstream white Christian political action is frequently driven by the narrative that America is a (white) Christian nation, which liberals, progressives, people of color, LGBTQ groups, and secular-minded folks have taken away, and white Christians need to regain control so they can make America great again. Their Christianity licenses them to "lord it over" others (Matthew 20:20–28). A Christendom mindset, even though formal Christendom no longer exists, is still very present in mainstream Christianity. And this contributes to the white Christian nationalism we see today.

Most white Christian nationalists genuinely seem to have trouble imagining that there might be a more faithful way to be Christian than dominating and coercively imposing one's religious convictions onto others. While democracy—or in America's case, a very flawed and barely democratic republic—is limited, flawed, and imperfect, and shouldn't be conflated with God's reign, I deeply believe that it provides a great opportunity for Christians to bear witness to the way of Jesus in the public square. In the United States, Christians are still in the majority. This should never have been an invitation to pursue a Christendom society. Rather, it is an opportunity to practice the basics of Christian discipleship. Radical discipleship invites us into a better way. It reminds us of Jesus' call to love our neighbors (whether metaphorical Samaritans or our enemies) and to practice mutuality through giving, receiving, and sharing with others. As we do so, we get to practice being slow to speak and quick to listen so that we are more committed to understanding others than merely being understood.

Christians who are a majority or a significant influence in society have a holy option to empty ourselves by not just taking on the form of a human but to enter into solidarity with the vulnerable enslaved person (Philippians 2:5–11). Anabaptists, while not perfect, have understood that Jesus invites us to practice servanthood rather than "lording it over" others. The memory of thousands of Christian martyrs living the truth of Jesus' story, at the hands of Catholics and Protestants on the underside of Christendom, is a story that, along with many other global stories, can invite us into new beliefs, scriptural interpretations, and ecclesial practices with the capacity of cultivating lives that follow, participate in, and make visible the life of Jesus for our watching neighbors.

Initially, Anabaptists did not call themselves Anabaptists. It was a pejorative and damning word. To be called an Anabaptist was another way of calling someone a heretic worthy of execution! Early in the first millennium, Augustine and many other Christians damned the North African Donatists as heretics for rebaptizing members who had been baptized by clergy whom the Donatists saw as failing morally. The "Anabaptist" label was one of many stigmatizing names that made Protestant and Catholic Reformers feel justified for the torture, executions, and persecution of early Anabaptists. Today, the word has been reclaimed as a badge of honor, sparking more positive conversation about Anabaptists' place in church history. You get a very different account when the martyr speaks, and not just the persecutor.

Anabaptism forces us to grapple with what a credible and faithful ecclesial witness looks like in society, especially while under the control and domination of other Christians behaving badly while hiding behind nuanced and eloquent doctrinal systems and confessionals. When the word "Christian" becomes so compromised that it has no relation to the birth, life, teachings, death, and resurrection of Jesus, what will worshiping communities do? Given the opportunity, will Christians become martyrs? By this, I don't mean whether Christians will die for their faith, though Jesus named martyrdom a risk to consider before genuinely following after him. No, I mean "martyr" in the original meaning of the word. Martyr means "witness." Across the centuries, Christians have been called martyrs because they fully bore witness to the Jesus story in their lives as others watched on. They became strange public spectacles as their lives provided glimpses of the Jesus story by following his way and yielding to the Spirit.

Anabaptism's gift, I believe, is that with all the ugliness and horror in church history, within the belly of the beast, and on the underside of empire, communities embodied a counter-witness to Christendom as they challenged the socioeconomic exploitation in their society, engaged in renewed scriptural reasoning together, and trusted that somehow, they might not just preach the gospel but embody it for their times.

– FOUR –

Has Anabaptism Failed in North America?

"Where have you Mennonites been?" Rev. Dr. Martin Luther King Jr. asked a white Mennonite leader in 1959.[1] Bro. Martin was aware of the Anabaptists' longstanding peace commitments and their important legacy within church history. And so, if Anabaptism was truly a radical tradition practicing the way of the cross, then he rightfully needed to inquire why they weren't present in the Civil Rights Movement. King believed and articulated a public theology rooted in the life of Jesus. Loving enemies, practicing forgiveness, speaking truth, as Jesus taught, were inescapably present through King's leadership in the Civil Rights Movement.[2] Brother Martin believed that this was how Jesus taught us to fight injustice. Yet in the early years of the movement this is exactly where many white Anabaptists and Dr. King parted ways.

Anabaptists have not had one consistent peace ethic from the sixteenth century to the present. They have evolved and adapted over time. In the mid-twentieth century, most North American Anabaptists believed that they were called to practice "nonresistance," drawing from the Sermon on the Mount. Many Anabaptists admired the nonviolent action embodied in the Civil Rights Movement but also thought that using nonviolence disruptively through protest was "coercive" and contradicted the teaching of Jesus. Over time, through the external witness of the Black freedom struggle and the internal prophetic witness within Anabaptist churches, the Civil Rights Movement significantly reformed the Anabaptist peace ethic and practice.[3]

White North American Anabaptism avoided the most egregious stories and patterns of antiblack oppression, like lynching people of African descent, but its on-the-ground witness in the early and mid-twentieth century was still frequently normed by racial segregationist practices, antiblack bias, and assimilation into white dominant cultural mindsets.[4] Too often, white Anabaptists sought to justify segregated worship rather than repent and do better through faithful Christian reasoning. However, by the end of the Movement, many white Anabaptists increasingly articulated and practiced a more radical peace witness while employing a more robust and careful reading of scripture that began to resist North American Mennonite political quietism.

To the degree that white Anabaptists were willing to vulnerably observe, listen, and reckon with the Black freedom struggle taking place, it led to the increased liberation of twentieth-century Anabaptism. Prior to that moment, white North American Anabaptism probably would not have been inclined to think of its tradition as *needing* to learn from Black Christians. White Anabaptists were the watching world, and Black Christians and their allies bore witness to God's reign through a wide range of nonviolent actions, enemy love, and truth-telling strategies and tactics that challenged and confronted Jim Crow *as* followers of Jesus.

I don't believe the radical discipleship stream within the Anabaptist tradition would be as robust as it is today without this courageous influence of so many Black Christians and others resisting oppression. Today, most North American Anabaptist theologians and ethicists typically describe their peace ethic in active terms, employing language like "peacemaking," "peace and justice," and "nonviolent resistance." Or they even use the word "pacifism" in more radical ways beyond early twentieth-century white liberal constraints. This significant transformation leaves open the question, What might happen if this posture of learning from their oppressed siblings in other ecclesial traditions was less episodic but was practiced as a consistent way of life?

One way to distinguish the failures and areas where North American Anabaptists need the most help is to evaluate how white Anabaptists responded to Western colonial conquest. Both are about five centuries old. Colonial conquest has always been part of Anabaptism's world, thus allowing us to see its strengths and weaknesses. Anabaptism growing under European Christendom is one thing; Anabaptism growing in North America is something else. Anabaptism isn't a fixed confession and practice of faith to be universally regurgitated for all time, for all people, regardless of context. As members of a living faith, Anabaptists should reflect an openness to yield to whatever God might be up to. And in light of the white

Anabaptist witness in North America, there are present strongholds that must die and be reborn by living in vulnerable solidarity and receiving wisdom from those who have lived with a white supremacist boot on their neck.

While Anabaptism emerged as an anti-Christendom ecclesial movement from within—and below—Western Europe, the same cannot be said of its witness in North America. Anabaptism still has many important gifts to offer the broader church today. Yet it remains complicit in white supremacy. I invite white North American Anabaptists, and other white mainstream Christians, to seek Jesus with bold curiosity. You, too, must be eager to become the student and not always the teacher in navigating white supremacist colonial settlerism and antiblack oppression in this land. Brother Martin's question still echoes today: "Where have you Anabaptists been?"

Has Anabaptism failed in North America?

About a decade ago, I was asked to present a workshop at a conference for Anabaptists. The neo-Anabaptist organizers were skeptical about my chosen workshop title—"Has Anabaptism Failed in North America?"—and they attempted to persuade me in a different direction. To the organizers' surprise, the conference room ended up with standing room only. Many of the participants were hungry to grapple with the shortcomings of Anabaptism.

During the session, I simply told stories. More specifically, I told stories about how white Anabaptists tell stories. I examined how Anabaptists frequently tell church history, as well as their own story. One of the things that I appreciate about Anabaptism, I shared, is how it holds discipleship in the way of Jesus together with the messiness of church history. Anabaptism emphasizes the need to take Jesus seriously in belief and practice by not seeking the easy out or taking detours whenever Jesus' life and teachings challenge us to break with societal norms. This is especially the case for renouncing the urge to "lord it over others" and instead practice the teachings of the Sermon on the Mount, like loving enemies, practicing forgiveness, speaking truthfully, and walking the narrow Way.

And just as importantly, as an anti-Christendom tradition, Anabaptists think about *how* church history has unfolded. Thinking about church history is one way that it expresses its anti-Christendom stance. I rarely encounter Anabaptists who don't have a hot take on Western Christianity within church history. Whereas many white evangelicals are unfamiliar with Constantine, many Anabaptists have inherited an interpretation of the meaning of his name. "Constantine" signifies something bigger than Constantine the human figure. Similarly, whereas most Protestants see the sixteenth-century reformers as the heroes of Western Christianity, Anabaptists are more critical, especially regarding where Anabaptists fit into that story.

In most North American Anabaptist communities I have encountered, they intentionally engage church history, combining scriptural reasoning and practical lived discipleship. For example, many Anabaptists in North America love to talk about the early church. Usually, they talk about how Christians in the first three centuries were persecuted and marginalized and had no power. It took courage and faith to be Christian. And they had no expectation that the state could or would support their way of life or kingdom pursuits. Instead, the early Christians embraced martyrdom and the third baptism—execution by drowning. In embracing the way of the cross, the church persisted and grew, even under the worst of conditions.

And then Anabaptists talk about Constantine and how he ended Christian persecution. But he didn't stop there. He poured money into the church. He gave the church worldly respect. And he gave the church worldly power through the might of the empire. And it is here, when the sword and the church are brought together, that the faithful witness of the church was marred. Christianity got into bed with empire. It went from being a prophet of the kingdom to a puppet of the empire. Love of neighbor was swiftly discarded for a more practical ethic of upkeeping the political life of the state. A church that was once on the margins had become the center, had become the persecutor of other minorities, and now wielded the power over society. A church went from a people to a building and institution. Mission was out "there" beyond the boundaries of Christendom. Orthodoxy (right beliefs) overtook orthopraxy (right behavior or practices) rooted in the story of Jesus. And because the emperor identified with Christianity, moving up the political ladder was tied to becoming Christian. So people flooded into the church. It took courage to remain a pagan. Converting to Christianity became the path of least resistance.

One of the notable dimensions of everyday Anabaptist accounts of church history is the importance of power dynamics. There is before and after Constantine, and that is a way of talking about the church under dominating forces and the church colluding with top-down, coercive, imperial power.

Now, most Anabaptists don't know much about medieval history, so they skip over that. But then comes the Reformation. Once again, everyday Anabaptists will talk about how the Reformation unveiled the power dynamics at work. The Catholics, Lutherans, and Reformed authorities were magisterial, top-down, coercive leaders who took for granted the marriage of church and state. These groups fought quite a bit as well, but the one thing they could agree on was disdain for the heretic rebaptizers and the need to persecute them.

The Anabaptists broke from the centuries-long marriage between the church and the state. They rejected infant baptism, using the sword, taking oaths, and any other imperially manipulated practice they believed had been adjusted doctrinally to be practical for political governance of society. They recentered the life and teachings of Jesus, reading scripture through the lens of the Jesus story. This Jesus-centered community focused on what it meant to live within Jesus' messianic reign. Thousands were tortured and executed. The Anabaptists sought to follow Jesus faithfully while the state had sought their extinction.

This overview might not have the nuance of a historian like Peter Brown. But for an ordinary understanding of church history by folks in the pews, these kinds of hot takes are not bad. These are important lessons, and any oversimplifications are doing legitimate work to point to a greater reality. And contemporary Anabaptists, having long been influenced by the thousands of persecution narratives in *Martyrs Mirror*,[5] are inclined to think about the early church, and other Christians who were persecuted, as part of a broader pattern and trajectory while exposing the church's complicity with the state. As I often tease Anabaptists, they are good at making other Christian traditions feel bad for the ways their traditions participated in Constantinian and Reformation Christianity through top-down, coercive, state-enforced Christianity.

Yet precisely after this portion of history my ears perk up. Having covered a millennium and a half of church history, how do white North American Anabaptists tell the rest of their story?

It's a very a different tale. I hear about European Anabaptists "arriving" in Pennsylvania. I hear about William Penn welcoming them in and providing land for them. There are stories about Germantown. Next thing I know I'm hearing about church splits and who is a descendant of whom. Lots of last names. That is very important. There are horses and buggies, shoofly pie, beards, and recipe books. And all those things are incredibly important cultural texture for understanding a people group. But I can't help but notice that this type of history, while important, does not do one of the main things that was done in rehearsals of earlier church history: scrutinize power. This storytelling seems to erase or distract attention from how sociopolitical power was shaping white Anabaptist experiences as they came to North America.

Why does the white North American Anabaptist church history narrative suddenly evade the power dynamics at work? I believe a large part of this has to do with European Anabaptist assimilation into the unfolding white supremacist and capitalist system. European Anabaptists weren't merely "welcomed" here—they came as colonial settlers to someone else's land. The land that they were "given" or bought for cents on the acre was stolen from Indigenous tribes. The land wasn't theirs to receive. And while white Anabaptists were not the ones physically displacing Native Americans, they sure did claim those lands before the blood that was spilt on them had fully dried.[6] In time, many white Anabaptists passed on intergenerational wealth from thriving businesses and farms that contemporary descendants and networks still benefit from today.

Anabaptist refugees and immigrants to North America flourished economically while espousing an attitude of being "the quiet in the land"—all within the antiblack chattel slavery economy that made the colonies, and then the United States, one of the wealthiest nations in the world. It is true that most white Anabaptist communities renounced the practice of slavery within their communities. To that, I often say that you don't get a cookie for *not* enslaving my ancestors. However when it came to the untold suffering, torment, and death of the deadly Middle Passage, of the auction block, of the murderous whip in the fields, of being branded like cattle, of the family members ripped apart to never be seen again, of the constant rape with no place to turn for protection, of constant terror and humiliation while being treated as nothing more than an expendable tool for white people's prosperity, how did white Anabaptists follow Jesus into this horror? They did not choose solidarity with their darker siblings. They did not share in our sufferings. And they did not empty themselves taking on the form of a slave (Philippians 2:7). Instead, there was political quietism and disregard from the late seventeenth century, when the first Anabaptists came to North America, until the Civil Rights Movement, when white North American Anabaptists slowly began returning to the roots of Christian discipleship.

I've been told that part of the reason there was such entrenched political quietism toward the enslavement of Black people, and then to Jim and Jane Crow white supremacy, is because Mennonites at the time didn't see Christian life implied through outwardly political life. The church was its own little polis before a watching world. Yet in the early and mid-twentieth century, many white North American Anabaptists found the political will to lobby the government against their conscription into war. When their own lives stood to be directly affected, they quickly became political lobbyists. This seems like a hierarchical system that valued some lives (their own white Mennonite lives) more than Black ones. And the truth is that even as white Anabaptists interpreted themselves as practicing nonconformity in North America in the early twentieth century, they had deeply internalized and adopted so much of white dominant culture. The first half of the twentieth century was marked by "deliberate segregation, overt participation in the racial order, and initial resistance to change."[7] For Mennonites, the Jim and Jane Crow era involved significant conformity to the antiblack prejudices and patterns of dominant culture.

This is certainly not the whole story of North American Anabaptism. Even so, when it came to being "brethren" with Native Americans and Black Americans experiencing the full force of white supremacist settler colonial conquest, white Anabaptism rarely embodied the Jesus story for their neighbors or made God's reign manifest. Many Anabaptists today are quick to teach that peace is not the absence of violence, it is the positive presence of God's shalom characterized by justice, peace, righteousness, joy, security, and interdependent thriving, with God holding it all together. If that is correct, which I believe it is, then what would it look like for Anabaptism to become a shalom church?

Toward a shalom church

If Anabaptists desire to be a peace church in the fullest sense, then they must not just intellectually articulate a broadened understanding of peace, but pursue it while healing their social imagination so they are capable of conceiving God's shalom in creation. The Old Testament is filled with glimpses of shalom that should be central for any Anabaptist discourse around peace in communities ravaged by colonial conquest and white supremacy. Isaiah's vision of shalom is particularly helpful.

For I am about to create new heavens
    and a new earth;
the former things shall not be remembered
    or come to mind.
But be glad and rejoice forever
    in what I am creating,
for I am about to create Jerusalem as a joy
    and its people as a delight.
I will rejoice in Jerusalem
    and delight in my people;
no more shall the sound of weeping be heard in it
    or the cry of distress.
No more shall there be in it
    an infant that lives but a few days
    or an old person who does not live out a lifetime,
for one who dies at a hundred years will be considered a youth,
    and one who falls short of a hundred will be considered
        accursed.
They shall build houses and inhabit them;
    they shall plant vineyards and eat their fruit.
They shall not build and another inhabit;
    they shall not plant and another eat,
for like the days of a tree shall the days of my people be,
    and my chosen shall long enjoy the work of their hands.
They shall not labor in vain
    or bear children for calamity,
for they shall be offspring blessed by the LORD—
    and their descendants as well.
Before they call I will answer,
    while they are yet speaking I will hear.
The wolf and the lamb shall feed together;
    the lion shall eat straw like the ox,
    but the serpent—its food shall be dust!
They shall not hurt or destroy
    on all my holy mountain,
        says the LORD. (Isaiah 65:17–25)

This text appears in the part of Isaiah written after the people of Israel return home after generations of exile in Babylon. Their nearly unspeakable yearning for Jerusalem has come to pass. Unfortunately, the reality on the ground is far from God's restoration. They are trying to rebuild Jerusalem. The people are in conflict, and some are even oppressing and exploiting others. Yet Isaiah stretches their eschatological imaginations through a prophetic and poetic vision of shalom that is coming but is not yet reality. Joy and gladness are characteristic of the people; holistic communal well-being practices celebration, praise, humor, and embodied movement like dancing.

One could write a whole book on Isaiah 65:17–25 alone, so I will highlight a few characteristics that should be intrinsic to the hopes and aspirations of any "peace" church. Isaiah begins by saying that God will create new heavens and a new earth. This is a radical transfiguration of everything, from our material existence to the cosmos. There will be no more weeping and crying, and instead people will live long lives. While longevity of life itself is important, length of years also implies people's well-being and a quality of life. I'm particularly struck by the vision of a society where everyone builds and lives in their own homes; they labor and plant fruit and are able to eat that fruit. The text explicitly anticipates an end to living as exploited people to the advantage of others.

Today, we live in a society built on stolen land and stolen labor. Our unregulated capitalist system permits and encourages the exploitation and plunder of people and our planet so long as it yields greater profits. But Isaiah prophesies that people will no longer bear children into a world of such horror. The passage enfolds more and more of creation into this vision, all held together by a present, attentive, and responsive God.

Before we can even call out, God responds, because heaven and earth have been healed, and the gap we often experience with our transcendent God will be bridged with a renewed intimacy. As the poetic vision wraps up in verse 25, even the wolf and the lamb, the lion and the ox, are living in harmony. This is important. This is not just a healing of human relationships, or relationships between God and people—all of creation (animals and our planet are vital) intertwines into one web of harmony, wholeness, and inseparable thriving. This peace extinguishes violence and harm.

In English translations of the New Testament, Jesus sometimes uses the word "peace," which translates a Greek word trying to signify God's shalom as described in our sacred scriptures. Peace can be applied in a variety of ways, but especially in the past several decades, many within the broad Anabaptist tradition have embraced the idea that peace should not be reduced to not committing individual, physical acts of violence. If mainstream Anabaptists were to embrace God's shalom in Isaiah as the paradigm vision that both stands in judgment of our present societies and propels us to struggle in our present toward an inbreaking future, it might lead white Anabaptists toward a true peace movement in North America.

This kind of radical discipleship in the way of Jesus would form followers of Jesus who are attentive to the suffering, plunder, material conditions of people, who learn how to live in harmony with their ecological watersheds, and who struggle against any horrors that diminish human well-being, joy, intimacy with God, and our interconnectedness as beloved community in creation. While some white Anabaptist scholars and pastors have begun to talk this way, my experience is that the normative beliefs and practices of ordinary white Anabaptists are typically far from this. Many are still practicing nonresistance. Any peace ethic grounded in the life of the Messiah must be anchored by a vision of shalom.

Grappling with whiteness

A further challenge for white Anabaptists is the need to collectively grapple with what it means to be white. Whiteness ought not be conflated with merely being of European descent or lacking melanin. Whiteness comes through racialized formation into identity, social imagination, and a way of being. It includes unexamined "universal" norms and standards. It is the conscious or unconscious hierarchical evaluation of human worth based on the logics and categories of race, it is the "proper" or "civil" way of talking, walking, dressing, interacting, inhabiting space, and just being. It is alignment with the social and economic order. It is the sense that your way is the right way, and that the worlds of others ought to rightly align with your truth and ethics.

Whiteness is imagining diverse ethical positions of people groups from around the world as "backward" or "forward" thinking as though some people are stuck in time. It is an overconfidence in one's own objectivity, and that one's finite and limited knowledge and experience is not merely a fragment but contains the whole picture. And it is organizing a society (including its myths, government, policies, institutions, production of knowledge, geographic boundaries, and access to opportunities) in such ways that overwhelming advantage people recognized to be white while most explicitly disadvantaging Black and Native American neighborhoods and communities.

White Mennonites and white Brethren communities have a complicated relationship with whiteness. On one hand, white Anabaptists from the historic denominations have sometimes transgressed what it means to be properly white. Some Anabaptists have (and some still do) refer to the broader world as "the English," rejecting the norm of white Anglo-Saxon Protestant identity and standards. Some have intentionally chosen nonconformity with dominant culture. They did so not because they were stuck in time but because they rejected mainstream forms of "progress" as better for human community. Most white Anabaptists have rejected at least parts of American nationalism and patriotism in their Christian faith and worship. And strangely, "ethnic Mennonite" and "ethnic Brethren" identity (as racialized and problematic as these terms are) have partly functioned to retain a distinct identity and sense of peoplehood. This is different from how whiteness claims a universal identity, asserting white culture and white people as the normative standard for humanity.

However, Anabaptist "ethnic" identities are also explicitly white supremacist. One of my friends from Philadelphia once clarified to me, "I'm not Mennonite, I'm an urban Anabaptist." Though he was part of a Mennonite congregation, as a Black Puerto Rican he did not find a sense of belonging or identity with the label "Mennonite." In contrast, I've also overheard white people raised in the Mennonite Church identify themself as "Mennonite" though they no longer identify as Christian nor participate in the church. On another occasion I overheard a "cradle" Mennonite from Canada say, "I'm not white, I'm Mennonite." On the spectrum between my Philly friend and these white Mennonites is the messy politics of racial belonging, identity, and marginalization within the church.

One of the best book to see this messy politics at work is Felipe Hinojosa's *Latino Mennonites: Civil Rights, Faith and Evangelical Culture*. He tells the story of how Latino

Mennonites fought alongside Black Mennonites for their place in the Mennonite Church, how they participated in Civil Rights, and how they forged their unique sense of identity. "It is often in the spaces between belonging and exclusion where the politics of religious life compel us to work for what is possible," writes Hinojosa.[8] A Brethren leader once shared with me that saying "Brethren" is another way of saying "white." This language, which isn't limited to white "cradle" Brethren, doesn't appear racial on the surface but still recenters whiteness through deceptive terminology.

On multiple occasions I've heard popular white neo-Anabaptists promote themselves as having moved beyond the racial and ethnic obstacles that trip up their historic Anabaptist denominational friends. Neo-Anabaptists embrace Anabaptist beliefs and practice in some form but engage those convictions outside of historic Anabaptist traditions and communities. It is a growing stream of Anabaptism, especially because of its post-Christendom implications. Ironically, I've found many of these communities to be more entrenched in the logics of white supremacy, not less. Many neo-Anabaptists have fled conservative evangelical spaces, claimed neo-Anabaptism after reading theologians like John Howard Yoder, Stanley Hauerwas, Stuart Murray, or David Fitch, and then imagine they have *solved* racism by espousing anti-hierarchical and anti-domination theologies. But this overlooks white neo-Anabaptism's own formation and complicity in white supremacy, just not from within Anabaptist history.

Neo-Anabaptism usually cultivates a vibrant pietistic faith expression (which has potential to resonate with Black and Brown Christians). Yet the white neo-Anabaptist movement has not engaged in serious collective lament and reckoning around white supremacy, revealing a deeply immature awareness of their own racial performance. White neo-Anabaptists overall (there are plenty of exceptions) have done less—not more—work as a community navigating our white supremacist and capitalist society than most traditional Anabaptist denominations (excluding the BIC and Mennonite Brethren). The frequently white, middle- and upper-class, and highly educated constituents of both white neo-Anabaptist and historic Anabaptist congregations make true solidarity and struggle leading to mutual liberation in the way of Jesus nearly impossible. And yet I know folks who are doing just that, so we confess that all things are possible with God!

Rethinking political engagement

A final challenge for white Anabaptists concerns political engagement and kingdom theology. While the sixteenth-century Anabaptist ecclesial witness was inseparably tied to the Poor Peasants' uprisings and liberation from economic exploitation, today, some streams of white Anabaptism are insufferably apolitical and neutral regarding the greatest concerns of our time. There needs to be more conversation around politics, liberation, and the kingdom of God in many Anabaptist circles.

It seems that some white Anabaptists still have not distinguished between partisanship and political engagement, as well as how their understanding of the kingdom of God might be reinforcing ways of living in society that run counter to the story of Jesus. Everything we do in society is political. The personal is political. Our decision to speak or remain quiet is political. There can be no opting out of political engagement (even if one tries to be apolitical or neutral), because we are always tied to a complex web of political realities. In John 18:36, Jesus tells Pilate and reminds his followers that his kingdom is not from this world—therefore they will not engage in violent revolt like others do. He also says that his kingdom has come on earth as it is in heaven. We are told that God's kingdom is here, among us, in our midst. Jesus points not to a disengaged apolitical citizenship in heaven, but to the distinct and upside-down character of God's reign that is breaking into our world but not yet fulfilled.

Jesus clashed directly with public powers like Herod or the Jerusalem establishment rulers, who had ties with the Roman Empire. We as Christians are called to follow and participate in the life of Jesus together as a community, and the prayer is that sometimes, through God's help, we too might make manifest the reign of God. The kingdom of God is not confined or controlled by the boundaries of the church. And we are to seek after the kingdom of God before anything else. Our pursuit of God's reign sometimes leads us into the proverbial house of Cornelius, a Roman centurion and thus an agent of the empire.

Even sixteenth-century Anabaptists typically understood kingdom theology in different ways. One is the Schleitheim Confession approach of Michael Sattler and the Swiss Anabaptists, which suggests a two-kingdom framework where the church and the world have dualistic and antagonistic vocations or ethical mandates. The church and kingdom can be overly conflated in this paradigm. The world is called to use the sword because it is outside the perfection of Christ, but the church lives by the way of Jesus. There is partial truth here, but it diminishes God's reign in creation.

Another sixteenth-century posture draws on Menno Simons, Pilgram Marpeck, and Balthasar Hubmaier. Among their positions exists a way of understanding God's inbreaking first and foremost in the church, but also as an uncontainable divine activity unfolding within the broader society. This Anabaptist orientation acknowledges God's singular desire for the whole cosmos to be ushered into a community of creation. God is shepherding our world toward shalom. While we live in the "not yet," we still perceive the Christological stitching of the cosmos made for peace, justice, liberation, and reconciliation. This is a good-for-all society vision rather than one just good for worshiping communities organized around the revelation of God in human flesh. The church is still called to embody God's dream right now, but the resulting peace, justice, and reconciliation are good for all humanity.

Now, the kingdom of God must never be conflated with a governmental or political structure, yet a spectrum of differences persists among the nations around the world, reflecting varying degrees of human flourishing. A death-dealing regime or "the greatest purveyor of violence in the world" should not be conflated with a nation-state that has increasingly learned to care for the most vulnerable and has rejected the rampant militarism of our time. Sixteenth-century Anabaptists like Simons, Marpeck, and Hubmaier could help contemporary Anabaptists consider what it means to invite the broader society to take the next step in the right direction toward God's shalom, participating in the common good as citizens. We ought to reject church-state fusions, invite others from our pluralistic society into dialogue, and hopefully work noncoercively toward a society that practices justice, mercy, and hospitality because we have caught God's dream of shalom. There is no better prophetic witness to society than when our calls to repentance are matched by the integrity of a people practicing the counter-politics of the Messiah in its own worshiping community.

One political posture that white Anabaptists have conveniently eclipsed from their language of "cores," "essentials," or "distinctives" of Anabaptist practices is needed for today: the recovery of an economic liberation ecclesiology seen among sixteenth-century Anabaptists. In the context of centuries of colonial conquest and antiblack chattel slavery, economic stances will need to go much deeper than "simple living" and periodically giving "mutual aid." White North American Anabaptists must speak of and practice redistribution of wealth, reparations for historic wrongs, and returning stolen land.

Additionally, white Anabaptists for too long have centered white male theologians, concealing the wisdom of people of color, and frequently that of white women as well. The Yoderian crisis came from exposing patterns of sexual abuse in the Mennonite Church thanks to the courageous leadership of Mennonite women who intervened and sought to break the cycle. This is a reminder that Anabaptists must not make "the mistake of separating theory from practice" and must practice a more inclusive dialogue that brings to the forefront the lived experiences of those who have historically been marginalized.[9]

How can white Anabaptists, in the aftermath of centuries of horror, become a healing, liberating, and restorative ecclesial witness in our present society? Where and with whom should they become proximate so they can have the vantage point of the crucified of our world? Many Anabaptists of color have, in part, embraced Eurocentric stories and enfolded them alongside their own people's stories to create something new. What new stories do white Anabaptists need to hold tenderly as a sacred and liberating gift to make vulnerable space for the possibility of ongoing radical reformation today? White Anabaptists must continue to engage with these questions so a new story of Anabaptism can unfold in North America.

— FIVE —

The Story of the Doctrine of Discovery and Antiblackness

I recently had a disorienting experience at the Atlanta airport. Anyone who braves air travel knows that unforeseen adventure can happen at any moment. On this occasion, I had arrived early and went to my gate, only to learn the flight was delayed. Staying on brand, the airline communicated as little as possible. Before my fellow passengers and I knew it, we were being sent back and forth to various gates across the airport. After the second gate change, an older white man turned to me to vent, and we began to talk, bonding instantly over airline practices.

After a few minutes, the conversation took a turn. My new friend began talking politics. He was soon mumbling about the deep state, how they want to assassinate Donald Trump, and how the CIA runs CNN. Conspiracy theories flew left and right. Seeking to create a bridge, I named that both political parties are biased, and neither reflects the full interests of the people. I gave a few examples of how Republican policies were hurting lower- and middle-class workers. When he began defending Trump, I gave some examples of Trump's lies and actions. I also said that both parties had problems, which I genuinely believe. I thought that the acknowledgment might allow him to truly hear what I was saying.

But after an exchange about how "politicians" need to stop letting our jobs leave the country, and my observation that politicians need to work together to stop multinational corporations from exploiting poor workers here and abroad, he pivoted once more. This time, he described how he grew up in an Italian neighborhood in New York City, where he witnessed his community overcome all kinds of obstacles, and now people were thriving. That's great, I said, and I'm sure they worked hard, but those opportunities to work hard and get paid for one's labor have not always been available to everyone. To this he said, looking me in the eye with a straight face and non-anxious presence, that Italians had been enslaved just like Black people were.

As you can imagine, I lost all will to play "common ground" mediator. I laid out all the historical facts of enslavement and the rebirth of Jim and Jane Crow white supremacy, and the ways that Black people were intentionally targeted, excluded, exploited, and oppressed in ways that Italians were not. I affirmed that Italians were sometimes discriminated against—but as "improperly white" folks. And then I gave examples of how antiblack oppression still shapes the social disadvantages and biases that permeate Black folks' lived experiences to this day.

Part of the problem is that there are so many absurd and imbecilic white myths that people have willingly adopted over time to help themselves conveniently forget the atrocities of the past five hundred plus years. Further, the desire to say and believe something so ridiculous as the myth that Italians were treated the same as Black people, including our experience of slavery and Jim and Jane Crow, shows the power of fake "history" and the social media algorithms that influence what we internalize and how we make meaning of our world. Just as I thought that I could not be disoriented any further, the airline associates announced that our gate had been changed once more, and we would now need to walk back to our original terminal. By this point all I could do was laugh at the absurdity I was experiencing in all directions.

If we want to heal and set things right, we need to reckon with how we got to where we are. So we need to pick up where our story of Christendom left off. Western colonial conquest and antiblack oppression were born in the womb of late medieval Christianity and coincided with the Protestant Reformation. Most mainstream church traditions within Western Christianity aided and abetted, if not outright committed, the crime of plunder and the racializing of our world's population. The history of white settler colonialism and antiblack oppression is a painful one that many have chosen to suppress with convenient lies and forgetfulness. But it will be impossible to make a radical break from these patterns without confessing the past that still haunts us.

Plundering faith

Western Christendom cultivated the mangled conditions and contexts from which Western Christian nations increasingly engaged in the conquest and enslavement of people beyond Western Europe. In many ways, growing anti-Judaism,

Islamophobia, and Orientalism, and the broader split between the Western Catholic Church and the Eastern Orthodox Church, cultivated binary thinking about the world. There were Christians (Western Europe) and heathens (those beyond Western Europe). There was a powerful fusion of Western society and culture with the very meaning of the word Christian. To be one was assumed to be the other. European Christians were developing a sacred "mission" to reshape the earth in alignment with the lordship of Christ—which looked like Western civilization, far so removed from the origins of the faith. They convinced themselves that their interpretation of Christianity was the sole "orthodox" take. They were guardians of the faith. If others wanted to come to Christ, they must come through the West. The Acts 15 council, which decided that Gentiles need not assimilate into all the practices of the Jewish community to be joined into the body of the Messiah, was abandoned. Western Christianity and civilization were *the* standard for Christian living for everyone.

The rise of Western Christendom trained Western European Christians to conceive of their faithful practice as done through domination, hierarchy, and coercion. This ideological way of interpreting Christian scriptures, belief, and practice proved diabolical the more they encountered others who did not conform to their expectations. The practice of Western Christian supremacy inclined followers to steal, kill, and destroy.

In 1441, a Portuguese crew stole ten to twelve Africans from the west coast of Africa, spinning together the sticky threads of Western conquest, plunder, slavery, and antiblackness all justified by Western Christian teaching. The crew was in search for gold but thought that these people would be suitable cargo to plunder and sell as commodities back home. By 1444, global

STORY OF THE DOCTRINE OF DISCOVERY & ANTIBLACKNESS / **131**

capitalist markets were in full swing as Portugal, soon to be a global economic power, saw the profits possible in plundering African people and making them into racial product.

We know a lot about this late Christendom moment thanks to Gomes Eanes de Zurara, the official Chronicler of the Portuguese Crown. His diaries narrate a horrific scene as West Africans are processed at auction. "Some kept their heads low and their faces bathed in tears, looking one upon another; others stood groaning . . . looking up to the height of heaven, fixing their eyes upon it, crying out loudly, as if asking help of the Father of Nature; others struck their faces . . . throwing themselves at full length upon the ground; others made their lamentations in the manner of a dirge. . . . And though we could not understand the words of their language, the sound of it right well accorded with the measure of their sadness."[1] Zurara describes how fathers, mothers, and children resist the horror of it all, trying their best to cling to one another as they are callously torn apart for sale by their captors.

While Zurara almost exposes his shared humanity and empathy, he quickly weaponizes Christendom doctrines to return to calculated confidence in the sovereignty of God, even over the enslavement, dehumanization, commodification, and exploitation of these people. Consider this interplay of empathy and antiblackness: "I pray Thee that my tears may not wrong my conscience; for it is not their religion but their humanity that maketh mine to weep in pity for their sufferings. And if the brute animals, with their bestial feelings, by a natural instinct understand the sufferings of their own kind, what wouldst Thou have my human nature to do on seeing before my eyes that miserable company, and remembering that they too are of the generation of the sons of Adam?" Zurara weeps and sees their shared humanity as children of Adam, yet he also compares Africans to brute animals and appraises their African bodies. Some are "white enough" and "fair to look upon." Others are "less white like mulattoes" and therefore lower on the purported ladder of goodness, beauty, and worth. Finally, "others again were as black as Ethiops, and so ugly, both in features and in body, as almost to appear (to those who saw them) the images of a lower hemisphere."[2]

From the earliest days of Western colonial conquest, humanity was categorized by the inseparable logics of white supremacy and antiblackness. It was a refusal to see everyone made in the image of God and therefore treated as though their lives mattered.

Zurara's chronicles in these early moments of Christian antiblackness demonstrate a striking use of theology. In *The Christian Imagination*, historian Willie James Jennings explains that for Zurara, a sovereign God was orchestrating the horrors and suffering for the end goal of Christian conversion. Jennings identifies the ironic parallels between the experience of Jesus in the passion with the suffering of the Africans—the very thing that Zurara and so many white Christians after him have been unwilling to do. Instead, their mental gymnastics around Jesus' "least of these" warnings in Matthew 25 prevent them from developing a Christological vision capable of seeing Jesus buried in the lives of suffering Black bodies. Here, both Jesus and these Africans are captive by the powers. Both are beaten and processed. The Africans also fall upon the ground, look up to heaven, and cry out to God. Of course, in Jesus' case, he triumphs over the cross through the resurrection. Evil and death do not have the last word. However, for these frightened, stolen, displaced, and extremely vulnerable Africans far from home, the powers and authorities appear to have triumphed. They encounter what many of their descendants for centuries will know firsthand, and which Israel testified to in its vast wisdom: so often, the "wicked prosper" (Job 21:7–13; Psalm 73:3–5; Jeremiah 12:1–2).

As Western Christendom gave birth to Western colonial conquest and antiblack enslavement, Western Christians were thoroughly entangled in the process. As Jennings explains, "Christianity in the Western world lives and moves within a diseased social imagination."[3] We have yet to understand all the ways that we still live inside and are comfortable with white supremacist settler colonialism and antiblackness. To understand that development, we need to remember how the church created official law and church doctrine (they were one and the same in Western Christendom) justifying global conquest and the transatlantic slave trade.

Piecing together the Doctrine of Discovery

In the past few decades, many mainline Protestant denominations in North America have begun to confess the church's sins in regards to colonial conquest and slavery. Many mainstream Christians, however, still don't understand Western and white Christianity complicity in the conquest of North America. After the pope crowned Charlemagne in the eighth century, Western Christendom grew increasingly violent beyond its borders. The Crusades socialized the church toward violent and coercive mission. In the fifteenth century, a flurry of papal edicts was used to justify colonization and plunder. This legal and theological framework is known as the Doctrine of Discovery. The church sanctioned by law and doctrine the right to claim heathen lands, plundering and enslaving along the way, in the name of Jesus. Within Western Christendom such decrees were immediately the law of the land and official divine teaching. Even after Protestants split from Catholicism, primarily Protestant nations and churches continued to take the Doctrine of Discovery as politically legitimate and theologically authoritative.

While most think Christopher Columbus initiated Western conquest, the church played a critical role in justifying plunder and enslavement before Europeans ever set foot in the "New World." In 1452, a papal bull called *Dum Diversas* "divinely" commissioned Portugal for the plunder and slavery it had *already* been practicing for a decade. This after-the-fact pronouncement from the church provided a clear and unequivocal mission to enslave heathens and "other enemies of Christ" and claim their lands for Jesus.

> We weighing all and singular the premises with due meditation, and noting that since we had formerly by other letters of ours granted among other things free and ample faculty to the aforesaid King Alfonso—to invade, search out, capture, vanquish, and subdue all Saracens and pagans whatsoever, and other enemies of Christ wheresoever placed, and the kingdoms, dukedoms, principalities, dominions, possessions, and all movable and immovable goods whatsoever held and possessed by them and to reduce their persons to perpetual slavery, and to apply and appropriate to himself and his successors the kingdoms, dukedoms, counties, principalities, dominions, possessions, and goods, and to convert them to his and their use and profit—by having secured the said faculty, the said King Alfonso, or, by his authority, the aforesaid infante, justly and lawfully has acquired and

possessed, and doth possess, these islands, lands, harbors, and seas, and they do of right belong and pertain to the said King Alfonso and his successors.[4]

Additionally, the Portuguese received blanket forgiveness for whatever "sins" they would commit—or had already committed—while reducing people to perpetual slavery. In 1455, the pope followed up with *Romanus Pontifex*. This papal bull deepened and emboldened adherence to the Doctrine of Discovery, and the right to claim "heathen" lands. It gave ethical cover for enslaving African people. *Dum Diversas* solely commissioned Portugal in conquest, but this provided a more expansive per-*mission* for other Western nations, mandating Spain to join in the plunder as well. *Romanus Pontifex* is a thoroughly "Christian" document, in the most mangled sense of the word, for how it grants the church spiritual authority and responsibility over the world, urging it to triumph over the heathens by coercion and domination.

Nearly four decades later, Christopher Columbus and his crew sought another route to India and China. They stumbled upon the Bahamas across the Atlantic Ocean instead. There they encountered vibrant Indigenous communities. Columbus, wrongfully thinking he was on the coast of India, called them Indians. Though Columbus initially recognized their generosity and kindness, it didn't take long before his Christendom formation led him to conceive of them as easy targets for forced exploitation. He also measured their beauty and worth against whiteness. For him there was "no comparison" in beauty because the Europeans' "skins are whiter." He thought that the so-called Indians "ought to be good servants" and (mistakenly) that they had "no religion."[5] After his first voyage, Columbus kidnapped several Indigenous people to take back to Spain. On subsequent voyages, Columbus escalated the brutality and violence, making plunder of resources through the forced labor of Indigenous people the central activity. All this was done in the name of Jesus.

When Columbus returned to Spain after his first voyage, he was hailed for claiming land and spreading Christianity. The Doctrine of Discovery expanded. In 1493, the papal bull *Inter Caetrea* incorporated not only Africa but the Americas within the mangled vision of Western Christendom's mission to the world. And now that Spain had joined the mission to conquer and plunder for Christ, there needed to be "rules of engagement that would minimize the blood and treasure Europeans would expend fighting each other"[6]—in other words, laws to protect Europeans from harming each other as they plundered other people's lands. In 1496, King Henry VII, not wanting England to be left out, issued a mandate "to find, discover and investigate whatsoever islands, countries, regions or provinces of heathens and infidels, in whatsoever part of the world placed." He permitted agents of the English Crown to "conquer, occupy and possess whatsoever such towns, castles, cities and islands by them thus discovered."[7] The king, in turn, would receive a fifth of the value of the loot brought back to England.

Eventually, many more Western "Christian" nations joined in coercively plundering, enslaving, and converting purportedly "heathen" people and their lands. It is not enough to name Christianity's complicity in racism. Western Christianity was central in engineering the origins of modern racism. From the earliest moments of its church and state alignment, Western Christendom constructed, blessed, encouraged, delineated, and expanded the greedy and inhumane plunder of people and lands. Western Christianity organized society through white supremacy and antiblackness, and did so within Christendom's mangled theological vision of creation and Europeans' relationship to other creatures made in the image of God. Increasingly, the idea of whiteness would be fused together with the word "Christian," and African, Indigenous, and other non-Western people would be understood as heathens in order to justify Western Christians' mission to the world.[8]

North American plunder
The transatlantic slave trade

In 1502, the Spanish brought Africans to Hispaniola (modern-day Haiti and the Dominican Republic). A short-lived Spanish colony on the coast of South Carolina in 1526 also had enslaved Africans. In 1565, Spain founded St. Augustine, Florida, which included enslaved Africans from the very beginning.

And then in 1607, the British joined the conquest and settling of Turtle Island (an Indigenous name for North America) by founding Jamestown, Virginia. In 1619, about twenty "negroes" were brought over for labor. They were technically indentured servants, because the British were late to slaveholding—though slaveholding was officially permitted by the Crown, it wasn't yet legalized. (A contemporary parallel might be how some jurisdictions have decriminalized but not legalized marijuana.) It would be a few decades before antiblack laws made these Africans and their children permanently part of the slave underclass. To be clear, 1619 in Jamestown wasn't the first time Britian participated in the transatlantic slave trade. Nearly sixty years earlier, Sir John Hawkins and his men pillaged three hundred Africans from Sierra Leone and sold them to Hispaniola. Queen Elizabeth provided Hawkins with the *Jesus of Lübeck* for his second such voyage. The ship was also known as "the good ship *Jesus*." "Forced aboard *Jesus*, African men and women probably had no idea that the ship bore the name of a man who had been crucified fifteen centuries earlier," write the authors of *The Color of Christ*. "They probably had no idea that the vessel outfitted with guns, chains, and dungeons was named for the 'prince of peace' who had come to 'set the captives free.'"[9]

By the early 1700s, Britain was the largest global human trafficker, aided by the blessing of its state church. The Anglican Church was another Christendom fracture, thoroughly organized by hierarchy, order, and alignment with the state. In the coming centuries, it bolstered the transatlantic slave trade and practiced settler colonialism, as the arc of its theology and practice bent toward a new organizing principle of white supremacy and antiblackness.

The Middle Passage was a horrific, often two-month journey from the shores of Africa to the "new world." The sheer numbers who underwent the Middle Passage are unfathomable. Between 1501 and 1866, around 12.5 million people were trafficked from Africa to Europe and across the Americas. Africans were chained and marched to the shore, beaten and branded, and loaded onto slave ships. They were crammed below with no idea what awaited them. Pale men brutalized and tortured them. Little girls were unchained and brought up to the deck to be raped. The horror was too much for some—some refused to eat, and others waited for opportune times to jump ship, choosing rather to die than submit to these pale brutal captors. They cried out to God, whether they held to Orisha practices, Islam, or Congolese Christianity.[10] The experience of this journey across the Atlantic on the ship was the first conversion to a white Christian racial hierarchy, coercively creating habits of master and slave.

Millions died in the Middle Passage. Millions more were sold into slavery throughout the Americas. By the end of the Civil War, four million displaced Africans were living in the United States.[11] As they arrived to this foreign land, the African spirit was unbroken, waiting for opportunities to struggle for freedom. A new peoplehood was born in the crucible of suffering.[12]

Virginia set the trajectory for racist policies in the British colonies. New laws codifying Blackness and slavery weren't established until the 1600s. Before that time, many of the Africans held the official status of indentured servant. This was not a position reserved only for Black people. Early on, Africans and poor Europeans had some common causes and concerns while doing forced labor under wealthy elites. European indentured servants joined African slaves and indentured servants in a revolt against the ruling class in 1676. As a consequence, white elites used racial identity and racial laws to divide and conquer exploited workers. Slavery was tied exclusively to Black people, and poor Europeans became "white," protecting them from ever becoming the bottom of the social hierarchy. Their new status encouraged poor whites to identify with white elites, because they knew they would never be treated like they were vulnerable and despised Black people. White supremacy and the 1660s antiblack laws successfully helped create a white identity that bamboozled poor whites to align with the political desires of the white elites who frequently exploited them.

While racial law was entrenching in the colonies, Christian belief and practice adjusted accordingly. Even though the

Doctrine of Discovery claimed that Christianizing heathens justified plunder and slavery, in reality, conversion of the enslaved didn't feel like a viable option for slave planters and masters. It wasn't even clear to them whether heathens could become Christian. Others were hesitant because they believed that Christianity made enslaved people "uppity." Finally, it had long been British custom not to enslave Christians. For many British settlers, "white" and "Christian" were interchangeable terms.

In 1701, the Society for the Propagation of the Gospel in Foreign Parts, commissioned by the Anglican Church, tried to convince enslavers and plantation owners that when Christianity is correctly taught, it produces more obedient and servile slaves.[13] Christianity was severed from social egalitarianism and freedom, and the practice of absolute obedience was taught as Christian orthodoxy while isolating, plundering, extracting, universalizing, and weaponizing Bible verses like "Slaves obey your masters," articulated by Paul in Ephesians 6:5 and Colossians 3:22. Baptismal catechisms were even adapted to make enslaved Africans confess that they were not seeking freedom through conversion and that they were called to servitude.

Of course, Western Christian Europeans didn't enslave Africans because they hated Black people. Deepening antiblack oppression was driven by the desire for wealth and power. The role of capitalism and greed is frequently understated in the development of antiblack oppression. Antiblackness helped white society justify and advance their wealth and status, especially in the newly established United States. After the cotton gin was invented in 1793, for example, cotton production and profits grew exponentially—as did brutality on plantations. The cotton gin was theoretically supposed to ease the process of producing cotton, but it merely increased demand for raw cotton. This resulted in the pressure to push enslaved labor to their productivity limits so producers could maximize profits. Greed fueled the expansion and brutality of slavery. Across the South, historian Edward Baptist reports, daily picking totals grew 2 percent a year up until just before the Civil War. Between 1800 and 1860, productivity increased by nearly 400 percent.[14]

This productivity, and the profits that came with it, was a direct result of what enslaved Africans called "the pushing system"—violently brutal supervision across rows hundreds of yards long so those who fell behind the set pace could be identified and publicly tortured.[15] This forced enslaved Africans to learn how to use both hands skillfully similar to the best pianists: "Enslaved people were only able to pick the required amount of cotton by learning how to unhook their nondominant hand from the tethers of bodily asymmetry and brain architecture that they had developed over the course of a lifetime," writes Baptist. "Only by using two hands that operated independently and simultaneously could they meet the rising quotas." What drove this mastery and "sleight" of hand? "Torture walked right behind them," writes Baptist.

> But neither their contemporaries then nor historians since have used "torture" to describe the violence applied by enslavers. Some historians have called lashings "discipline," the term offered by slavery's lawgivers and the laws they wrote, which pretended that masters who whipped were calmly administering "punishment" to "correct" lazy subordinates' reluctance to work. Even white abolitionist critics of slavery and their heirs among the ranks of historians were reluctant to say that it was torture to beat a bound victim

with a weapon until the victim bled profusely, did what was wanted, or both. . . . No one was willing, in other words, to admit that they lived in an economy whose bottom gear was torture.[16]

Mainstream Christians in the United States encouraged this torture. They allowed overseers, slave masters, and everyone who benefited from the slavery-fueled economy to interpret their actions as participating in some divine order. Throughout his autobiographies, Frederick Douglass highlights the distinct brutality, meanness, and violence of Christian slave masters. They vandalized and inverted the name of Jesus to do the opposite of what we see from Christ's life in the Gospels. That Western Christians could so easily adapt into a slaveholding religion, with only a minority of resistance among white people, exposes the terrible wrongs within the worship and formational habits of white American congregations. Even in the North, most white Christians were not against slavery being practiced in the South; they just wanted to limit its expansion into new territories to hold a balance of political power in the national government. Most were content with the booming economy built on tortured stolen labor because it was intimately connected to northern banks, insurance companies, factories, other industrial manufacturing, and cheap goods. Black people were expendable if it made white Christians' prosperity possible.

White preachers, theologians, and early universities created false yet sophisticated theological and biblical arguments that deemed Black people created for slavery and not fully human. When tensions increased over slavery in some denominations, Christians split. The Southern Baptist Convention, for example, would not exist except for their claim that slavery was "biblical" and that Northern abolitionists had no book, chapter, or verse to say otherwise. More plundering of isolated, extracted, universalized, and weaponized verses set the stage for the kind of biblical interpretive methods that would be deemed "faithful" among white conservatives even today. As Western colonialism unfolded in the United States, Jesus himself was colonized and refashioned. Severed from his first-century, Afro-Asiatic, Jewish, and oppressed status under Roman rule, Jesus morphed into a white Savior who sided with white domination and control.

The colonization of Turtle Island

As antiblack plunder and oppression ramped up, the Doctrine of Discovery simultaneously facilitated white settler colonialism through ongoing displacement, forcible removal, and genocide of Native American people. In the late nineteenth century, Protestant Christians openly pushed Christian conquest as a divine mandate. For example, Protestant Josiah Strong wrote *Our Country*, which claimed that Anglo-Saxons had a special gift to spread around the world: a genuine spiritual Christianity and civil liberty. Strong saw the numerical increase of Anglo-Saxons as a divine foretaste of their trajectory. "North America is to be the great home of the Anglo-Saxon, the principal seat of his power, the center of his life and influence," declared Strong.[17] The American Anglo-Saxon, he wrote, was oriented and energized for this mandate to go west and take the whole continent. He praised the disappearance of "the aborigines of North America, Australia, and New Zealand . . . before the all-conquering Anglo-Saxons" and speculates that would become the case in Africa and India as well—"God's final and complete solution of the dark problem of heathenism among many inferior peoples." Anglo-Saxon conquest and expansion, he declared, would culminate with "the coming of Christ's kingdom in the world."[18]

Early on, Western Christians believed that Indigenous people in the Americas would leave their ways of life and adopt Christianity (and thereby Western civilization). The so-called heathenism and paganism of Indigenous peoples—that is, these peoples' traditions and practices—were categorized as bad behavior. As time progressed, optimism turned into discouragement. Most Indigenous people were not voluntarily adopting Western ways and Christianity from the white European settlers. Eventually, this resistance was racialized as something inherently and unchangeably "Indian." In the late eighteenth century, military force and martial coercion were used to Christianize the land and its people and take control. This, argued the colonizers, was the only way the colonies could flourish.[19]

Christians broke treaties, forcibly removed Indigenous people, and even resorted to intentionally marrying and then poisoning Indigenous people to seize their property, wealth, and land.[20] They purposefully exposed Indigenous communities to new and devastating diseases that decimated their populations. Blatant disregard for Indigenous sovereignty only increased. In 1830, President Andrew Jackson signed the Indian Removal Act, which displaced massive numbers of Native Americans for the rest of the century. Reservations were established, usually far from people's sacred tribal lands. Later, if a reservation suddenly became desirable to white settlers, the land would be reclaimed again. Churches in both the United States and Canada established Indian Residential Schools, where children were taken away from their families and often violently assimilated into

Western culture in an effort to destroy Indigenous cultures, customs, and languages by attacking a vulnerable generation. As late as the mid-twentieth century, the government constructed policy that further eroded Indian tribes and sovereignty. The US Indian Relocation Act of 1956 tried to move Native Americans to urban centers, promising housing, opportunities, and a better life. Many moved out of necessity, only to encounter more government lies, experience discrimination, and be limited to low-wage jobs.

To this day, the US government transgresses these already unjust arrangements whenever it wants to further "develop" or use the land to run pipes for oil extraction. The Doctrine of Discovery remains alive today, justifying the disregard of the original inhabitants and stewards of Turtle Island. We can't understand white supremacy outside of the interconnected way that antiblackness and Indigenous displacement were reformulated as God's mission in the minds, hands, and faith of white Christians, thereby constructing the death-dealing world that we now inhabit.[21]

From Jim and Jane Crow to our police and prison industrial complex

While there were early promises of racial equality and reparations after the Civil War, they did not last. The Reconstruction era (1865–1877) held promise, but that decade of possibility devolved into a new form of white supremacy. In the 1880s and 1890s, white Northerners increasingly reconciled with white Southerners, offering amnesty and forgiveness to Confederates who rebelled against the United States. Formerly Confederate states and politicians were allowed to dismantle all the Reconstruction efforts that offered protection and support to the freed Black community. Roughly ten years after slavery was abolished, Black people were expected to pull themselves up by their nonexistent bootstraps. Northerners left Black people completely vulnerable to Southern resentments and hatred as they refashioned society according to a new white supremacist order, better known as Jim and Jane Crow oppression. These new laws and customs violently forced the newly freed back into a permanent and terrorized underclass. To be truly American was to be white and Protestant. Antiblackness mutated as neo-slavery and alternate forms of public torture arose. White unity was forged by treating Black people as expendable.[22]

Just as American racialized chattel slavery is often sanitized in American memory, the Jim and Jane Crow era is frequently domesticated into something much more tolerable for us to imagine. When students first come into my classroom, they seem to know very little about this time other than that Black people drank from separate water fountains and sat at the back of the bus. These humiliations, they imagine, were the final barriers to full equality. There is no awareness of how society was restructured according to white supremacy and antiblackness to further exploit Black labor and provide advantages for poor whites so they would continue to align with white and wealthy elites. In the South, new laws established multiple streams of neo-slavery. Draconian Black Codes made loitering, or Black men having a relationship with a white woman, or not getting permission from a white man to change jobs punishable, serious offenses under the law. Law enforcement, judges, and politicians helped create this Black vulnerability. When Black people could not pay their court fees, they were leased (without any oversight) to white businesses for hard labor. People were often stuck in the convict leasing system for decades and frequently under more brutal conditions than slavery, with much higher mortality rates, and very similar torture methods. The convict leasing system was much cheaper than purchasing and insuring enslaved people. Other neo-forms of slavery included exploitative sharecropping arrangements, chain gangs, and even peonage. Other than peonage, which was practiced but illegal, all the other forms of exploited and forced labor were perfectly legal.[23]

Black people had no place to turn for protection. Black women were frequently raped by white men, and Black men were frequently lynched. Governor Blease of South Carolina actually said, "I have . . . very serious doubt as to whether the crime of rape can be committed upon a negro."[24] Like the many centuries prior, Black women were completely vulnerable to the corrupt desires of white men. Lynching happened to all Black people, including women and children, but Black men were the most explicitly targeted. The Equal Justice Initiative has recently discovered an additional two thousand documented cases of racial lynchings, putting the total to six thousand and five hundred fully documented race-based lynchings between 1865 and 1950. It is believed that thousands more have not been documented.[25]

In the earliest years of race-based lynchings, thousands of white people, including children, would come to watch, as though it were a town fair. People ate meals, took photos, and left with souvenirs (body parts). Black people were often tortured over extended periods of time while white people jeered. As the twentieth century progressed, lynchings became less "civilized" of an activity for the masses, occurring more frequently at night among smaller groups. In either case, white people documented the lynching of Black people, frequently posing in photos with their suffering victim.[26] In the early twentieth century, journalist Ida B. Wells-Barnett targeted the myth that lynchings occurred because Black men were raping white women. Her reporting revealed how most lynchings were not in response to rapes at all. Instead, antiblack racism and white terrorism fueled the spike in lynchings. White people used fear and the public spectacle of lynched Black bodies to oppress Black people.[27]

It is convenient for white people in the North to imagine that antiblack oppression occurred only in the South. Nothing is further from the truth. Across the country, antiblack prejudice and narratives shaped public policy and allowed whites to justify the targeted discrimination of Black Americans. For example, the early twentieth-century "progressive era" in modern urban America saw a rise in crime among both white foreign-born Europeans who recently immigrated and Black Americans who had fled Jim and Jane Crow terrorism in the South. The response to rising crime differed in surprising ways. Italians, Irish, Polish, and Jewish immigrants, for example, were described as *victims* of industrialization, and a variety of programs were created to help them navigate these obstacles and build a life for themselves.

Black people, in contrast, were stereotyped as being innately *criminal*, even though they were living under similar conditions—but with less wealth, education, or opportunities—as their European contemporaries. Blackness and criminality were being fused together in white consciousness, justifying oppressive policing and unjust policy.[28] Black people across the country were forced into substandard public housing ghettos and were excluded from job opportunities and neighborhoods with quality housing. They faced socioeconomic discrimination through sundown towns, racial zoning, racial covenants on property deeds, redlining of black neighborhoods, and decimating Black businesses by intentionally running new interstate highways through Black neighborhoods all across the nation (to offer a sample of examples).[29] Black people had been excluded from the Homestead Act and were now regularly denied access to New Deal policies, government housing subsidies, and credit systems that broke cycles of poverty, supported property ownership, and generated wealth for ordinary white Americans. They were also excluded from GI benefits offering a range of aid like housing loans, educational supports, and unemployment benefits. Overall, these twentieth-century programs opened the door of opportunity for home ownership and intergenerational wealth, creating a brand-new white middle class while simultaneously shutting and locking those same doors for most Black Americans.[30]

Throughout the twentieth century, European immigrants streamed into the United States. Rather than recognizing that the opportunities they sought for themselves were made possible because of the oppression and plunder of Black and Indigenous people, many chose to become white. Many Europeans were not initially deemed properly or fully white. However, they chose to assimilate, identify, and perform whiteness in such ways that they were enfolded into it, leaving Black and Indigenous people behind. They voluntarily severed themselves from their original languages and culture, they sought to move into white segregated neighborhoods, and they pursued jobs held by white people and refused jobs associated with Black people. Along with reaping the benefits of New Deal and progressive era policies that lifted up a strong white middle class, these Europeans immigrants distanced themselves from people of color and participated in antiblack racism on their path toward true whiteness.[31] To be a white Anglo-Saxon Protestant was to be properly white. Even many non-white people of color from the majority world have come to this land conveniently forgetting or ignoring Black and Native American suffering over many centuries. Some see Turtle Island as a place of opportunity while trying to imitate and approximate whiteness, even though they will never be deemed properly white by the standards of white supremacy.

The Doctrine lives on

The Doctrine of Discovery lives on today with the nearly two million people locked up in our prison industrial complex, which disproportionately incarcerates Black and Brown people.[32] The Doctrine of Discovery lives on when police brutally take the life of unarmed Black people and many white people respond with disregard and Blue Lives Matter apparel. It lives on when municipalities use poor Black people as a source of revenue, perpetually plundering them of their resources by over-policing minor infractions that are ignored in other communities (or creating new policies to accomplish these goals).[33] The Doctrine of Discovery lives on through disparities in access to safe and economically invested neighborhoods and fully funded schools. If you are Black or Native, your quality of life is more likely than not intentionally disinvested.

The Doctrine lives on in disproportionate infant mortality rates, deaths during pregnancies, and the likelihood of exposure to harmful elements like lead in paint, asbestos, or terrible air quality because incinerators have often been intentionally placed near Black neighborhoods. The Doctrine lives on when the government disregards Native sovereignty so it can further plunder their lands for resources. The Doctrine of Discovery lives on through the generational accumulation of wealth stolen from plundered lands and enslaved labor—wealth that is hoarded in mostly white hands. Meanwhile, those whose communities suffered directly and continuously for over five hundred years are excluded from many of the economy's benefits. Today, there are massive racial disparities in wealth. The racial wealth gap has barely budged from when Black Americans were first freed from enslavement.[34]

And the Doctrine lives on most egregiously through white American Christianity. Being white and Christian in the United States actually increases, rather than decreases, the likelihood that someone will hold racist views. White Christians—evangelical, mainline, and Catholic—are more likely than white non-Christians to hold racist views.[35] In many ways, white Catholics and mainline Christians are the original racists who, over several centuries, taught and socialized evangelicals into their racialized views. The great horror of white American Christianity, and those who adhere to it (not all white people adhere to it, and some people of color have adopted it), is how closely it aligns with Josiah Strong's dream for a white Christian nation. His political vision is a direct predecessor to the white Christian nationalism that fuels the faith and political desires of so many people today.

White supremacy and antiblackness have diseased the imaginations and desires of so many people who call themselves Christians. This distorted faith is seen when justice for the vulnerable is considered "wokism," when our shared humanity and cultivating spaces of belonging and inclusion is seen as liberalism, and when intentionally and equitably healing and repairing historic harms is judged as Marxist. After centuries of plunder, oppression, and alienation, too many have lost sight of the way of Jesus and how his messianic reign ought to be good news to address the urgent concerns and lasting wounds of our society. Instead, it feels like the past holds us captive. The past is not past at all but lives on in our intergenerational and communal sins. History might not completely repeat itself, but as some suggest, it does rhyme.

Given this history, one might wonder why anyone would put their faith in the gospel. Without a concrete lived and embodied faith that bears witness to God's love, liberation, and justice, there is no compelling pathway into following the way of Jesus. That is, if you believe that the Jesus way ought to be an overall good for society. That the church, however imperfect, is still the salt of the earth. That faith without good works is dead. That hope is made visible in the midst of despair by people who dare to live God's dream right now. That love for the disinherited, the despised, and the downtrodden is the mark of God's people. Thankfully, the Doctrine of Discovery is not the whole story. Christians across the globe have encountered Jesus for themselves, and when they followed after him, they cultivated counter beliefs and traditions right under the nose of white supremacy.

— SIX —

The Black Church, an Antiracist Tradition

Every fall I teach an undergraduate African American theology course. At the start of the semester, students are assigned to attend several churches from a variety of Black Church traditions. The goal is to engage a small sample of traditions, congregation sizes, liturgies, and expressions of the faith as an introduction to Black and womanist theology. Many students, especially white students, have never stepped foot in a Black church.

Though the format varies from year to year, I can usually count on one thing. Many of the white students are nervous prior to their visits. Some students have even been brave enough to articulate their concern, with visible anxiety, wondering how they will be received in Black worshiping communities. Will they experience welcome or hostility? It's happened so often that I have a canned speech to orient them to their first Black church visit. "You will be more welcomed in these congregations over the next few weeks than most of you have been welcomed in your own home congregations," I say. Part of the issue, I observe, is that they expect Black folk to treat them the same way we have been treated in white congregations. Nothing could be further from the truth. Almost always, Black worshipers overextend themselves to make white people feel welcome. In fact, as I tell my students, if the Black Church has erred at all when it comes to white visitors, it has been too welcoming, loving, inviting, and trusting of white people when white Christians have and continue to mistreat Black people. This openness has led to antiblack violence in our sanctuaries as well as the ahistorical disparagement of the very existence of the Black Church.

Without fail, after each visit, students return to my classroom moved by their experience, full of insightful takeaways about Black worship practices. My white students often tell me about the hugs, love, and welcome they received. Many express how they might start attending this or that church, though it's mostly empty talk. They experience the gift of the Black Church, yet most won't break from their white worlds. Stepping out of that boat is too hard.

Black faith and the Black Church arose in the aftermath of antiblack chattel slavery, Jim and Jane Crow, and subsequent forms of white supremacist oppression. The Black Church—which is a shorthand for the significant plurality within Black worshiping communities—has been a vital antiracist Christian expression cultivated on the underside of white Christian death-dealing belief and practice. This especially includes the prophetic, liberative stream of the Black Church that has participated in the Black radical tradition and struggle for justice, survival, healing, joy, truth-telling, liberation, and dignity in the presence of God. The Black Church tradition is an invitation to encounter and know the God who is a father to the fatherless, a mother to the motherless, and a waymaker to those who have been hard-pressed on every side. It is a gracious call to know and follow Jesus from the underside of white supremacy, colonial conquest, and antiblackness.

The invisible institution

In his groundbreaking book *There Is a River*, Vincent Harding reminds readers that Black people's struggle for liberation started the moment enslavement began on the shores of Africa, persisted through the Civil War—and continues today.[1] Harding describes the story of Black survival and resistance as a " long, continuous movement, flowing like a river, sometimes powerful, and roiling with life; at other times meandering and turgid, covered with the ice and snow of seemingly endless winters, all too often streaked and running with blood."[2] The river is people, it is activism, it is hope, it is creativity, it is movements, it is meaning-making, and it is the ongoing reconstructing of peoplehood that is always more expansive than just the Black community. To understand the breath, width, beauty, power, and significance of the Black Church, we can only know it as we step into these waters, rather than remaining as bystanders on the riverbank.

Mainstream American Christianity, built on the foundations of the Doctrine of Discovery, was inherently white supremacist and antiblack, and enslaved Africans didn't mindlessly assimilate into that death-dealing religion. Enslaved Africans were not intellectually compliant to whatever white Christians sought to impose on them. Don't get me wrong, the white Christians tried. They hired preachers who pushed a slaveholding religion, and over time they developed a white supremacist slaveholding theology and biblical hermeneutic. However, Africans already had their own memories of encounters with God and ways of conceiving and interacting with the sacred cosmos. And they had agency to adopt, adapt, or reject anything based on their own lived experiences, intuitions, and reasoning.

Many expressions of Christianity were rejected by Africans in this land, especially early on. Most practiced indigenous African religions, and a smaller percentage were Muslim, or even Christian. Very few responded to white people's preaching of Christianity initially. It wasn't until the religious revivals of the First and Second Awakenings that masses of Africans began converting to Christianity, drawn to its egalitarian and liberative implications. They saw that the gospel meant more than spiritual freedom—it meant freedom from enslavement as well. The Black Christian faith that emerged over time creatively and dynamically reinterpreted and synthesized West African sacred cosmology and religious practices with current experiences and conditions, interpreting everything through a discerning lens of what was of ultimate concern for their present situation. Many Africans eventually placed their faith in Jesus, but most rejected the white man's slaveholding religion.

The Black Church began with what scholar Albert Raboteau calls the "invisible institution" rather than any formal Black Christian denomination or tradition.[3] If we only pay attention to visible institutional religion, we will miss a lot. So why did many Africans become Christian? Well, conversion to Christianity was not a big leap. Western Christianity and West African cosmology (the way of explaining the natural order of things) had plenty of similarities. Each saw God as a supreme creator, and each held to intermediary spirits, gods, angels, or demons that interacted with humanity. West African veneration of ancestors parallels some of the more ancient forms of Christianity in the East and West that value the communion of saints and the great cloud of witnesses. Ecstatic and embodied communal worship and the role of spirit possession were similar to Great Awakening conversions and inner experience of the Spirit resulting in outward response. Storytelling and wisdom in scripture is similar to many African oral wisdom traditions. West African cosmology and religious life were closer to ancient Judaism and first-century Christian social and cosmological imaginations than most Enlightenment or modern Western European and North American beliefs! Those who adopted and adapted the gospel message did so because it resonated with them.

Beyond the watchful eye of the master's surveillance and sanctioned slaveholding church services, enslaved Africans stole away to gather (illegally) to worship God based on their own encounters with God, Jesus, and Spirit while retaining African cosmology and rituals. They improvised and created something new. In these secret hush harbor gatherings, they encountered a very different God from white people's racist, status-quo god and religion. They encountered a living and present Jesus. Jesus suffered with them. He was a friend in hard times and an ever-present help in times of need. Occasionally, Jesus was described as white—but as a short and little white man. "Black slaves," explain Edward Blum and Paul Harvey, "took the new white Jesus, shrank him, and made him into a trickster of the Trinity" who led them in subverting the white world.[4] In West African tradition, tricksters (often animals) in moral tales use wit, cunning, and subversive tactics to outsmart the powerful or overcome tough situations.

Jesus as a little white man identified with the enslaved and could slip pass white enslavers without notice.

Though white people intentionally denied (eventually by law) most enslaved Africans the opportunity to learn how to read and write, Africans developed biblical oral traditions and storytelling that would be rehearsed in community, providing good news. Spirituals were communal songs for praise and prayer, often infusing interpretations of biblical stories and their cosmology into song. Gatherings incorporated the West African ring shout, with foot stomping, clapping, and dancing as participants moved together in a circle. This was not a colonized liturgy. Many Old Testament stories resonated with their experiences in slavery and oppression under white Christians. In particular, the story of Hebrew enslavement in Egypt became a powerful motif for its resemblance to their own experience. If God could liberate the Hebrew slaves, then God could do it for them. God was a liberating God who responded to the enslaved and oppressed and would lead them to freedom. Jesus was the new Moses come to liberate the oppressed (see Luke 4:18–19).

Fear of unsupervised Black worship increased during the antebellum period before the Civil War. Black people worshiping on their own without white control and surveillance was dangerous and could lead to resistance in many forms, including revolt. Sometimes Black people stole away to freedom, some broke farming tools or burned fields, some learned to read and write, and others told dangerous stories of resistance, struggle, and overcoming. Others became abolitionists of slavery, while some worked the Underground Railroad. Some preached or wrote about justice and freedom, or nurtured a liberating faith in others. And yes, people revolted, all the way through the Civil War.

Black preachers were notorious for igniting slave revolts. Gabriel Prosser, a Christian leader, organized hundreds of people to revolt, but a storm delayed them and they were betrayed by a fellow enslaved African, leading to the execution of Prosser and many others. Denmark Vesey, an African Methodist Episcopal (AME) preacher in Charleston, South Carolina, organized a revolt to overthrow white authorities with the goal to flee to Haiti, which had successfully overthrown slavery nearly two decades earlier. The Charleston revolt was expected to have thousands involved, but word of the plot leaked before it happened, and Vesey and many other leaders were executed. Then in 1831, preacher Nat Turner had an apocalyptic vision, igniting a slave revolt in Virginia. Over fifty white people were slaughtered as enslaved people went house to house, trying to liberate themselves. Unfortunately, they were outnumbered against massive gun power backed up the white social order. They were hunted and eventually executed.

These preachers were inspired by Haiti's successful revolt and newfound independence. But Haiti's numerical advantage did not translate into the same success in the United States. Nonetheless, the uprisings sparked because of Black faith proved Black worship and its liberationist commitments to be a dangerous and subversive force for white supremacy and slaveholding society.

Schools sometimes teach about Black historical figures without acknowledging them as people of faith and how that influenced their resistance to antiblack oppression. Almost everyone knows about Harriet Tubman, but strangely, many have ignored the Christian faith that fueled her as a great conductor of the Underground Railroad. Tubman had deep faith and interpreted her work as a divine vocation from God. She had sustained a severe head injury as a child, but the profound and vivid dreams she received from God as an adult helped her avoid capture and discern which routes to take. She helped free over seventy enslaved people on around thirteen missions. She also spied for the Union army and helped lead an armed revolt that freed over seven hundred more Black enslaved people. Her courage over her life is why she became known as our Black Moses.

Frederick Douglass, the most well-known abolitionist in the country during his life, was also a devout Christian. He escaped enslavement in 1838 and quickly became a powerful orator against slavery. His slave narrative unmasked the horrors of slavery as well as the hypocritical and slaveholding Christianity of this land. He constantly referred to Scripture in his speeches and urged people to genuinely follow Jesus as he railed against American racial oppression. While Tubman and Douglass are perhaps two of the best-known abolitionists, the Black Church (invisible and institutional) cultivated many other resisters who also joined the river of struggle.

The institutional Black Church

In 1787, white elders at St. George's Methodist Episcopal Church in Philadelphia constructed segregated balcony seating for Black members, making clear their second-class status in the church. Mind you, Methodism was founded by John Wesley, who opposed slavery, but that didn't prevent white supremacy from infiltrating its gatherings in the North. Proximity under the same steeple doesn't necessarily mean hierarchies have been dismantled. Tensions snapped when church officials forcibly pulled Absalom Jones from his knees in the middle of prayer on a Sunday morning because he wasn't in his assigned place in the newly segregated section. Not only did this disruption deny Jones's dignity and worth as one created by God, it also violated the good news of Jesus that was supposed to be visible in the church. In response, Black folk were not having it. In an act of courageous faithfulness, Jones and Richard Allen led the Black congregants in an immediate walkout. The white American church needed a prophetic witness. Bad religion had to be rejected.

The first thing they did after withdrawing from St. George's was found the Free African Society, a mutual aid organization, to support the Black community in Philadelphia. Richard Allen remained committed to Methodism, so he founded Bethel African Methodist Episcopal Church, now known as Mother Bethel AME. Mother Bethel in Philadelphia wasn't the first institutional Black Church, but its break from mainstream American white supremacist Christianity symbolized a new stage for the Black Church. Mother Bethel planted the seed for the African Methodist Episcopal denomination, which would build up faith and leadership in many Black people. They were organizing an antiracist space where Black people could worship in spirit and truth without the willful imposition of white supremacy and antiblackness, whether in building design, ecclesial polity, doctrine, or social practice.

I've heard white people ask, Why should there be a Black Church in the twenty-first century? Shouldn't there just be one church? Doesn't the existence of the Black Church cause division and perpetuate segregation? This is a classic example of asking the wrong questions. First, and fairly straightforwardly, we need to distinguish between white supremacist segregation and withdrawal from white supremacy. White congregations habitually practiced hierarchy and segregation, even when Black people worshiped with them. Rejecting institutional white supremacy in the church is not practicing segregation. From the very beginning, Black worshiping communities consistently rejected racial hierarchy. When Richard Allen started the AME tradition, he powerfully affirmed our shared human equality while simultaneously empowering Black African people to live in our antiblack society. His work met a direct need for Black Americans. The "African" in their name demonstrates self-affirmation. Yet they also insisted on the full equality of people, socially and spiritually, regardless of race or ethnicity. Beyond the church walls, Allen remained open to working with white abolitionists and leaders.

The goal of the Black Church has never been to create a racial hierarchy where Black people enslave white people or flip Jim and Jane Crow policies to terrorize and exploit white people. Even today, white people find belonging in a Black church (often, as I remind my students, without working very hard to earn such trust). The Black Church doesn't practice *reverse* segregation, externally or internally. Rather, Black Christian separation from the white church has meant a radical break from racial hierarchy and segregation, seeking to faithfully and contextually embody the good news of what Jesus has done and is doing in this land.

Rather than asking whether the Black Church should exist today, maybe the better question is whether white churches, whose legacies stand on the shoulders of the Doctrine of Discovery (explicitly or implicitly), ought to exist. What should we do with these traditions that have never repented for nor made repair for its centuries of horrific harm and vandalizing of the name of Jesus? Strangely, in renouncing and withdrawing from white supremacist Christianity, the Black Church is framed as the source of segregation rather than the mainstream

American Christian traditions descended from death-dealing and deeply racist traditions. If any tradition deserves interrogation for perpetuating ongoing racism, it is not the Black Church.

From their earliest emergence, Black congregations were gatherings where white people could have chosen to die to the false white identity and unchallenged social lives. White people could have yielded to God and Black ecclesial leadership, renouncing all domination and paternalism, thereby rejecting the lie of the Doctrine of Discovery in their lives. Today, many white Christians desire multicultural and multiethnic worship spaces, and want Black people to join them. And while that might *sound* good, most of these congregations still organize their gatherings so that white norms, comfort, beliefs, and practices remain supreme. Black people (and Indigenous and other People of Color) are expected to assimilate into white norms.[5]

People think that merely diversifying leadership and throwing in a gospel song here and there somehow suggests a radical break with white supremacy. This superficial and shallow understanding reflects the limited degree to which people have questioned how white supremacy and antiblackness have shaped their doctrines, practices, and preferences. The great irony is that the Black Church has always been an intercultural and expansive community of belonging. In its mere existence, it has already done the hard work of creatively weaving together West African and Western European practices. If the category "Black" were practiced in the same way that "white" has functioned, then Blackness would be about purity, hierarchy, and segregation. Blackness, however, is a broad way of being, seeking to survive within, live among, and resist the dominating realities of white supremacy. Everyone has something to learn if they are willing and ready to have their white-dominated worlds undone.

The three main streams of the Black Church

Leading up to but especially after the Civil War, Black people organized Black churches where they could worship without white interference in their lives and practices. Again, "the Black Church" is shorthand for a diversity of expressions of African American worshiping communities. Black faith has been practiced in a plethora of Christian traditions in North America. And over the past few decades, Black people have increasingly participated in a widening range of traditions.

Nonetheless, the majority of Black Christians are connected to nine historic Black denominations: African Methodist Episcopal (AME) Church, African Methodist Episcopal Zion (AMEZ) Church, Christian Methodist Episcopal (CME) Church, National Baptist Convention, National Baptist Convention of America, National Missionary Baptist Convention of America, Progressive National Baptist Convention (PNBC), Church of God in Christ (COGIC), and Full Gospel Baptist Church Fellowship. Several other denominations include sizable numbers of Black members as well. To understand the gift of the broad Black Church tradition is to understand that it is not a monolith. Still, one helpful way of making sense of the diverse Black Christian worshiping traditions is to broadly categorize them into three groups—Black Baptists, Black Methodists, and Black Pentecostals.

Black Baptists

The Black Baptist tradition surfaced in the South, initially often under the surveillance of worried white Christians who wanted to limit free Black worship and what that might inspire. However, the numbers exploded after the Civil War as Black people created worship communities free from the inherent racism of white American mainstream Christianity.

The Black Baptist tradition practices the separation of church and state, believers baptism, and local autonomy. Black Baptists are organized as conventions rather than denominations because the power is based in the local church, offering significant autonomy. The tradition is more decentralized; furthermore, there is significantly more democratic governance of congregations, which choose their own pastors. Formal education is not a requirement for clergy ordination—you can imagine why this was an appealing and empowering tradition for Black believers coming out of enslavement. They controlled their own communities and discerned for themselves who was called and who had the capacity to tell the old story afresh without needing to meet white standards and criteria. Preaching has always been very important in the Black Baptist tradition. And many Black Baptists continue to empower and develop their own leaders internally.

The Black Baptist tradition has navigated white supremacy in significant yet sometimes conflicting ways. Given congregational autonomy, local Black Baptist pastors were free to engage in social action. Many Black Baptist congregations hosted the Civil Rights freedom struggle across the South in the 1950s and '60s. But many others were not. The Progressive National Baptist Convention, for example, started because not all Black Baptists believed they should or could get involved in the struggle for equality. In contrast, Dr. King and the Progressive National Baptist Convention believed the church needed to be involved.

Pockets within this and other streams of the Black Church retained African cosmologies of one integrated and interconnected reality of our natural and spiritual world. Other congregations assimilated into white, Western dualistic frameworks that divided sacred from secular, physical from spiritual, body from soul. The rhythmic preaching that sometimes climaxes with whooping or singing, as well as the charismatic worship and leading of the Spirit, reflects African retentions. In contrast, many doctrines and popular hymns represent white American evangelical theologies that interpret being "born again" in hyper-individualistic ways. For some, the gospel is primarily a spiritual message; social justice and civic engagement, while good and important, are not always understood as central to the gospel itself. This is not the case for all Black Baptist congregations. There is significant diversity among the different conventions as well as within each congregation.

Black Methodists

Black Methodism originates from the Wesleyan tradition and began because of racism among white Methodists and in the broader society. Like their white counterparts, these Black denominations are highly organized structures. Clergy are placed by bishops, and authority is more centralized. This structure has provided Black Methodist denominations the opportunity to coordinate educational efforts like establishing schools and colleges for African Americans. Social justice efforts can also be organized more easily through these structures. The Methodist denominations are known for being more egalitarian than other Black traditions. The AME Zion denomination has been ahead of all the Black denominations on this front, ordaining women early in the twentieth century. The Black

Methodist denominations, especially AME and AME Zion, have strong ties with abolitionist struggles against slavery.

Since these traditions are rooted in Wesleyanism, holiness is important. For Black Methodist congregations, holiness can range in meaning from focusing primarily on individualistic moral purity and behavioral standards to being set apart to seek social reform and justice while participating in the liberation of God. Some Black Methodists adhere to Black social gospel teachings that meld the spiritual and social, whereas others operate out of more evangelical theologies while still valuing social justice on some level.

Very early on, some influential leaders demeaned traditional Black African worship practices that were practiced during slavery. They wanted Black people to adopt white hymns and methods of singing. And they duplicated the doctrine and structure of the white denominations. While there is significant difference among Black Methodists congregations, and most retain and value Black worship orientations, there is no question that many African Methodist denominations began as bourgeoisie assimilated communities that wanted to be respectable in the eyes of white majorities. So the tradition has had to navigate African pride alongside the lure of white cultural assimilation. The contemporary landscape of Black Methodists is diverse, and it remains a vital witness to God's justice with an affirmation of Black identity.

Black Pentecostals

Black Pentecostalism is best known for its emphasis on the Holy Spirit and the gifts of prophecy, healing, and speaking in tongues. The most well-known Black Pentecostal tradition is the Church of God in Christ (COGIC), but there are many other Pentecostal and Apostolic expressions, including in many urban centers and in storefront churches.

While Black Pentecostalism is the youngest of the Black denominations, it is rooted in Black African worship under slavery. In Black Pentecostal worship, people are regularly seized by the Holy Spirit. My Black Pentecostal friends tell stories of people being delivered from demonic possession after barking like a dog, and some even saying they have seen people levitate. More often, speaking in tongues and charismatic, Spirit-filled worship are central to Black Pentecostalism. COGIC doctrine includes a second experience of receiving the Holy Spirit after one has received salvation. When one receives the Holy Spirit, the evidence is manifested through speaking in tongues. The charismatic dynamism in Pentecostal worship is probably similar to what W. E. B. Dubois observed and referred to as "the frenzy" as he described the power and genius of Black people.[6] The Black Pentecostal tradition has also been at the forefront of creating Black gospel music and innovating new sounds rooted in old African sensibilities.

Like the other traditions, Black Pentecostalism has helped Black people navigate white supremacy in intricate and perplexing ways. Black Pentecostalism has often attracted poor and socially disadvantaged Black people. The tradition is known for offering spiritual uplift and personal deliverance for those needing divine healing from God. Pentecostal worship usually rejects colonized norms, disregarding Western rationality where faith is primarily about the mind. Black Pentecostal Christians do not care about appearing respectable in the eyes of those in the dominant culture. There is no concern about whether white people will look down on their worship. Worship can be undignified in the eyes of humans so long as it ascribes all honor to God.

The spiritual life—especially being seized by the Spirit—of Black Pentecostals retains connections to older enslaved African practices. However, Black Pentecostalism has often adopted what some have called Neoplatonism, with a goal of ascending beyond and above material concerns. It has frequently embraced Western dualisms between the material world and the spiritual realm as opposed to African cosmologies where material and spiritual are integrated and whole. Black Pentecostals are also the least likely to be involved in direct social activism as an expression of faith, and are more oriented toward spiritual deliverance and personal self-help. The tradition's holiness teachings are frequently interpreted and practiced as strict communal morality, dress standards, and behavioral codes. These practices can be legalistic and patriarchal, but they also have helped people avoid harmful and unhealthy habits. Black Pentecostalism, like all the other Black Church traditions, has played a distinct role in helping Black people experience God and navigate a society bent toward their death.

The liberative spirit and prophetic witness of the Black Church

We cannot talk about how Black Americans survived centuries of oppression in this land without honoring the role of the Black Church in its plurality. It was there for Black people during slavery, as we got up and out from it, as we navigated Jim and Jane Crow and mutated antiblack systems of oppression like neo-slavery and exploited labor, white terrorism and lynching, and segregation and exclusion from economic opportunities. It was there while Black people resisted antiblack stereotypes like minstrel shows with blackface and white supremacist films like *Birth of a Nation*. The Black Church was an inseparable part of the struggle to survive and pursue freedom against all odds. And it remains a refuge for millions today in the age of mass incarceration, police brutality, vast disinvestment of predominately Black neighborhoods, underfunded schools, and disproportionate access to jobs with livable wages, healthcare, quality housing, clean air and water, and grocery stores with fresh and healthy food. Through it all, the Black Church still proclaims that the doors of the church are open.

Black faith has traditionally held to a deep trust in the God of the cosmos. A term like "the Trinity" can't capture the fullness of the Black Church's journey with the Creator, Sustainer, and Liberator who created the heavens and the earth and "has flung the stars and planets" into the universe and yet intimately knows us and cares for us. It is in and through God that we "live and move and have our being" (Acts 17:28). This is the God of the exodus and the One who takes us through exile. God is our Waymaker, our help when our backs are against the wall, who can turn things around right at the midnight hour. The Black Church does not believe in a distant and removed God—God has been with us through the storm. We confess that God is here and promises to never leave us alone. God will guide us into freedom.

At the center of life in the Black Church is Jesus Christ as our deliverer and savior. Jesus is preeminent in our lives. He is the center of joy. He is "the way and the truth and the life" (John 14:6). For those in the prophetic stream, we see in his life a first-century, dark-skinned, Afro-Asiatic Jew living under the Roman Empire in what we now call Palestine. Jesus came to set the oppressed free and invited us to follow after him as he centered the disinherited, the disadvantaged, and the downtrodden, and as he reigned right under the nose of Caesar, speaking truth to power everywhere he went. He was falsely arrested by policing-soldiers, brutalized, experienced an unjust "justice system," and then was issued a state-sanctioned death sentence that deemed that his life didn't matter. But the powers and authorities didn't have the last word, and on the third day he rose in all power.

The brilliance and beauty of the Black Church is most notably in its attentiveness to the Holy Spirit. Whether in the church's gathering or its scattering, believers have often demonstrated a profound willingness to let go of control and let the Spirit lead, generating moments of profound communal contemplation. Contemplation is more than Western individualistic practices of silence. As theologian Barbara Holmes reminds us in *Joy Unspeakable*, the Black Church has cultivated contemplation through communal worship, allowing for deep reflection and intimacy with God.[7] This contemplative practice is attuned to the presence and movement of the Spirit as people dwell in the presence of God and interact with mind, body, and soul. These Spirit-led lulls in Black Church liturgies are different from the common conceptions of only "shout'n" or "getting happy" when seized by the Spirit.

Of course, the Holy Spirit's activity is not limited to Black communal worship. The Spirit is at work in the world. "The Holy Spirit inspires the dance of God, calling all to participate in the dance of divine love, creativity, healing, justice, and renewal," writes Karen Baker-Fletcher in *Dancing with God*.[8] We can see that dance in everyday people who are inspired to love, to speak up, to act courageously, and to participate in the healing presence of the Spirit rather than cycles of harm that continue to wound so many. "Women like Mother Mamie Till-Mobley, Mother Rosa Parks, Mother Ella Baker, and First

Lady Coretta Scott King could have hated, but walked in love," Baker-Fletcher writes. "They could have sunk to violent rage, but instead they walked in holy indignation and holy dignity. They led others as they followed Christ in the comforting, encouraging, healing power of the Holy Spirit. God in Christ bore them up on wings like eagles (Isa. 40:31). They showed the world the meaning of resurrection, Holy Spirit power."[9]

Black preaching is a vital part of a Black Church worship gathering. Shaped by West African oral traditions and communal habits as well as Protestant emphases on the sermon, Black preaching has instructed, inspired, corrected, and encouraged attendees while also opening space for prophetic truth-telling. The community expects to encounter God as they reflect and interact with the preached word. Black preaching is not a passive experience—the congregation dialogues with the preacher and responds to God verbally. Preaching, explains scholar and minister Dale Andrews, is an invitation "to experience revelation and to experience the Spirit of God."[10] Black preaching invites the whole congregation into a holy experience. And the best Black preaching addresses the spiritual needs, material concerns, and sociocultural realities of the community.

Black preaching participation unfolds through call-and-response. It intentionally engages the whole being of congregants, not just the mind. This is *nommo*, an African term to describe the communal experience and power between speaker and hearer. "In *nommo*," writes Andrews, "expression and content are held together."[11] The form, feel, and sound of preaching matters as well as the content. And the content usually comes through storytelling—like most of Scripture itself. Abstract systematic propositions that have led to church division, such as how exactly God is present at the Lord's table, are the product of the Western church. Systematic doctrines severed from story and context don't shape our formation, identity, and ethical understanding in the same way as the Black congregational experience.

Storytelling remains important in traditional Black congregations. Black preachers are expected to "tell the story" of sacred scriptures—make it touch the lives of the worshiping community so they begin to live these scriptural stories and can see how God can make a way, offer healing, provide revelation, and so on, in their own lives. Traditionally, Black preaching ends with communal celebration and/or participation. It can even be lament. This is possible only if the preaching resonates deep down within the souls of listeners or the Spirit is at work from the inside out, within that communal moment. This is always the goal.

The prophetic stream of the Black Church

While the Black Church has been an important antiracist witness in society, the tradition as a whole has not always consistently committed to the liberation of all people from all oppression. Some Black churches have been unable to intentionally cultivate a faith that leads to racial and economic justice for their own communities beyond the pews. Institutional and communal antiracism that rejects white supremacy and antiblackness because of our shared belonging in Christ, and because everyone is made in the image of God, is important. Good news, however, must extend from the pews to the streets.

There is a stream of the Black Church that cuts across all the major Black denominations and has embodied the struggle for freedom and justice from enslavement to this present day. This same stream often challenges and resists the interlocking oppressions that are embedded in our societies' policies, structures, and institutions. To recognize the power and promise of the Black Church is to single out the prophetic tradition that resisted slavery, subverted and challenged Jim and Jane Crow, and today continues to unmask the powers of empire and its desire to dominate, plunder, and violate many of the inhabitants of the earth (and often the earth itself).

The word "prophetic" could be confusing. Mainstream American Christians, and even some corners of the Black Church, use the term to denote someone who has a special revelation and knowledge from God to predict the future, offer a special message to someone, or peer into the spiritual realm. By contrast, in more justice-oriented Black congregations, this language draws on the example of the Hebrew prophets like Micah, Amos, Isaiah, and Jeremiah—how the prophets challenged idolatry and injustice. The prophets speak truth to power, pull back the curtain on empire, and critique empty religiosity tied to exploitation and oppression. The prophetic stream of the Black Church offers a collective call to social repentance, to challenge the nation to turn away from its immoral value system, and to pursue liberation from all that keeps everyone captive. It's an oversimplification, but some see prophetic as *foretelling the future* whereas others understand it to mean *forthtelling God's truth* to the powerful or the whole society. I mean the latter option when talking about the prophetic stream. Many Black churches have some degree of prophetic inclinations, yet not all fit within the prophetic stream of the Black Church.[12]

The hard truth is that not all Black congregations participated in the Civil Rights freedom struggle, though most contemporary Black churches collectively take credit for that activity. And while most Black Christians believe that justice is a good thing, not all could explain how justice and liberation are an essential part of the gospel of Jesus Christ. So while we celebrate the antiracism witness of the current Black Church, it is also worth making distinctions so we can celebrate the wing of the Black Church that courageously resisted white supremacy and antiblack oppression and became a mouthpiece for God's truth and commitment to justice for vulnerable and suffering people. The prophetic stream has understood that as we draw on the biblical story fulfilled in Jesus, the church is called to embrace the prophethood of all believers. The prophetic tradition dares to reveal imperial religion, racist practices, militaristic nationalism, greed and exploitation, patriarchy and sexual abuse, and the ecological destruction of our planet. The Black prophetic tradition has been one of the most important Christian traditions around the globe to emerge from the devastating underside of the Doctrine of Discovery.

In the face of antiblackness and patriarchy, Sojourner Truth said, "Ain't I a woman?" Over a century later, Cheryl Townsend Gilkes said, "If it wasn't for the women . . ."! During the early stages of Jim and Jane Crow, minister Henry McNeal said, "God is a negro." During the rise of the Black Power movement, James Cone said, "Jesus is black." This is the prophetic tradition, inspired to courageously speak truth and challenge harmful, death-dealing ideologies by unveiling their hypocrisies and pronouncing God's judgment.[13]

Jesus embodied the prophetic tradition in his own life. The gospel writers make it clear that he was a Jew formed by Judaism who cited and embodied the Hebrew prophets afresh for his day. Today, when we participate in the body of Christ, we are called to join the prophethood of Jesus' ministry. Again, I'm not talking about a special role for those who have esoteric spiritual knowledge to dispense. Individuals and communities step into the prophetic tradition when they faithfully join in God's delivering presence, healing justice, and truth-telling in the way of Jesus Christ. This is part of what it means to be the church, full stop. The prophetic stream of the Black Church has embodied this holy calling before a watching world, demonstrating faithful resistance in the aftermath of colonial plunder, white supremacy, and antiblack oppression.

Why the Black Church matters today

Rev. C. T. Vivian was a pastor, a dear friend of Dr. King, and a vital Civil Rights leader who organized protests and sit-ins. As a survivor of Jim Crow white supremacy, he shared personal stories and insights with several generations coming after him. On two occasions, I heard him observe how the Civil Rights Movement was "a clash of two Christianities" expressed in the public square. It's fairly simple: one expression of Christianity practiced and pursued God's justice and peace for all God's children while the other version of Christianity maintained and bolstered Jim and Jane Crow oppression and the belief that white people's bodies and culture ought to be put above other people's bodies and culture, especially over Black people.

I immediately recognized "a clash of two Christianities" as a prophetic, precise, and provocative way of unveiling that not everyone confessing the name of Jesus worked collaboratively in pursuit God's beloved community. However, it took a few years for Rev. Vivian's insight to fully sink in for me. It's obvious that the faith of Dr. King, Ella Baker, Rev. Fred Shuttlesworth, Diane Nash, and Rev. Vivian diametrically opposed the kind of faith animating the KKK and the White Citizens' Council. That difference is overt. However, when I thought about the white moderates whom Dr. King called out in his "Letter from Birmingham Jail," I began to see the forest and not just the trees. It wasn't just the white Christians hiding under hoods and burning crosses in yards who were clashing with the faith of the Black Christians and their allies. Most mainstream and moderate white Christians were also clashing with the faith of the freedom struggle as well.

To this day, different expressions of faith continue to clash in the public square. The divergence of faith expressed through a political vision for society has been especially apparent in electoral preferences. Paying attention to race, faith, and political desire together is especially telling. For example, during the 2024 presidential election, white Americans who regularly attended church supported Republican candidate Donald Trump in significantly high numbers, yet the opposite was true for Black Americans. Those who attended religious services overwhelmingly supported Democrat Kamala Harris.[14] During slavery, Jim Crow, and still today, Christians continue to clash across lines of race, faith, and politics. The Christianity of the Black Church remains distinct from mainstream Christianity.

It's hard for me to talk objectively about the significance of the Black Church. I am who I am because of the congregation that loved me, mentored me, stretched and challenged me, believed in me, and nurtured my faith. My church taught me that Jesus was the center of my faith. My church kindled a love for God within me. The habits of reading my Bible, prayer, and singing songs of worship and praise were cultivated in my church, along with growing in Christian character and faithfulness in private and in public. And while I know this is not the testimony of all children of the Black Church (especially some in the LGBTQ community), my Black church instilled in me the deep belief and understanding that I was "fearfully and wonderfully made" by God. I learned to read, pray, teach, and preach publicly because of my congregation. It's hard to imagine who I would be without my home church. And I say all that while also acknowledging that my church was part of a Black evangelical stream that uncritically adopted and perpetuated parts of the "white man's religion" in our worshiping community. Too often Black women and girls were excluded from full inclusion and belonging or opportunities for leadership. The Black Church is diverse and complex when moving from ideal to reality.

Yet through most of Black people's existence in this land, the Black Church has been a deeply liberating and prophetic community as we sought to carve out a space for ourselves to live on this side of antiblack chattel slavery. The Black Church was our refuge. On Sundays we could find rest in God's presence as we gathered together regardless of what indignities and disrespect we encountered throughout the week at the hands of white people. There, worshiping God was a healing practice for traumatized people who didn't have access to therapy. The community was a network of mutual aid for those who couldn't make ends meet. Our community was empowering, encouraging us to hold our heads high even as antiblack discrimination defined the broader society. And this worshiping community sought to be the presence of Jesus as we followed the lead of the Holy Spirit.

To this very day, so much of what has made Black culture(s) so powerful and distinctive is threaded to the tapestry of the Black Church. From spirituals to gospel music, the Black Church has left its mark on Black music, repeatedly infusing soul into the lives of Black people and the broader society.

The cadence of West African rhetoric now expressed through English morphed into all sorts of poetry and spoken word, rap, and rhetorical power. The Black Church helped to sustain this genius. Many of the most iconic Black leaders, artists, innovators, and politicians got their start, and support, from within the Black Church. Its prophetic witness is needed today in the Black Lives Matter era and amid the entrenchment of white Christian nationalism. When myths, systems, policies, and institutions are organized by the principles of white supremacy and antiblackness, the memory of the Black Church's liberating activity is inspiring. My prayer is that God will use it again in the twenty-first century.

For many centuries, American mainstream Christians persisted in the path carved out by the Doctrine of Discovery. Black people found themselves captive inside this antiblack death-dealing religion and society. Nevertheless, many courageous Black people dared to become fugitives, making their escape from captivity and in pursuit of freedom. Stealing away to Jesus and freedom cultivated a liberative faith. This Black fugitive faith is one of the greatest gifts that the Black Church has offered the rest of the body of Christ. Christianity doesn't have to remain a white supremacist, antiblack, settler colonial tradition. The way of Jesus leads to freedom. The Black Church is needed more today than ever before.

── SEVEN ──

Is the Black Church Dead?

In 2010, scholar Dr. Eddie Glaude posted an article titled "The Black Church Is Dead." Yeah, that started something. A big debate busted open online about the merits and limitations of his turn of phrase and argument. Some people focused on a straightforward analysis of his title. They scoffed—while seemingly ignoring his thesis and main arguments—because clearly the Black Church had a higher proportion of Black people regularly attending church than white Americans.

But Glaude was not concerned about that. His provocative article highlighted several concerns. First, he said, the progressive and prophetic myth of the Black Church was not legitimate. Most contemporary Black churches, pastors, and congregants were theologically conservative. They were not all participating in and pursuing God's justice and liberation. Some were even caught up in the prosperity gospel, where it is taught that if you have enough faith, you can "name it and claim it" and receive direct health and financial prosperity from God. Second, Glaude asserted, Black churches were no longer central to the Black community—they were one institution alongside many that competed for Black people's commitment, energy, and focus. And that included white congregations, which were competing with Black churches for Black people.

Glaude argued that we needed to acknowledge "the routinization of black prophetic witness."[1] The contemporary Black Church loved to recount the Black Church's historical role in the Black community, thereby using nostalgia to justify its existence in the present. It was all too common to explain and legitimatize the present witness of the Black Church through its *past* witness and deeds. By always pointing to the glory days of the Black Church, whether under slavery or during the Civil Rights Movement, we were obscuring how such a past is no longer alive in the present. I can testify to this: I've seen Black Christians who have no intention of struggling for justice themselves rely on such arguments. The nostalgia hides their lack of involvement in similar sociopolitical activity today. If we are honest, sometimes they are part of congregations that refused to be involved in the 1950s and '60s struggle as well.

In announcing the death of the Black Church, Glaude was seeking not to demean Black worshiping communities but to create an "opportunity to breathe new life into what it means to be black and Christian."[2] Despite all the criticism—some of it legitimate—of his proclamation, most did not disagree with his key claims: most Black churches were not preaching a liberating gospel. Their prophetic witness was minimal or missing. They did not live out an inclusive and ever-expanding practice of beloved community where all oppressed people belong, matter, and can thrive. The prophetic stream of the Black Church participated eagerly in God's justice and deliverance, but the majority of Black congregations were not in that living tradition.

Fifteen years later, these concerns seem even more pressing than when Glaude published his article. The Black Lives Matter movement has helped expose and confront how Black suffering and oppression is built into American institutions. Slow death occurs through policies that crush the possibility to thrive for most Black neighborhoods, and quick death occurs at the hands of police and others who want to control Black people. The resurgence of white Christian nationalism has not only revealed white mainstream Christians' opposition to the way of Jesus, but also unveiled how the preaching, theology, discipleship, liturgy, and overall ministry in some Black churches is severed from the death-dealing realities that many Black people are confronting every day. That is, they have internalized a slightly tweaked version of the white American gospel that provides no good news to the communities they are called to serve.

I can list many Black congregations that do not fit into this box. And many more that fit in some ways and not others. But I do think that the *idea* of a prophetic Black Church in the twenty-first century rarely lines up with the reality of what people are experiencing on the ground. The story of the Doctrine of Discovery, and its organizing principles of white supremacy, antiblackness, Indigenous erasure, and ongoing plunder, is still unfolding. The Black Church needs its own come-to-Jesus moment. Can the doors of the church be opened for and to the Black Church so that it can revive its revolutionary witness for the radical and liberative way of Jesus and the delivering presence of God in our world?

Renouncing the white American gospel

There are significant differences between the lived beliefs and practices of the Black Church and mainstream white American worshiping communities. The Black Church cannot pursue and be beloved community in and for the world while leaning on unexamined doctrines that promote or remain neutral to the bad news that white Christians have spoken and practiced.

I can hear the inevitable pushback from those who preach an Americanized gospel. Many Black Christians compare themselves to their white Christian counterparts and highlight real differences between their faith and that of white religionists. On many fronts, Black Christians tend to be more loving, kind, generous, and compassionate to those who are disproportionately suffering than many white Christians who preach love yet are known to support mean-spirited and harmful policies that devastate vulnerable people groups. Many might think there is no need to interrogate the inherited beliefs that are woven deeply into the sacred rhetoric and God-talk of many Black churches. Comparing oneself to a low bar helps no one. As James Cone once said, "The black church looks good when compared with the sick history of the white church. But what about our relations with our brothers and sisters who believe that black churches are destructive forces in the struggle for political freedom?"[3]

Especially in the era of Black Lives Matter and the reactive rise in white Christian nationalism, the Black Church has moved slowly, with nonstrategic spectacle marches, ecumenical prayers, and nondisruptive protests that do not confront the strongholds and systems that have a foot on many people's necks. Yes, there are prophetic exceptions. But right now, those most committed to racial justice and Black liberation largely view the Black Church as irrelevant to Black well-being. The Christianese prayers and cliches (like proclaiming "God is still on the throne" right after a tragedy) offered without substantive action prompt some to interpret the Black Church as the problem. Folks are out here saying they are too blessed to be stressed, but I believe that God's heart is agonized over the suffering happening all around us. The holiness of Jesus didn't lead to being unbothered—it meant compassion, lament, and sometimes tears in response to the need and wounds of others.

Many Black preachers and teachers continue to push a non-liberative white evangelical gospel. This gospel reduces the revolutionary character of the liberating story of Jesus to "He died for you, so you can go to heaven." This gospel is extremely individualistic, spiritual, other-world oriented, and severed from the messianic announcement of the kingdom of God that has come, is here, and is in our midst. The simplistic, mainstream gospel focused on heaven is unmatched by the gospel of Jesus, who brought God's kingdom from heaven to earth.

White mainstream Christians have found clever ways to plunder Bible verses out of context and arrange them anew to make the Word of God fit their discipleship-less gospel. They reduce our faith to believing doctrine without needing to truly embody the way of Jesus. Consider the popular "Romans Road" Bible verses used to lead someone to Christian conversion. This method isolates verses scattered throughout the book of Romans that appear to be focused on sin and salvation, then realigns and stitches them together to provide a "biblical" path to conversion.[4] However, once you study Romans on its own terms and understand as much as possible about the ancient context to which Paul's letter responds, we see that Paul wrote to help Roman Christian communities overcome Jewish-Gentile tensions, resist imperial power, and practice a faithful embodiment of Christ's love and justice. By plundering verses from their context, the Romans Road method domesticates the Bible and distracts us with a less radical challenge to our lives. This irresponsible selectivity is no different from when slaveholders told enslaved Africans that God commanded, "Slaves, obey your masters."

Most in the Black Church are aware of more holistic implications of Jesus and his kingdom found in the Bible, yet many are still socialized to describe the gospel itself in narrow ways that conform to white evangelical doctrine. Holistic teachings like God's justice and healing are present, but are categorized as secondary instead of central to the gospel itself. God's liberating justice has been compartmentalized so that the white evangelical interpretation of the gospel is the one teaching that remains untouched and not held up to the scrutiny of the full biblical witness.

We need to study Scripture afresh, immerse ourselves in the story of Jesus, and define the gospel out of our own study and Spirit-filled readings. Theologian Lisa Allen makes it plain: "If our understandings of the gospel of Jesus Christ are centered on personal salvation and an individual righteousness, we have missed Jesus's message and ministry."[5] The gospel has implications for us individually, but overemphasis on these lacks the full scope of Jesus' invitation in the Gospels. Our experiences as Black people under white supremacy and antiblack oppression provide more insight into biblical books written under the thumb of the Roman Empire than the neutered readings that have lacked power to disrupt slavery, Jim and Jane Crow, and subsequent forms of oppression today. The Black Church must boldly renounce the domesticated American gospel so it can faithfully and consistently preach (and embody) the liberative, prophetic, transformative gospel of Jesus that is still turning our world upside down.

Liturgy and justice

If the Black Church is going to be a life-giving and liberative community, it needs to become more conscious of its liturgical life and its relationship to participating in God's justice. By liturgy, I don't primarily mean high church practices, but rather any communal worship practices and habits—everything that happens when we gather. In Black communal worship, Black people have been able to create refuge from the ongoing assaults they often encounter every day. Yet without intentionality, communal worship can lose sight of what we ascribe worth to (worship) and how we faithfully participate in what God is doing (discipleship and formation).

Over the past couple of decades, I've witnessed ongoing shifts in the worship life of the Black Church. This includes the adoption of white mainstream contemporary Christian music that further dilutes the biblical teaching on God's compassionate justice for the vulnerable and our vocation to love our stigmatized and overlooked neighbor (vital to knowing God and pursuing faithfulness in the way of Jesus). We must keep watch for how content and form shape people who do justice, love mercy, and walk humbly before God.

In *A Womanist Theology of Worship*, Lisa Allen considers how Black Church liturgy shaped Black worshipers throughout slavery and Jim and Jane Crow and up to our present day, with an eye toward its relationship to intersectional justice and African cosmology. Unfortunately, the historic witness of the Black Church has continually eroded, as seen through its disregard for a robust theology of worship practice. Allen, for example, compared contemporary church services with accounts of post-antebellum Black worship. "There was one jarring revelation," she writes. "The link of liturgy with justice that infused and imbued the worship of the historic Black church is all but missing today. There are preachers who preach justice and liberation in Black churches, to be sure, but do entire worship services in these churches undergird and underscore the important link between worship with justice?"[6]

Unfortunately, I have found Allen's observation to be true. Something about the sound of gospel music speaks to my soul. However, if I want to listen to Black music that reflects God's justice for poor and oppressed people, it's easier to find among so-called conscious rappers than in catalogs of contemporary gospel music. I am increasingly concerned about how Black worship leaders (and gospel artists) are uncritically incorporating contemporary Christian music (CCM) into the Black Church. White CCM is known for feel-good lyrics, commercialized sounds, and a tendency to prioritize vague inspirational messages that lack ethical depth or prophetic critique. Give me the power and the simplicity of the songs born out of Black people's experiences with God instead! Even some Black gospel artists are diluting the good news of the gospel.

It takes effort and time to pull together worship music that appropriately ascribes God's worthiness while not erasing the character and activity of God who has been revealed in Scripture as one who prioritizes justice for the widow, orphan, foreigner, poor, and oppressed. The focus of the Black Church's worship, and in this case, its music, is overly determined by colonial white doctrines and music industry practices geared for broad commercial appeal—this will not set the captives free.

Theologian Robert Beckford sees the same problem in his British context. "Theological ideas in most Black churches are 'policed' by colonial Christianity," he writes, naming how liturgy and worship—including contemporary Black British gospel music—continues to be influenced by perverse ideas about God communicated to enslaved Africans by white colonizers.[7] We need to find ways to decolonize the music itself, not of its sound, but of its primary message and orientation. This requires writing gospel music that emerges out of the life of the Black Church rather than music pushed by music executives and trend analysis. It must contemplate how the old story is good news for those whose backs are against the wall in our communities today. Beckford also recommends improved communication and creativity between theologians, songwriters, and musicians: "Only through more dialogue and conversation, especially in the context of music production, can we find creative commercially viable ways of confronting colonial Christianity in Christian music."[8]

The reality is that the *entire* liturgy of our gathering ought to be organized in such ways that it forms us to desire, and participate, in God's justice. If the Black Church is to recover its vocation as beloved community, it will need to relink biblical emphases on justice with all our liturgy while decolonizing the mainstream dominant cultural theology and music industry consumer trends that have seeped into our communities.

Liberating *all* oppressions

Most Black churches have no tolerance for the explicit white supremacy and antiblackness frequently generated in mainstream white American congregations. And most Black churches are, in some form, oriented toward embracing antiracism. But one challenge for the twenty-first-century Black church is whether its historic orientation of liberation of Black people from racist systems will expand to reflect the depth and width of the gospel of Jesus Christ and its good news for all oppressed people. This includes recognizing the liberative significance of Jesus' life for everyone, recognizing the inherent dignity of each person, and practicing the rule of the kingdom, where the last are first and the first are last (Matthew 19:30; 20:16; Mark 10:31; Luke 13:30). God's liberation is not limited to race and poverty. It extends to gender, sexuality, abilities, and any time people are stigmatized, socially rejected, or discriminated against.

There are many more Black women pastors today than just a couple decades ago. But it is still typical to encounter patriarchy in the Black Church. This habit is inherited from centuries of patriarchy emboldened by Christendom. By internalizing this particular biblical interpretation, many have, without careful scrutiny, reversed Jesus' social upheavals of his own patriarchal society. In Jesus' reign, women are taken seriously as disciples studying at his feet, they embody God's reign, and they proclaim his resurrection.

I'm grateful for the many Black women pastors in my life who have preached the gospel and discipled others faithfully over the years. I am a recipient of their ministry and gifts. Yet many Black women who have a calling to pastoral leadership end up leaving for more progressive or liberal white denominations because there aren't enough Black churches willing to receive their gifts and leadership. This is nothing new—James Cone made this point four decades ago. "In many contexts the black church is as backward and obscene on the issue of sexism as is the white church," wrote Cone. "It is truly amazing that many black male ministers, young and old, can hear the message of liberation in the gospel when related to racism but remain deaf to a similar message in the context of sexism."[9] That might sting, but it is true nonetheless.

Sexism will persist until Black men in the church are willing to break from white patriarchal assumptions and reread our holy scriptures, led by the Spirit, as we understand how the liberation of God extends to women and requires their full participation. I was a part of an all-Black and male pastoral team in my twenties. I was frequently discouraged by our collective lack of discernment about a situation involving a case of marital abuse. My frustration with the older male pastors, whom I loved dearly, was coupled with a conviction that the conversation would have been much different if Black women, who made up a majority of the congregation, were eligible to provide guidance and pastoral wisdom. But that table was set only for Black men. Too frequently I hear Black Christians justify the second-class status of Black women in the church by applying a scriptural method that sounds eerily similar to the methodology used to justify the enslavement of Black Africans.

As with other topics, individual Bible passages might suggest that women in church should not speak (a standard that is never actually upheld) or lead men. However, there are lots of problems with those selectively plundered readings. In Paul's first letter to the Corinthians, for example, he appears to tell women not to speak in one chapter (1 Corinthians 14:34–35), then instructs them how to speak and prophesy in the church in another chapter (11:5–13). People will draw on a very confusing passage in 1 Timothy to insist that women cannot lead—but never then teach that women are saved by childbearing, which is in the same passage (1 Timothy 2:11–15). Many scholars have noted that Paul was probably writing about interactions between husbands and wives, not all men and all women.

These letters are by no means the only voice on the matter, and many other passages are explicitly liberating for women living under patriarchy. Jesus' ministry consistently undermines patriarchy. In Luke 10:38–42, Jesus defends a woman's right to study as a disciple, saying that Mary has chosen "the better part" (v. 42) by sitting at his feet to learn rather than being confined to gendered domestic duties. Women are the first to proclaim the resurrected Jesus to men who were afraid and hiding and yet didn't believe them (Matthew 28:1–10; Mark 16:1–11; Luke 24:1–12; John 20:1–2, 11–18). Galatians 3:28 imagines life in Christ to have destroyed the hierarchies of ethnicity, freedom, and slavery, as well as that between men and women. They are all one in Christ. Romans 16 provides a window into the life of the early church, where women serve in every capacity in the life of the church. And in the book of Acts, the Spirit of God falls on *all flesh*, women and men (Acts 2:17–18). As we read the whole Bible, we must notice how liberative patterns in scripture converge and are fulfilled in Jesus Christ and how the Spirit leads us into full liberation.

This same Spirit remains at work today, breaking down boundaries of race, ethnicity, and class. As in the book of Acts, the Black Church must vulnerably follow the lead of the Spirit as it seeks to embody life in Christ, where everyone belongs, everyone matters, and everyone can thrive. Too frequently, the contemporary Black Church has followed the patterns of mainstream white American Christians on issues of gender, relying on a small handful of verses (which often don't mean what we think they do). We do this while claiming to hold to a "biblical" view on gender while ignoring the larger liberative patterns throughout the biblical canon and the ongoing work of the Holy Spirit that leads and guides us into God's dream.

The greatest challenge facing not only the Black Church but the global church in the twenty-first century is discerning whether God's liberation is radically inclusive for all people, including LGBTQ people, or whether that group can be singled out for exclusion and denied full belonging in the body of Christ. Conservative Black Christians believe that a shift toward embracing LGBTQ people in the church is merely Western society's moral degradation and an unwillingness to do things God's way. Progressive or liberationist Black Christians, in contrast, suggest that the Black Church needs a consistent liberationist ethic for all oppressed people. "Traditional" sexual ethics and practices that exclude or marginalize LGBTQ people stem from white Christian colonization of Black people—these moral standards are largely taken for granted, imposing alien morals onto our community. Western views on sexuality have influence around the globe, including in Uganda, where colonial logics have led to laws making "aggravated homosexuality" a crime punishable by death.

While few in the North American Black Church believe that LGBTQ people should receive the death penalty, most of those who do not support inclusion are unwilling to consider how their views are shaped more by Western reasoning than by careful Spirit-led scriptural and theological wrestling over what most reflects the way of Jesus. The Bible doesn't say a lot on this subject, especially compared to other subjects like the evils of greed and hoarding wealth or the call to redistribute our resources to the poor. Teachings on wealth and poverty saturate our sacred text but seem to carry minimal weight in many conservative congregations—especially compared to churches' hyper-focus on sexuality. Furthermore, we rarely talk about the specific circumstances that the biblical writers were addressing in their minimal commentary on sexuality and gender. Most Bible passages that people fight over do not directly address the questions or concerns raised today. Without understanding the gap between their ancient concerns and our contemporary debates, our ethical reasoning is forcing a square peg (an ancient concern) into a round hole (our modern context).

In the twenty-first century, a primary social concern has been addressing the laws, policies, and attitudes that have legalized discrimination against LGBTQ people—laws and biases largely constructed by the hegemony of American Christians. White progressive Christians' stance on LGBTQ concerns sometimes feels like virtue signaling. Still, the Black Church must do some soul-searching as it surrenders to the liberating God we worship. No matter the particular tradition, churches' hyper-focus on sexuality doesn't seem healthy for thriving communities. The church of Jesus Christ must practice the full belonging and inclusion of marginalized peoples, loving them in their bodies and as they are as God's beloveds.

If the Black Church is to be a liberating presence for all people, it needs to stop outsourcing biblical study and theological reasoning to mainstream white Christians. When we set aside the white interpretations, how might our own discernment rooted in Scripture, the leading of the Spirit, and our remembering God's liberating activity and presence in the Black experience over the past several centuries shape our ethics of what God desires of us? While Jesus does not directly address our questions concerning the LGBTQ community, he demonstrates a deep attentiveness and concern for the differently-gendered bodies of eunuchs during his day. Ancient eunuchs, like intersex people, were outside the normative categories of male and female. Jesus says, "For there are eunuchs who have been so from birth, and there are eunuchs who have been made eunuchs by others, and there are eunuchs who have made themselves eunuchs for the sake of the kingdom of heaven. Let anyone accept this who can" (Matthew 19:12).

This one verse doesn't resolve all questions, and it would be strange to uphold one verse and universalize it as the only scriptural perspective since I've warned against extracting and cherry-picking Bible verses! At the same time, that is our record of what Jesus has to say on the subject. I hope to broaden and deepen our compassion and curiosity to match the character and commitments of Jesus, who consistently took sides with and demonstrated concern for the least, last, and little ones stigmatized by society. How can the liberation of God that we participate in orient the Black Church toward the *kin*dom practice of Jesus that leads to radical inclusion and love for all oppressed and marginalized people? As theologian Marcia Y. Riggs writes, "Black liberation in the twenty-first century must be centered in the justice of God so that it does not have too narrow a focus for the ministry of God's redeeming and reconciling radical love of inclusion."[10] If the Black Church is to pursue being God's beloved community before a watching world, it must grapple anew with its beliefs and practices around gender and sexuality and offer a more faithful, loving, courageous, Jesus-shaped, and Spirit-led way forward.

Transforming nation-state logics and partisan politics

Christian discipleship is inherently political, but *how* it is to be political is not so obvious. Some may be confused to see the word "political" tied to Christianity. Many Christians operate within the Western split between spiritual and sociopolitical realities. The two, they think, are unrelated. This gets complicated when we talk about the separation of church and state (which I believe is important), and how US churches, as tax-exempt entities, are not supposed to endorse political candidates. But separation of church and state does not mean that Christianity isn't political. Calling Christian discipleship *political* can be confusing because many people conflate partisanship with being political. Supporting political parties and engaging in electoral politics (partisanship) is only a very slim part of political activity. Politics, says theologian James Logan, includes how "we humans organize our common lives in contexts of differential power."[11] Politics is about how we organize our lives together and how we treat one another collectively. Christianity is deeply concerned about how we treat one another, individually and collectively. And Scripture's eschatological visions of shalom—the new heaven and new earth and the new creation—provide a glimpse into God's dream for all creation.

Our lives are political because we live in, navigate, and interact with society. And our faith is political because it shapes how we live in and engage society. Jesus teaches and models how we are to live by centering our concern on the poor, the oppressed, Samaritans, vulnerable women, the hungry, the sick, and the neglected. That has profound political implications. Taking seriously Jesus' teachings on forgiveness could drastically influence our views on capital punishment. The jubilee ethic emphasized in the gospel of Luke should shape how we think about poverty and our response to it. Certain reflections on the crucifixion of Jesus can sensitize followers of Jesus to other crucified people in the world. Jesus preached about God's kingdom while living within Caesar's Roman Empire. His followers called him "Lord"—a term reserved for Caesar. The word "gospel" was typically used to announce imperial activity, such as the presence of the empire or a military victory. These were dangerously political acts. From its inception, Christianity was understood to be not only political, but subversive, with people seeing the community and movement as "turning the world upside down" (Acts 17:6).

The question is not whether the Black Church is a political entity, but how it should be political today. There is no easy answer to this, and it can't be answered once for all time. What I do know is that our political praxis *ain't* working. Our political imaginations, grassroots popular education, and collective will to collaborate across coalitions needs to be transfigured. My prayer is that the Black Church, after undergoing its own rebirth, can help guide others into a better, more faithful, and subversive way of engaging politically.

From my vantage point, our post–Civil Rights political imagination has been stifled primarily because we have been hoodwinked to believe that our only viable options are what the state offers as official forms of political activity. For most of us, getting political means running for office, supporting someone's campaign, or voting. Thank goodness Jesus didn't limit his activity to authorized activity according to the Roman Empire! The Black Church needs a more robust historical memory so it can be inspired by the wide array of political activities engaged in by its members over many centuries.

It is common today for Black leaders to focus on voting as the singular birthright of post–Civil Rights struggle. I get it—we need to mobilize folks who are not engaged politically. Voting rights are regularly being stripped, antiracism and racial justice work is being banned, and our history is being erased from public education across the nation. This is happening as our nation persists in perpetuating racial inequities and terrible living conditions for too many people of color. Voting is one way to engage. I vote; voting has its place. I certainly prefer our broken and flawed democracy to a dictatorship.

However, many in our community feel that voting doesn't make a difference. Whether under Republican or Democratic leadership, the fundamental policies and institutions that advantage the haves and disadvantage the have-nots remain untouched. Policing is tweaked, sometimes for better, sometimes for worse. Neighborhoods and schools remain disinvested. The prison industrial complex and its abuse and humiliation of inmates persists. Wages remain low, and corporations prioritize the wealth of stockholders over the well-being of workers. Our planet continues to be plundered, and environmental racism still leads to terrible health outcomes for many Black and Brown neighborhoods. So when people say voting doesn't matter, there needs to be a better answer than, "Well, if you don't vote, you have lost the right to speak on these issues."

The Republican Party has been blatantly racist, and its policies are broadly devastating for the poor. At the same time, many Democratic leaders have done very little to address the issues that are most pressing for the Black community. The Black Church has voted consistently. The Republican Party had Black support during and after slavery, but Black support switched to the Democratic Party when the Republican Party embraced racist candidates and opposition to the Civil Rights Movement. Starting in the 1930s and throughout the twentieth century, Democrats were more likely to support policies that helped poor and working-class people and also benefitted Black people. And Democrats increasingly embraced Civil

Rights legislation. It took a lot to move the Black Church away from the party of Lincoln. But automatic support for any political party limits our capacity to have a prophetic witness in society, and allows for Black people to be used for electoral politics without any corresponding strides toward meaningful justice for our neighborhoods.

Political imagination in the Black Church needs to expand, and it currently needs more prophetic distance from the political machine and the Democratic Party. One of the most important Black-led political struggles in my generation has been the Movement for Black Lives. One lesson that the Black Church could learn from the movement (and yes, some have) is that we have a wide range of political options outside of the formal channels that we must utilize for organized, deliberate, and pointed action. The Black Lives Matter (BLM) movement forced an untouchable subject into American public discourse, compelling everyone to take a side. In some cases, the movement failed to organize for long-term and ongoing impact, but it still shifted public opinion enough that the largest racial protests in the country occurred in 2020. This is a marathon and not a sprint, so we'll need carefully designed and disruptive mass protest strategies and grassroots community organizing efforts that engage with a variety of social change methods.

Above all, the Black Church must remember that "the vote" is not how Black people became free. Freedom and the right to vote were won through a range of activities under slavery and during Jim and Jane Crow, when we were mostly locked out of the electoral process. Let's remember the lessons from centuries of faithful action that moved the needle. As already established communities, Black congregations have the potential to embody a prophetic witness in society while drawing on the lessons and wisdom of those who came before us. This must include our capacity to hold political leaders accountable through prophetic truth-telling, which happens regardless of who is in office. If we can't tell the truth to Black Democratic leaders and hold them accountable, it would be better to not have Black people in those roles. The Black Church can't be the beloved community that seeks God's *kin*dom in our world unless it knows how to be political and maintain its prophetic witness to the political machine of the empire.

Reckoning with faith and Afropessimism

As with other demographic groups, younger Black people have been leaving the church, and sometimes Christianity altogether, in unprecedented numbers.[12] And while some bigger American trends help to explain this (like a decrease in trust of clergy, and revelations of church scandals), other challenges make Black faith difficult in this moment. What happens when what we observe around us does not appear to align with what we have been taught to believe? How might the ongoing antiblack police violence, mass incarceration, disproportionate poverty, and overall lower markers of well-being impact Black faith? How does the persistence of antiblack racism impact faith in a God who is purported to be able to do all things? How does the continual mutation of antiblack oppression from the fifteenth century to the present lodge unavoidable skepticism of a liberating or almighty God?

Many Black pastors continue to preach and teach as they always have, but for many ordinary Black people, optimism concerning racial justice which existed in the era before Barack Obama's presidency has converted into pessimism. Middle-class

Black Americans have woken up to the widespread and severe antiblack oppression impacting the broader community; the loss of Civil Rights momentum through attacks on affirmative action, DEI initiatives, and voting rights protections; and the emboldening of white Christian nationalists. Despair has increased especially in the past decade with the overall conscientization of most Black people.

To be clear, the antiblackness was present before the mid-2000s, and many of us have been talking about it consistently; more people have awakened to its scale and scope. This happened while seeing white Christians lose their minds over the election of our first Black president, the cultural shift that came with having smartphone cameras that can record and share antiblack police brutality, the Black Lives Matter movement that forced a national conversation, the rise of Donald Trump and more explicitly racist political rhetoric and behavior in the public square, and a pandemic that fragmented, isolated, and pressured our already antagonistic society. School districts around the nation have stopped teaching basic information about how our nation was founded on conquest and slavery. Many people can no longer hold to the optimism of the Civil Rights era that purported our ongoing and inevitable march toward racial justice and freedom.

In recent years, increasing numbers of Black people have adhered to Afropessimism. Afropessimism argues that antiblack oppression and social death are baked into modern society and that genuine Black thriving is impossible within these conditions. Despite this rise in Afropessimism, the Black Church seems oblivious to it and similar perspectives. Afropessimism inevitably raises serious theological question of ultimate concern that arise directly out of Black experience.

It asserts that our (global) society is built on antiblackness; minor tweaks do nothing to fix it. Society treats Black people as expendable and not fully human, an organizing principle so baked into the fabric of our society that accepting the permanence of antiblackness is the only honest way of reckoning with our situation. Within this reasoning, integrating into this burning house may help individuals, but it is not a liberating strategy because it accepts antiblack structures on their terms. If white theological questions and answers persist as the norm for theological reasoning and spiritual discernment in most Black churches, we will fail to deliver a word of good news for those in our community who are caught in despair. The Black Church must come alongside those of us seeking to find pockets of thriving and joy in the spaces we cultivate ourselves from below.

Despite massive shifts from slavery to the present, antiblackness has remained in morphed forms. To make a radical break would require that white people confess to, repent of (not feel sorry for but turn away from), and make amends for white supremacy, antiblackness, and Indigenous conquest. We would need the collective will to thoroughly transform our current society to fully abolish the built-in inequities and unjust policies. Is it possible for the United States to recognize and treat Black people with genuine dignity and as full members of society without reckoning with America's white settler transgenerational and corporate sins of plunder, torture, and dehumanization? And what would it mean to accept and work through the communal moral and psychological injury that comes from knowing one's entire community is built upon the intentionally justified, centuries-long, and intense suffering of Black and Indigenous people caused by white Americans? Our national narratives and myths, criminal justice and prison system, public education systems, housing and land arrangements, healthcare, political governance, capitalist markets and access to opportunities, policing, and other dimensions of society would have to die and be reborn. Afropessimists say don't hold your breath.[13]

Writing before the rise of Afropessimism perspectives, Black philosopher William R. Jones penned a provocative book titled *Is God a White Racist?* His perspective may be helpful for any out-of-touch leaders in the Black Church to understand how and why Black faith can be difficult right now. To be clear, Jones did not believe that God is a white racist; he didn't believe in God at all. His book uses Western philosophy to expose the absurdity of Black faith. Black liberation theology, he writes, doesn't question basic Western assumptions about God. For example, Black theologians believe God is good, and more than that, that the God revealed in Scripture is actively liberating the oppressed and is committed to bringing justice for the most vulnerable. Black liberation also has typically taken for granted that God is all-powerful and sovereign. As we say in our tradition, God is able! But when we look at Black experience over many centuries, Jones argues that we do not find a God who is both good and liberating and who has taken sides with Black oppressed people and rectified the prolonged and intense and disproportionate suffering we have endured. Jones contends that if we assume that God is in control over everything, then when we analyze history, God looks more like a white racist than a God of liberation. Where, asks Jones, is the concrete evidence of this all-powerful, good, and liberating God in human history? Barring such evidence, he believes that it is time to either let go of God or at minimum embrace a more humanocentric theism that takes seriously human action and responsibility for the world as it is. Otherwise, our God-talk will stifle actual liberative struggle against oppression.[14]

Many Black theologians have not shied away from such questions. But it remains for the Black Church to seriously engage these questions and allow them to inform its ministry in the twenty-first century out of love for those who are struggling with their faith. Typical cliché answers will not do if we hope that young people keep the faith.

We can look to Black Christians who are grappling with and writing about these concerns, such as scholar Kelly Brown Douglas, who asserts that "Black faith is, in and of itself, a theodicy. It resists any notion that the evil that oppresses Black bodies will have the last word." For Douglas, this requires not getting stuck at the cross, but moving through the full story of Jesus that ultimately ends with resurrection. In 2020, Douglas saw the resurrection hope of God in real time during the protests in response to the killing of George Floyd as people came together "for a world that looked more like God's just future" and how "they were embodying that very future."[15] But actual change will require resurrection-level reparations, not just improvement. And it will need to be embodied faith that prays with its feet through action, as many of our ancestors did in previous times.

We must face these questions courageously, vulnerably, wisely, and empathetically while drawing from the gifts and insights of our theologians and biblical scholars. Being a beloved community is inherently intergenerational, and it requires the humility to listen and take seriously the emerging questions of the next generations.

Can these bones live?

Ezekiel 37 is a popular passage in the Black Church tradition. It's not surprising, given that it offers spirit-filled opportunity to explore God's hope, restoration, and liberation after severe suffering. The passage was written during the Babylonian exile—a time of conquest, defeat, and forced displacement. Israel, now a conquered people, found themselves living under the rule of a dominating empire that sought to dictate the terms of their existence and assimilate them into Babylonian life. As is often the case, history was written by the victors; through the lens of Babylonian exceptionalism, conquest and captivity were framed as justified and inevitable. The empire believed all should be colonized into its way of life, a process that led to the cultural, sociopolitical, and spiritual death of the captives' traditions. Read the story in Ezekiel 37:1–10 and see why it has resonated so deeply with Black Christians:

> The hand of the LORD came upon me, and he brought me out by the spirit of the LORD and set me down in the middle of a valley; it was full of bones. He led me all around them; there were very many lying in the valley, and they were very dry. He said to me, "Mortal, can these bones live?" I answered, "O Lord GOD, you know." Then he said to me, "Prophesy to these bones and say to them: O dry bones, hear the word of the LORD. Thus says the Lord GOD to these bones: I will cause breath to enter you, and you shall live. I will lay sinews on you and will cause flesh to come upon you and cover you with skin and put breath in you, and you shall live, and you shall know that I am the LORD."
>
> So I prophesied as I had been commanded, and as I prophesied, suddenly there was a noise, a rattling, and the

bones came together, bone to its bone. I looked, and there were sinews on them, and flesh had come upon them, and skin had covered them, but there was no breath in them. Then he said to me, "Prophesy to the breath, prophesy, mortal, and say to the breath: Thus says the Lord God: Come from the four winds, O breath, and breathe upon these slain, that they may live." I prophesied as he commanded me, and the breath came into them, and they lived and stood on their feet, a vast multitude.

As Black people, we have our own dry bones. We, too, have our own exilic experience. We, too, have felt persistent suffering and oppression systemically organized by an empire that narrates our suffering as necessary for American thriving. As Black people, our exile has been physical, and it has also ripped us from powerful traditions and cosmologies of our ancestors. Exile has torn us from our sense of identity, ushering us into alienation from our homeland and assimilating us into the dominant identities and narratives of those who plundered and tortured our community for centuries. Many of us have become comfortable with the antiblack disrespect and have normalized the denial of our dignity as people made in the image of God. It has been this way for so long. We, too, have been brought into the valley of very dry bones.

Sometimes God speaks to us through answers, but sometimes God speaks to us through questions to wrestle with. In this passage, God asks Ezekiel a powerful, scary question—"Can these dry bones live?" By all human logic, the answer would be no. Of course the long-dead, very dry bones lying out in a valley can't live! What does it mean to sit with God with these kinds of dangerous questions? To bring our doubts, our skepticism, our pessimism, and our human reasoning and to endure a soul-searching season with the One in whom we live and move and have our being, the One who is the very ground and source of life and existence.

Can these bones live? We see the persistence of Black suffering, second-class status, and discrimination in society. Can these bones live? How can they live when our loved ones are at the mercy of unjust policing and courts, when our children can easily be funneled from underfunded schools to overfunded prison systems disproportionately filled with Black, Indigenous and other People of Color? Can these bones live? That seems ridiculous—we can't even receive the basic respect as fellow siblings created by God. Sometimes even we don't honor what we have endured for centuries in this land, so how can we expect those who have oppressed us to do so? In Ezekiel 37, Israel is exiled from their homeland, from their identity, from their language and culture, and from being treated with full dignity. Black people have also been severed from land, identity, and language. And our nation has perpetually disrespected us and denied our inherent dignity. It's dangerous to ask whether these dry bones can live when you are still in the valley.

Ezekiel could have responded with despair or optimism, but he instead chose trust in a God who is somehow, despite the circumstances, still able to do for the people what God has done in the past. Rather than an easy religious cliché, Ezekiel's answer dared to have faith in the transcendent God over the cosmos. "O Lord God, you know," said Ezekiel, even while grappling with devastation but refusing to allow the Babylonian conquerors to have the ultimate word over their existence. God tells him to prophesy over the bones. In doing so, Ezekiel is now creating *with* God. Ezekiel must not only sit and wait to see what

God will do. God's life-giving, empire-altering, history-shifting activity will take place through Ezekiel. He is prophet. A mouthpiece of God who embodies and performs God's word and judgment. When Ezekiel speaks in alignment with God's say-so, he participates in the new thing God is doing. Ezekiel prophesies life where there is death, hope where there is despair, God's justice where imperial domination and control are reigning. He speaks the breath, the very Spirit of God, into those dry bones. And as I look over our present valleys today, I also wonder if the Black Church can live again and rediscover its prophetic calling while we live in our Babylon.

When Ezekiel amid exile and despair speaks with the same breath as God, the prophet sees the breath rattle those dead bones, bring them together to make skeletons, and then cover them with flesh. One more time, Ezekiel takes up his prophetic calling and sings the breath of God to a death-dealing world, and those bodies find new life. And there before him stands a great multitude.

A great beloved multitude

The truth is that the Black Church, and our entire society, faces serious challenges. The bones in our society seem very dry. Easy answers won't help us. But I do believe that God is present in all we have been through and seen. It may be that some of our assumptions and doctrines of what the word "God" means might be inadequate to explain the life-giving Source of all things who holds everything together. We'll need to discern how to rearticulate the God who helped us make it through past storms. I still have faith that God will have the final say, and that the Black Church has a role to play if only it can recover—or for some, sustain—its prophetic vocation.

As a disciple of Jesus, I yield to the Spirit and consider myself a church theologian before I'm a public one. The Black Church can't live in nostalgia. It needs to continually recommit its own way of liberating love so that it is always Jesus-shaped and Spirit-led. Our lives ought to bear collective witness to the story of Jesus from birth to resurrection, taking seriously the solidarity and commitments embodied in the life of Jesus. Dr. King didn't invent the language of beloved community, but he popularized it for the Black Church. That powerful image can guide us toward our calling as the church, as well as our prophetic task in a society marked by intergenerational systems of oppression. Beloved community exists when a people group pursues, participates in, and extends mutual love, holistic liberation, and healing justice. When that community subverts hierarchy, domination, control, and exclusion while embracing all of God's children.

Beloved community is a metaphor for God's shalom, God's kingdom, and God's ultimate future. It is also God's dream for us breaking into our world. My hope is that the Black Church—in all its messiness and problems that come with such a restrictive concept—can be the visible beloved community for the world to show that a loving, liberating, and life-giving God exists. That witness is Jesus, existing as the body of Christ in the world.

– EIGHT –

Seven Signposts for Anablacktivism

What does Anabaptism have to do with Black faith, Schleitheim with Harlem, or Menno Simons with Frederick Douglass? Those unfamiliar with Anabaptists tend to think of Old Order Amish communities living separatist lives, riding horses and buggies, and wearing plain and old European dress. People who haven't spent much time in the Black Church think first of movie depictions or televangelists, where the preachers and gospel choirs offer inspiration, sometimes trying to bamboozle congregants out of their money, and lots of emotionalism. One community is thought of as rural and reserved; the other is assumed to be urban and loud. Anabaptists are presumed to have a safe and sectarian pacifism that contradicts but doesn't disrupt America and its militarism. The Black Church is associated with the Civil Rights Movement that nonviolently got in the way of Jim and Jane Crow.

These two traditions are both examples of American Christian traditions outside the mainstream, and one could easily wonder what actual interaction and exchange has occurred between these very different traditions. In other words, are there *any* historical convergences of Black faith and Anabaptism that might illuminate how to live faithfully in the way of Jesus in the aftermath of centuries of Western Christendom and colonial conquest?

The simple answer is yes. There is real-life convergence. I want to consider seven signposts on the road to Anablacktivist faith. This isn't a romanticized version of Black and Anabaptist convergences—life is messy and people are contradictory even as communities take courageous steps in the right direction. I offer these chronological signposts as a curated journey of the vibrant, diverse ways that Black faith and Anabaptism can inform Christian faith more broadly.

Counter-witness to slavery: The 1688 petition

European Mennonites settled in Germantown, Pennsylvania, in the early 1680s and immediately adopted antislavery ethics as a community. Some Mennonites and Quakers worshiped together in a Germantown meetinghouse until they each had their own spaces. At the time, Mennonites were discouraged that Quakers practiced slavery. They saw it as hypocritical because each group had come to Germantown for religious freedom. Nonetheless, Mennonites and Quakers interacted, with some parties changing religious affiliations from one tradition to the other.[1]

In 1688, as they observed the growth and racialization of the enslavement of Black people, four Quakers produced the first written antislavery petition by any Christian tradition in the colonies. They directed it toward the Quaker meetings, hoping to challenge the practice of slavery within their tradition. Three of the four signers were former Mennonites who had become Quaker.

A few strange dynamics are in play here. Quakers, who are associated with antislavery and abolitionist movements, did not become so until around the time of the Revolutionary War. Quakerism in the early colonies was still a tradition that practiced slavery. The other strange reality is that Mennonites, while already holding to antislavery positions, tended not to be very activist and vocal. Thus it was not, nor would it become, the norm for Mennonites to be known for public antislavery petitions and demonstrations. It seems that an Anabaptist counter-witness and counter-ethic, coupled with a Quaker public witness, made possible this antislavery petition. As these Quakers and Mennonites watched the practice of enslavement and disproportionate suffering, they couldn't help but place themselves in the shoes of Black Africans. The petitioners drew on the teachings of Jesus simply and straightforwardly and provided white people an opportunity to imagine themselves under slavery by citing Jesus' golden rule. Other arguments followed, like religious hypocrisy, the cruelty of separating African families from one another, and the inherent equality of all people.

Moving forward, most Anabaptist groups continued to ban the practice of slavery within their communities. The Anabaptist tradition became the first non-Black religious tradition in the colonies to reject the compatibility of practicing slavery with following Jesus. There were exceptions to this rule, especially down South, where some Anabaptists went against the consensus of broader Anabaptist bodies. While I don't want to overexaggerate the effect of the petition, it still marks a drastic distinction that began unfolding the moment Anabaptists settled in the colonies. Grounding themselves in the teachings of Jesus, they saw and affirmed the humanity of Black African people. And they showed the potential of an Anabaptist faith that combined its ethics with public activism.

People sometimes excuse those who participated in American antiblack chattel slavery as merely "people of their time." Very early on, Anabaptists demonstrated an active counter-ethic immediately after white supremacy and antiblackness had been written into law. Followers of Jesus should take seriously the teachings of Jesus, empathize with those most oppressed or vulnerable in their communities, and act to do something about the evil and suffering happening around us.

Liberative ecclesiology: The freedom of Samuel Weir

Samuel Weir was born into slavery in Virginia, in 1812. At age twelve, he was sold to the McClure family for $280. After the McClure family experienced a collective religious conversion years later, they applied for membership at the local Brethren (Dunkard) congregation in town. The Brethren combined Anabaptism and radical pietism. Like the Mennonites, the tradition had renounced the practice of slavery (although some individuals in the South disregarded that position). This Virginia Brethren congregation insisted that if the McClures wanted to join the church, they would first have to emancipate Samuel Weir. The McClures did just that. Weir also joined the congregation (though he was not greeted with the holy kiss, which was the Brethren custom of that time).[2]

Virginia law dictated that Samuel Weir could face enslavement as a free person if he remained in Virginia beyond one year. So a white Brethren member from Ohio escorted him to his state. Weir was received into fellowship in Paint Creek

Brethren Church, where he was the only Black member. The Bryant family took him in for two years to get him settled. Weir wanted to learn to read, and he took lessons alongside the Bryant's granddaughter. While he studied many subjects, once he was able to read the Bible for himself, he was satisfied. He read the Bible voraciously. He also received the call to preach. At first he only went to the "colored" meetings to preach, but in 1849, he received an opportunity to preach for the Brethren, and there they affirmed his calling and ordination—though they commissioned him to preach "to his own race" rather than imagining that he might be a gift to them directly. Nonetheless, Weir had a powerful preaching ministry for the rest of his life. He died in 1887 or shortly thereafter.

The life of Samuel Weir and his encounter with the Brethren during antebellum slavery highlights the promise and pains of early encounters between Black people and white Anabaptists. The anti-Christendom ecclesiology of Anabaptism, and their willingness to not conform to mainstream American Christianity, ended up producing Weir's freedom. What unfolded could be called a limited liberationist ecclesiology. It wasn't full liberation that led to comprehensive reconciliation, but it marked a radical contrast to most white mainline, Catholic, and evangelical traditions of the day. The ethically grounded discipleship in that community meant something, and it made enslaving others incompatible with the life of a Christian. Weir's freedom, education, and (partial) commissioning to preach the gospel of Jesus Christ were possible because a faith community engaged, albeit in limited ways, in God's freedom for the enslaved.

Sadly, they did not fully exorcise racial logics from their faith. Since Anabaptism at the time was a mostly rural tradition and white Anabaptists' encounters with Black African people were few (white enslavers and planters did not want enslaved laborers interacting with Christians known to have antislavery views), engagement was limited. The margins of the Anabaptist community—what I call the radical discipleship wing—engaged in abolitionist work and played a role in the Underground Railroad, but most Anabaptists would have just renounced slavery internally. Still, Samuel Weir's life demonstrated the liberative possibilities of Anabaptism.

Nonconformity, confession, and practice: Denominational statements

Between 1940 and 1976, US Mennonites made nearly two dozen race-focused statements.[3] The Church of the Brethren made similar denominational statements on race. In the twentieth century up to the present, US Anabaptist statements demonstrate a growing clarity on racism. They also offer an opportunity to reflect on the coherence between denominational statements and our lives.

The 1955 statement titled "The Way of Christian Love in Race Relations" became the most famous and prominent Mennonite statement on race and racism in the twentieth century. It made biblical arguments, named racism and discrimination as sin, called for more education, and claimed that Mennonites had conformed to worldly patterns. The topic of conformity was significant, since Mennonites highly valued nonconformity. However, Mennonite practices of nonconformity in the early twentieth century frequently prioritized minor issues (such as plain clothing and head coverings). Nonconformity should lead to fully resisting oppressive systems. Mennonites could have done the former without neglecting the latter, but they missed the mark.

The 1955 statement occurred during the beginning stages of the Civil Rights Movement. The statement is fairly vague on race, with generic "prejudice" or "discrimination" language and often lacking prophetic clarity. Historian Tobin Miller Shearer argues that basically all the Mennonite statements on race during the Civil Rights Movement lacked explicit confession of their participation in whiteness.[4] Even if one accounts for the use of language more common at the time such as "race relations," the Mennonite statement failed to robustly diagnose white supremacy. The wording could easily lead to expecting Black and Brown people to assimilate into white Mennonite normative cultural practices.[5] Many whites who believed Black people were inherently equal to white folk still believed that Black people's culture was inferior to white people's culture. This kind of white supremacy still leads to forced cultural assimilation.

In 1963, the Church of the Brethren made a pointed statement entitled "The Time Is Now." Where Mennonites spoke of nonresistance and love, the Brethren emphasized racial justice and methods of nonviolence. Even before theologian James Cone argued that liberation must precede reconciliation, the Church of the Brethren's statement proclaimed, "The time is now to understand that racial reconciliation is built only on the foundation of racial justice, that justice delayed is justice denied," while also pointing out that "few white Christians have suffered with their oppressed Negro brothers in efforts to obtain racial justice." The statement urged Church of the Brethren congregations to respond through "confession, repentance, and dedication" in this work.

However, the most commonly quoted statement in the Church of the Brethren today in regards to race and racism is the relatively recent "Separate No More." This 2007 statement is anchored in intercultural practices, and invites the denomination, districts, congregations, and individuals to transform their practices and approach. This certainly bucks assimilationist and colonizing assumptions! However, the statement doesn't provide any historical context for why the Church of the Brethren would need to change in the first place. It doesn't acknowledge the history of colonial conquest and white supremacy that defined American society.[6]

As the twentieth century progressed, Mennonites went through dramatic shifts of their own. Their growing focus on ministering to different racially minoritized groups, though often coupled with paternalism, led to significantly more Black, Brown, Asian, and Native Mennonites in the United States than in other Anabaptist denominations. Mennonites of color in recent years have profoundly guided dialogues on white supremacy and racism among the corporate body. In 2014, an ad hoc Mennonite group formed a coalition for dismantling the Doctrine of Discovery. Since then, there has been increased focus within the denomination and externally to educate people about, challenge, and dismantle the Doctrine of Discovery.[7] The primary emphasis is on settler and Indigenous relations and far less on Black plunder and oppression, but some Mennonites are working to address the overlaps and intersections of the Doctrine of Discovery for Indigenous and Black communities in North America, as well as its global impact.

In a 2023 denominational statement, the Church of the Brethren lamented the Doctrine of Discovery. There is no faithful way forward for Western European Christians without confessing that death-dealing history. The commitments of the

2023 statement, however, feel mostly educational. The statement briefly acknowledges the broader consequences of colonial conquest, but mostly limits its focus to settler/Indigenous concerns.[8] This reflects a common gap in understanding the interconnected and overlapping plunder of Black and Native peoples—denominational "race" statements typically focus on one or the other.[9] Ultimately, the question is whether these statements are being embodied on the ground in local communities. Are they mostly empty signifiers and virtue signaling without the accompanied formative practices toward a new way of being in the world? Denominational statements mark important developments over time, but to what degree have they helped white Anabaptists move into solidarity in the struggle for justice and liberation and subvert and dismantle their whiteness?

The Black Church's very existence, in contrast, is its most meaningful statement. The decisive action of withdrawing and persisting, despite the powerful lure of white dominant culture and mainstream white American Christians' hegemony, reflects a subversive commitment to loving Black people. Each Black Church tradition—really, each Black congregation, despite human imperfections—affirms the dignity of Black people. Even when some have unknowingly and overly assimilated into white supremacist American theology, their persistence under extreme constraints has birthed Black faith. By Black faith I don't mean racialized faith or even merely faith by people of African descent, but a faith forged out of a new peoplehood in the aftermath of slavery, people who are oriented to join the liberating and loving God who "can make a way out of no way" through slavery, Jim and Jane Crow, and subsequent forms of antiblack oppression.

Black and Anabaptist congregations are liberated *and* always in need of liberation. On the road to Anablacktivism, we must scrutinize the tension between our confession and our lives.

Black Anabaptism, strategic resistance, and the Lark Vision: Rowena and James Lark

Despite resistance, Rowena and James Lark played a vital role in cultivating a genuinely Black Anabaptist communal tradition. They saw a path forward for being both Black and Anabaptist under the constraints of white racism, Mennonite colonizing mindsets, and in a world that was undergoing seismic shifts because of the Civil Rights Movement.[10]

James and Rowena, both born in the late nineteenth century, became Mennonite in 1935. They were impressed with the tangible way that the Mennonites served their neighbors and saw the powerful potential of the Anabaptist tradition for the Black community. Rowena quickly became a visible powerhouse for evangelism, outreach, and programming in African American neighborhoods while representing the Mennonite denomination. She knew she had to contextualize the Mennonite tradition for Black people.

White Mennonites in the early twentieth century didn't engage in some of the more explicitly violent forms of oppression that many other white American Christians did, but they still internalized and practiced key dimensions of white supremacy and antiblackness. In the North, this often looked like white paternalism, including mission posts *to* African Americans rather than *with* them, also neglecting to imagine new belonging together in Christ. Sometimes white congregations would start a separate "mission" church for Black people only blocks away from their own, rather than looking to form an integrated church as equals. When the Larks began ministering in the Virginia Mennonite Conference and Black Mennonites joined the church, conference leaders created segregationist practices for the holy kiss and communion. White Mennonites often held Black Mennonites, especially women, to stricter nonconformity dress standards. There may have been glimmers of potential for a liberating and holistic faith, but white Anabaptists frequently took on a colonizing orientation, seeking to make Black people in their own image and insisting that the *white* Mennonite way was the right way.[11]

Despite these constraints, Rowena Lark persisted. White women at the time increasingly resisted Mennonite hair coverings through subversive practices, like making the coverings smaller or more decorative, and eventually replacing them with more fashionable options. Rowena and many other Black women did the opposite—while also creating space for Black faith, identity, and culture within the tradition. Rowena wore Mennonite coverings and plain dress but also encouraged Black women to embrace their natural hair (very countercultural at that time), performed solos (normative in the Black Church but taboo in white Mennonite spaces), and even unofficially preached sermons at church (undermining white Mennonite patriarchal customs). Despite resistance from white Southern racists, she discipled Black Mennonites who embraced being fully Black and Mennonite. Black women in particular used plain dress to identify themselves as Mennonite, but then added their own touches, some even wearing gold hoops with their plain clothing.[12]

The Larks eventually left Virginia for Chicago, where James advocated for what is known as the "Lark Vision"—a precursor to what would much later be called Christian community development. James believed that Mennonites had a great opportunity and responsibility to respond as Black people fled white supremacist violence and oppression in the South. Despite limited support from denominational bodies, he started multiple Black or multiracial congregations in various parts of the country. He had a vision for Black Mennonitism. He wanted to empower self-determined and sustainable Black congregations in every city in the nation. In Wichita, Kansas, James "mapped out a four block by six block 'area of influence' and developed a proposal for a community vegetable and flower garden, child care center, baby-sitters for mothers who attend health clinic, a preschool, and noonday meal for aged indigents." Longer-range plans included "a church-related camp, a home for the aged, and other outposts on the fringe of the area of influence as needed. All projects would be under pastor and church council management with an advisory board." His ministry focused on empowering the Black community, and repeatedly asked, "Is it building the black church?" to keep their priorities focused.[13]

The Larks were not the only people who started Black or multiracial Anabaptist congregations in the mid- and late twentieth century. However, their work symbolizes and epitomizes the important work of carving out space for the birth of an authentic tradition within a tradition. Black Anabaptists, and the convergence of genuinely Black faith and the Black Church with Anabaptism, took communal root in this era. Many contemporary congregations have histories tied to this era. I still remember first encountering third- and fourth-generation Black Anabaptists in Black congregations. Someone had to dig a hole, plant, and water for that to be possible. The Larks embodied this work. Even more so, Rowena demonstrated the strategic resistance and creativity required to make space for authentic ways of being Black and Mennonite within the Mennonite Church, and James's ministry pointed to the still powerful potential of Black Church within Anabaptism—making Anablacktivism possible.

Anablacktivist precursors and the Civil Rights Movement: Vincent Harding

The twentieth-century freedom struggle, particularly the Civil Rights era of the '50s and '60s, brought together the edges of the prophetic stream of the Black Church and the radical discipleship tradition within Anabaptism, especially in the life of Vincent Harding. The Civil Rights era, and Harding within it, nurtured Black Anabaptism and sought to empower Black people living under the hells of systemic oppression. They demanded a conversion of white Anabaptism itself toward a more proactive justice-oriented and peacemaking practice that embodied nonviolent activism. That was the difference between the Larks' Black Anabaptism and what I call Harding's Anablacktivism. As Tobin Miller Shearer puts it, "Whereas Lark worked from a church base to bring converts off the streets and into pews, Harding stood abreast both the church and the movement to get church members off pews and into the streets."[14]

While not all Black congregations participated in the Civil Rights freedom struggle, Black churches were the backbone of the movement. Though it is often ignored by mainstream historical accounts, Black activism was alive at every point of the twentieth century and beyond. Yet there was something particular in the air when Black soldiers returned from fighting Nazism in World War II only to experience Jim Crow anti-blackness at home. Then came *Brown v. Board of Education* in 1954, and Emmett Till's torture and execution in 1955. Till's mother compelled the public to confront the evils of Jim Crow terrorism by insisting on an open casket at the boy's funeral. In that moment, writes historian Henry Louis Gates Jr., "the Black Church in America, that nation within a nation, extended its reach well beyond the front steps of the sanctuary" because it held to "the unshakable belief that the liberating God of their fathers and mothers was on their side."[15]

Born in Harlem in 1931, Vincent Harding was raised in a Black Seventh-Day Adventist congregation. He served in the military and then pursued graduate school in Chicago, eventually obtaining his PhD. While pastoring an Adventist congregation in Chicago, he learned about the compelling historical witness of the sixteenth-century Anabaptists. Shortly thereafter he encountered Mennonites in Chicago, and he later joined Woodlawn Mennonite Church on the South Side, where he also met his future wife, Rosemarie. In 1958, Woodlawn called him to serve as an associate pastor. That summer Harding and several others made a pilgrimage down South to learn and understand what was happening on the ground. Harding met Rev. Dr. Martin Luther King Jr., who invited him to return to join the work.

Dr. King's nonviolent methods and philosophy, further affirmed by Harding, demanded Mennonites' attention. At this time, most Mennonites, including prominent Mennonite theologians like Guy Hershberger, espoused "nonresistance" as their peace ethic. In contrast, Dr. King taught and practiced nonviolent resistance. White Mennonites appreciated the nonviolence but felt that they couldn't join a coercive and disruptive nonviolent practice. Ideologically, they were stuck. Hershberger offered some limited ways for Mennonites to participate in the movement but didn't budge on nonresistance. The Hardings, however, moved to Atlanta and started a Mennonite House close to Dr. King's home. For the next few years, Harding had a foot in both the Mennonite world and the Black freedom struggle. In his "dual demonstration" in the streets and to the Mennonite Church, Harding worked to support and advance the movement, from being jailed or working on negotiating just policies with white leaders to drafting speeches for Dr. King. His participation in the Black freedom struggle and in the Mennonite Church made him the go-to leader in the Mennonite Church regarding the unfolding racial revolution.

Harding grew increasingly frustrated with the Mennonites. He drew on Anabaptist theology and terminology, believing that the Anabaptist understanding of discipleship to Jesus and nonviolence called for activist participation that confronted injustice. His words to the white Mennonite Church were sharp and prophetic; he grew increasingly tired of so much inaction. Ironically, the more Harding turned away from the Mennonite Church, the more they turned toward him.

Harding never saw the level of participation he wanted from Mennonites, but a growing number of white Mennonites participated in Civil Rights protests and activism. However, in 1966 and 1967, Harding began his departure from the Mennonites and deepened his engagement with the Black Power movement and the broader Black community. Frustration played a big role; also, he confessed to marital infidelity and decided to step back from both his movement involvement and the Mennonite world. He needed to repent, repair his marriage, and reestablish integrity in his "thoughts, words, and deeds."[16] Harding went on to teach at Spellman College, lead the King Center, advise the *Eyes on the Prize* Civil Rights documentary, and write one of the most important books on Black resistance under slavery.

Both Mennonites and Brethren have some stories of Anabaptist participation in the Civil Rights Movement. However, Dr. King's external witness and Vincent Harding's internal witness among the Mennonites played a significant role in reframing Anabaptist theology toward activism. Many today take active peacemaking and justice for granted in Anabaptist theology, but Black faith played an important contribution in that development. Harding helped strengthen a radical discipleship tradition on the margins of the Anabaptist community that overlapped with the Black freedom struggle. Black faith and Anabaptism were overlapping, sometimes even in the streets.

Black theology and Anabaptism: Hubert Brown

During my doctoral studies, I stumbled upon Hubert Brown's 1976 book, *Black and Mennonite: A Search for Identity*. In the book, Brown discusses his initial encounters with Mennonites, including their white paternalism and prejudice in Norristown, Pennsylvania. The First Mennonite Church of Norristown started in the late 1920s as a mission. Brown remembers how when he was young (in the 1950s), Mennonites helped his struggling family. In 1960 he joined Bethel Mennonite Church, which was for the "colored" families. A few years later, he became Bethel's pastor.

However, as much as he appreciated contemporary Mennonite theology, he found that it couldn't address his questions the way Black theology could. "The Mennonite Church has failed miserably in being a radical manifestation of God at work in the world," Brown concluded. "We have failed in creating an atmosphere of the first- and sixteenth-century protest. Particularly we have failed to bring about radical obedience to

Christ which was evident in the sixteenth-century Anabaptist thrust."[17] Brown was also discouraged that "Mennonite theological thought has refused to take seriously the black liberation movement."[18] However, he still recognized something special in Anabaptism that he was confident was necessary and vital for faithful discipleship in America.

In the 1940s, Harold Bender, a white Mennonite scholar, presented "The Anabaptist Vision," a galvanizing essay that refashioned, refocused, and simplified Anabaptist identity, belief, and practice in Mennonite streams. Since that moment there has been ongoing debate about what it means to be Anabaptist. Bender's definition of Anabaptism meant discipleship and obedience to the teachings of Jesus, a voluntary church separated from the world, and the practice of love and nonresistance. This was the normative framework for Anabaptism of Brown's generation. Thirty years after Bender presented his "Vision," Brown controversially differentiated Mennonites from Anabaptism, suggesting that the former had drifted away from the latter. "The Mennonite community today has lost much of the historical spiritual quality of the Anabaptists," wrote Brown. "Mennonites today have drifted from the Anabaptist model of life and from the Anabaptist Christ. In fact, present-day Mennonites have replaced the Anabaptist Christ with an American one whose attitude toward blacks is obnoxious and abrasive."[19]

Brown exposed the gap between the ideals of Anabaptism from the lived Mennonite reality that was not living out those convictions. "The Anabaptist Vision" was supposed to challenge Mennonites with their own history, but Bender probably never anticipated that a Black person would go as far as revoke the Anabaptist "card" from Mennonites for not engaging oppressed Black people struggling for freedom.

Brown described sixteenth-century Anabaptists as a persecuted "community of protesters." They lived by scripture and the Holy Spirit, and Christianity led to the transformation of one's life. Anabaptists rejected "the dominant values of the sixteenth century," and the "Anabaptist Christ led the Anabaptists to reject compromise and to live by a new set of values, a new set of economics." Anabaptism, wrote Brown, was "a movement of poor folks, oppressed peoples seeking liberation and the ushering in of God's kingdom for His will to be done on earth as it is in heaven."[20] Brown's understanding of Anabaptism aligned with, and possibly was influenced by, Vincent Harding's challenges to white Mennonites in the 1950s and '60s.

Brown reasoned since Mennonites had drifted away from and lost their Anabaptism, those seeking to recover this radical tradition could do so through the Black Church and Black theology. "Blacks with the emergence of black theology represent a dynamic resemblance of the Anabaptist past," he wrote. "Mennonites seeking to find themselves ought to look to black theology and to those black theologians who penned new theological consciousness amidst an American revolution." Those seeking to "recover the Anabaptist Vision can learn from the black church."[21]

Brown revoked the Anabaptist card from white Mennonites, brilliantly decentering white power and racist control over Anabaptist identity, belief, and practice. He concludes his book by calling for a *diunital* both/and approach to being Black *and* Mennonite. For Brown, this meant following the "Black Christ" and the "Anabaptist Christ" through Scripture, the Spirit, and discipleship. It also meant that the broader church should recognize Black theology's critique; affirm the liberation theme of the gospel; confess Jesus as Lord and Liberator; embrace that

Christianity has radical and revolutionary implications for life and society; create a counter-community of faith; and cultivate a sense of celebration informed by liberation theology.[22]

Black Anabaptism: A manifold witness

Black Anabaptism in general, and what I define as Anablacktivism more specifically, is alive and well today. In fact, the Anabaptist world has shifted dramatically from its sixteenth-century beginnings. White Anabaptists are the minority in what is now a global tradition—most Anabaptists around the world are Black or Brown. Today, even within Black Anabaptism, a manifold witness to the work of the Holy Spirit takes up a range of expressions. And it has included an ever-expanding embrace of God's reign where the first is last and the last is first. This often includes a multidimensional understanding of interlocking oppressions and the liberating power of intersectional justice.

Anabaptist womanists have frequently led the charge in cultivating intersectional awareness in Anabaptist spaces. Womanism centers Black women's experiences of racism and sexism while challenging all oppression and pursuing individual and collective survival and thriving. I don't know how often she uses the term, but I remember hearing Michelle Armster, a Black Mennonite and executive director of MCC Central States, describe herself as an AnaWomanist after I used the term Anablacktivist. A creative assertion—Anabaptism would not be where it is today if it were not for womanist insights and interventions. A small sample of other AnaWomanist friends whom I've admired and appreciated since my Anabaptist turn include Gimbiya Kettering, Regina Shands Stoltzfus, Calenthia Dowdy, Osheta Moore, and Nekeisha Alexis. They represent different Anabaptist streams, and some worship completely outside of historic Anabaptist traditions, yet their lives and convictions have each been influenced by womanist and Anabaptist traditions.

The first explicitly womanist and Anabaptist literature I encountered was from Nekeisha Alexis. Alexis sought to free the language of the cross from ideological usages that glorify, domesticate, or facilitate oppression and involuntary suffering. In an essay written at a time when John Howard Yoder was still dominant in Anabaptist theological reflection, she put both Yoder and womanist thought in conversation, offering interventions in both directions. She challenged the common womanist habit of conflating the language of the cross with forms of political suffering that were not truly equated with state-sanctioned execution or oppression. Such terminology, she feared, left room for the ongoing domestication, spiritualization, and glorification of the cross of Jesus in Western mainstream Christianity. While she noted that womanists don't necessarily engage in such usage themselves, use of "the cross" ranges broadly and should be deployed with great care. Her intervention "subverts the hermeneutics of sacrifice that sanctifies Black women's pain and encourages resistance to oppression as a way to follow Jesus."[23]

Alexis also troubled Yoder's language of "revolutionary subordination."[24] Yoder proposed this as a subversive faithfulness from below, but the language is deeply problematic. He was theoretically trying to affirm the agency of oppressed people under constraints, and elsewhere argued for "maximizing freedom" when possible. But the theological execution (and language itself) was counterproductive, leaving the status quo in place. As a Black woman, Alexis noted that this was unsatisfactory. "Does not maximizing one's freedom also entail making an effort to transform the social order that makes continued oppression possible?"25 Considering womanist concerns about using the cross to justify Black women's subjugation, she instead called for "creative transformation" that is more liberative and places more emphasis on challenging and changing the systems of society. This Anabaptist and womanist lens takes seriously the ways that theology has been weaponized ideologically against Black women, and in this case frees the cross from interpretations that support domination and oppression.

Other forms of Black Anabaptism exist today. For example, my friend Leonard Dow, a Black Mennonite leader, describes himself as a "Mennocostal" (Mennonite + Pentecostal). His ministry brings together Black Philly Mennonitism, charismatic spirituality, racial and economic justice orientations, and pastoral and community development experience. I'm also mindful of many friends who bridge the Black Baptist and Anabaptist line. Even more broadly, I'm reminded of the ongoing Black African and Anabaptist conversations that provide global perspectives. The Meserete Kristos Church, an Anabaptist denomination in Ethiopia, intertwines a charismatic faith reliant on the Holy Spirit with evangelism that is shalom-oriented and justice work that prioritizes people on the margins of society. This holistic approach is very similar to yet distinct from many BIPOC (Black and Indigenous People of Color) Anabaptists in the United States, perhaps in part because Ethiopians have not experienced the same intensity of colonial imposition as other Black Africans and the diaspora on the continent and around the world.

I'm also deeply moved by the Black South African Anabaptism of folks like Mziwandile Nkutha, who grapples with his country's legacy of colonialism and conquest. "I have this in me a kind of Christianity that is impacted by a story of colonization," he shared in a podcast interview. "What does that mean for someone like me in South Africa who has been shaped by a Christianity informed by coloniality?"[26] Nkutha is forging creative ways to distinctly disentangle Christianity from the post-apartheid context in conversation with Black South African and Anabaptist theologies. He has provided leadership for the Anabaptist Network in South Africa, and his research puts Black South African theology and Anabaptism in conversation with a concern for decoloniality. Antiblackness is local and hyper-contextual, as well as global and baked into the systems and logics of modern society more broadly, making these broader Black Anabaptist ecumenical exchanges vital for living in the aftermath of Christendom and colonial conquest.

— NINE —

Salvaging the Way

We live in the aftermath of centuries of Western Christendom as well as five centuries of colonial conquest, slavery, and ongoing oppression. For the church to become a community and movement of healing rather than a harmful institution that bolsters empire and the status quo, we need a way forward. And I really mean *a way* that is capable of breaking free from the cycles of violence, systems of oppression, and even our corrupted minds.

For too long, mainstream Christians have understood the gospel from inside the reasoning of Christendom, white supremacy, antiblackness, and colonial settlerism. Anablacktivism is a way to take seriously two very different living traditions born on the underside of these historic forces. When we learn from them together (especially where they overlap), we are compelled to fix our eyes on the particularity of the story and person of Jesus, to attend to the Spirit's activity, and to become a prophetic and radical body of the Messiah. When we see our reflections in the Black fugitive and the Anabaptist martyr, we can take up a new mode of living that improvises on how our ecclesial ancestors have followed, participate in, and made visible the life of the Messiah, and in doing so, salvaged *the Way*.

The particularity of Jesus

Faithfulness begins, is sustained by, and ends with the person of Jesus Christ. Sojourner Truth famously said, "I has just one text to preach from, an' I always preaches from this one. My text is, 'When I found Jesus.'"[1] Many enslaved Africans were illiterate because of draconian antiblack laws that made reading (especially the Bible) illegal because it threatened white power. This created barriers to enslaved Africans reading the Scriptures for themselves. Nonetheless, Sojourner Truth and others internalized the oral retelling of biblical stories and their own encounters with Jesus, who was their ever-present help in times of trouble. White people could not contain and control the liberating presence of Jesus.

Menno Simons is said to have claimed 1 Corinthians 3:11 as his favorite verse: "For no one can lay any foundation other than the one that has been laid; that foundation is Jesus Christ." The foundation of Anabaptist faith has been grounded in knowing and following after Jesus. By immersing ourselves in the specifics of the Jesus story and encountering Christ in the present, disciples can subvert the appropriations of Jesus that claim his name and attach it to domination and plunder.

Mainstream American Christians often present a generic Jesus with a narrative that includes elements of his story (he was born, crucified, and resurrected), but marginalizes or omits important particularities of his life and teachings. This abstract Christology doesn't resemble the ethics and sociopolitical commitments of Jesus and his reign. There is little concern about embodying the radical and prophetic way of Jesus who once walked the earth, so long as one believes Christ died for you. But when we separate believing in Christ from embodying Jesus' Way, we end up with a hazy spirituality void of what makes Jesus distinct. We overlook Jesus' social status, teachings, and prophetic posture toward the powerful and rich, as well as his solidarity with the poor, oppressed, socially stigmatized, and the most vulnerable of his time. Believing in a generic Christ without participating in the particular vocation of Jesus erases his full significance for us today, allowing the "Christ of faith" to be a mere ideological projection concocted by the socially advantaged who don't want to account for the revolutionary implications of the kingdom of God.

"He was not a 'universal' man but a particular Jew who came to fulfill God's will to liberate the oppressed," writes James Cone. "The authenticity of the New Testament Jesus guarantees the integrity of his human presence with the poor and the wretched in the struggle of freedom."[2] Jesus' ethical way of life and social identification with those living under Roman imperial occupation are not random and interesting facts. They disclose his holistic commitments and reveal his ongoing present character and activity in our world.

In the late 1960s, James Cone blazed a trail for Black theology as an academic discipline when he named and denounced white supremacy's entanglements with Christianity. Across decades of deeply persuasive writing, Cone illuminated how Jesus thoroughly identified with the poor and subjugated in his society and promised to "liberate the oppressed" (Luke 4:18–19). Cone believed that the revelation of Jesus' meaning for us today was so bound to the least, last, and little ones that the best Christological title for his context was Blackness. The Blackness of Jesus isn't primarily about his skin color but rather a translation of Jesus' present identification and solidarity with the oppressed in our contemporary white supremacist and anti-black society. Jesus is Black because he is who he was and is who he will be. The risen and coming Liberator will put an end to all suffering. A Black Jesus is often offensive to mainstream American Christians, especially those whose lives are sustained by past and present systemic plunder and oppression. Yet Black theology takes the birth, life, teachings, death, and resurrection of Jesus much more seriously than domesticated Christendom doctrines, and doesn't need to find creative and fancy interpretations to explain away the enormous volume of social teachings and actions of the Crucified and Risen One.

Mennonite theologian J. Denny Weaver also insists that the whole story of Jesus is necessary for theological reflection, ethics, and salvation. People have often substituted the death of Jesus for a robust Christology rooted in the whole gospel narrative. "Jesus' mission was to live as a witness to God and to the reign of God," writes Weaver. "His life made visible what God's rule looks like on earth. It cares for all people, particularly the marginalized. It is not passive; it confronts injustice, but without resorting to violence. The resurrection put on full display that the life of Jesus was the life of God and a living presence of the reign of God on earth."[3] Weaver puts less emphasis on the contemporary living presence of Jesus in comparison to Cone, but they both agree on the significance of focusing on Jesus' whole life and deeds in Scripture. Anabaptists have commonly confronted mainstream Christians' attempts to detour around the radical life and teachings of Jesus. By marginalizing the life of Jesus and primarily holding up Christ's death, the word

"Christian" ends up having little relation to being like Jesus in terms of his ethics and sociopolitical practices like loving enemies, speaking the truth, forgiveness, and nonviolent action.

Combining Black theologies and Anabaptism makes me think about the similarities and differences between Luke and Matthew's narratives, especially their presentations of the Beatitudes. Luke often resonates deeply with Black people's lived experiences since the gospel account emphasizes Jesus' focus on people's social conditions and status. Drawing on Leviticus 25 and Isaiah 58 and 61, Jesus announces in his prophetic statement in Luke 4:18–19: "The Spirit of the Lord is upon me, because he has anointed me to bring good news to the poor. He has sent me to proclaim release to the captives and recovery of sight to the blind, to set free those who are oppressed, to proclaim the year of the Lord's favor." In Luke 6:20–26, Jesus announces that the poor, those who are hungry, those who weep, and those excluded and reviled are the ones who are blessed—while the rich, those who are full, those laughing, and those well-spoken of, receive Jesus' woes. Luke's account of Jesus' life engages in constant subversive social reversals where the poor, the Samaritan, vulnerable women, and those most socially stigmatized are now at the center of God's reign.

For many Anabaptists, the gospel of Matthew provides significant spiritual formation, and the pinnacle teaching is found in Matthew 5–7, known as the Sermon on the Mount. Jesus' teachings are presented as more authoritative than Moses as he delivers the fulfillment of the Law and Prophets to the people. Jesus teaches inner and external transformation, enemy love, non-retaliation, speaking the truth and having integrity, humility and authentic piety, kingdom-seeking and sabbath-oriented trust in God for needs, self-examination over moral condemnation of others, the golden rule, and to make these teachings the rock and foundation of their way of life.

Though Jesus' Beatitudes in Matthew and Luke are similar, a closer look reveals striking differences. Where Luke describes Jesus as focusing on people's sociwal conditions, Matthew shows Jesus' concern for their social posture and practices. Where Luke 6 contrasts blessings for the poor, the hungry, and those who weep with woes to the rich, the full, and those who are laughing, Jesus in Matthew 5 announces that the poor in spirit, those who mourn, the meek, those who hunger and thirst for God to set things right, the merciful, the peacemakers, and those persecuted for the sake of God's righteous justice are actually blessed, and the kingdom is theirs. Overall, both texts demonstrate Jesus' concern for vulnerable people, call people into radical and costly discipleship to Jesus, and demonstrate that Jesus' announcement of his reign is central to his vocation and significance—yet their differences unveil varied emphases that also are visible in Black and Anabaptist theology.

As such, it is not surprising that for Anabaptists the ethic of peace has traditionally been important. Historically and in some parts of the world today, Anabaptists have sought to live faithfully as disciples in a world that sought to persecute, torture, and banish them. Meanwhile, Black Christians have held to the historical and eschatological goal of freedom in response to being enslaved, oppressed, and racialized as nonhuman for merely existing. Despite those differences, theologies of peacemaking and theologies of liberation can and do converge. This is especially the case for Anabaptists in the radical discipleship tradition and Black Christians influenced by the Black Church prophetic tradition.

Participating in God's peacemaking invites us to break cycles and systems of violence. Joining in God's liberation calls us to break every chain of oppression and seek the end of all social practices of domination. Peacemaking and liberation can apply to individual situations and broader social structures. An Anablacktivist theology invites us to practice liberative peacemaking that pursues God's shalom in creation with an explicit focus on liberating oppressed people. It also means practicing a peaceable liberation, because as we seek liberation for the oppressed, disciples of Jesus actively and attentively seek every creative possibility for cultivating peace and healing as we break the chains of oppression.

I often prefer the language of "peacemaking" to "nonviolence" when describing Jesus' ethic of peace. I don't believe our theology should prescribe systematized rules of behavior that oversimplify our complicity in cycles and systems of violence. "Nonviolence" and "pacifism" as theological terms evoke ethical systems; "peacemaking" is a more open-ended orientation and vocation. Some pacifists would agree with me about peacemaking, but some employ the term "pacifism" as a rule expressing their commitment to never use violence under any circumstance. Following Jesus doesn't merely come down to systematizing our ethics into rules. In contrast for me, nonviolent action and nonviolent resistance are social strategies that implement Jesus-shaped liberative peacemaking through grassroots resistance. During the Civil Rights Movement, for example, pacifists and those who believed violence was sometimes necessary were able to link arms while employing the social strategy of nonviolent resistance. Through the ethic of liberative peacemaking, disciples seek to follow Jesus faithfully in every situation and attend to what the Spirit is doing, looking for openings for where God's shalom might be creatively expanded.

I also sometimes prefer the term "God's deliverance" to "liberation," because it feels more holistic and not limited to sociopolitical concerns. Of course, "liberation" is often used holistically, as I have done throughout this book. I take very seriously the concreteness of the gospel as intervening in the here and now. We should never erase the gospel's explicitly sociopolitical and economic liberation. Still, though it is a churchy term (and was common in my Black church upbringing), "God's deliverance" feels more comprehensive to our entire human condition. All of us are caught in intergenerational webs of sin and are captive to forces seen and unseen from which we need healing and salvation. This includes trauma, our mindsets and psyches, hard-heartedness, and habits, as well as broader evil patterns, structures, and forces shaping our society that keep us captive. We need God to deliver us from sin and death.

Every generation must follow, participate in, encounter, and make visible the story of Jesus in our lives. And we must develop the language to best describe a Jesus-shaped life and the ethics and practices he calls us to. Our language must arise from within our current crises and concerns and how the gospel relates to them. There is no one-size-fits-all language, but Black theology and Anabaptism, together, take seriously the social status, disposition, teachings, and practices of Jesus in a way that can help us make a break from the legacy of Christian domination, oppression, and mangled reasoning at work in our world today.

Dependence on the Spirit

Anyone can practice following the life and teachings of Jesus, but to commune with him, participate in the life of the Messiah, and live in such ways that Christ is living in and through us, individually and collectively, requires dependence on the Holy Spirit. It's unfortunate that the Holy Spirit has been so domesticated that engaging with the Spirit is often expressed primarily as personal religious experience void of social significance. In contrast, the book of Acts describes the Holy Spirit as a decolonial force: it leads people groups to speak and be heard in their distinct languages and ignites radical economic redistribution of wealth and justice for those who want to live as one in Christ. The Holy Spirit in Acts leads them to break the walls of hostility between Hebraic Jews and Hellenized Jews, Jews and Samaritans, and Jews and Gentiles.

Our world is filled with myths, ideologies, and lies. Only when we refuse to trust our human capacity to be objective and all-knowing (as though we could be like God grasping absolute truth) can we learn why we need both our mind and the Spirit of God that "will guide you into all the truth" toward God's ultimate reality (John 16:13). Dependence on the Spirit is the antidote to making an idol out of our ability to reason, perceive, and know in creation. As finite creatures who only see dimly and in part now, we trust that the Spirit will guide us toward God's truth.

Dependence on the Spirit, in Anablacktivist experience, neither follows those white Anabaptists who have eclipsed the role of the Spirit nor those Pentecostals who have severed the activity of the Spirit from radical participation in life of the Messiah in our world. Luke's gospel explains how the Spirit fell on Jesus, who then proclaimed his messianic manifesto of liberation and social reversals. Jesus demonstrates a life dependent on and empowered by the Spirit.

Pentecost in the book of Acts similarly sparks God's revolution through the church. We need the Spirit. As I understand the apostle Paul, the Spirit indwells us so that we are clothed in Christ, and Christ's presence within and among us enables us to overcome evil with good.[4] I appreciate the framing of radical pietism among some Brethren, because it expects and necessities devotion to God, encounter with the Spirit, regeneration of the inner and outer life, and obedience to Jesus. Radical pietism is complementary to Anabaptist emphases on discipleship to Jesus but necessitates the work of the Spirit.

I'm indebted to how most of the Black Church has always taken seriously the activity of the Holy Spirit, expecting and anticipating that the Spirit can and usually will disrupt business as usual. The Spirit breathes life into scripture for our inspiration, it intercedes for us when we only got groans in response to the pain and suffering we endure, it emboldens us to speak when our own words have run out, it reveals what is of God and what is not, and it guides us on life's journey.

There is helpful tension between some Black and Anabaptist ways of living with the Spirit of God. Anabaptism calls us to live a life of yieldedness to God. This emphasis in Anabaptism can lead to complete resignation or abandonment of this world—renouncing materialism, embracing God's call to do difficult things, or a willingness to endure through opposition. The fullest expression leads to sharing in Christ's death with our very bodies. In the sixteenth century, this attentiveness and trust in God and the Spirit's guidance in one's life frequently led Anabaptists to take an unflinching stand when faced with persecution and torture. The Negro Spiritual "Give Me Jesus" communicates a similar focus: "You can have all this world, just give me Jesus." A posture of yieldedness to God and abandonment to the world cultivates courageous and sometimes revolutionary boldness as followers of Jesus.

That said, some Black and womanist theologians are concerned with more than abandonment of the world. Anabaptism invites people to practice a voluntary abandonment of the world, while to be Black has often meant already being abandoned by the world. If Black social death is indeed baked into modern society through a pervasive antiblackness, such yieldedness on its own only further entrenches that reality. Voluntary rejection of the world makes sense when you have an abundance and don't want to have two competing masters—God and mammon. Voluntary rejection of the world is insufficient when you need to courageously challenge the structures in the world that restrict your communities' capacity to thrive. Therefore, we must also consider what theologian Karen Baker-Fletcher calls "dancing with God in a world of crucifixion."[5] She draws on both actual charismatic dance and the fancy theological word *perichoresis*, which is borrowed from ancient Christians, to describe our embodied life with God, even when death is near. The Spirit "moves in the world in perichoresis—a type of sacred dance, within God's own nature. God is a Spirit who moves in and through creation."[6]

The world continues to crucify vulnerable and oppressed people in new ways today, thus we can dance with the Spirit and take "one dynamic step at a time" so that we too can "dance with the Trinity in the power of the Spirit!"[7] By joining this divine movement in creation, we can live courageously and participate in God's love and healing work in the world to the fullest extent possible. We must yield to the Spirit, and whenever possible we must dance with God, creating new realities together with God. Sometimes the death-dealing forces in our world restrain what is achievable, yet we still hold fast to God while renouncing the old order.

The prophetic and radical church

Being discipled through the convergence of the prophetic stream of the Black Church and the radical edge of Anabaptism has the capacity to transform the pitiful, mangled, status-quo Christianity that too many of us take for granted today. It's a strange thing to acknowledge that Jesus has so frequently been preached in the United States, yet the mainstream church in the West barely resembles anything related to Jesus' story. Where Jesus renounced "lording it over others," the domesticated American church has grasped for sole control and power over society so that it can impose its polluted morals onto everyone else. As Jesus fulfilled the covenant of Torah and the Prophets through his integrity, speaking truth to power, eschatological hope, and healing justice for the most vulnerable, the church of the empire has been disingenuous, deceitful, and fear mongering, fashioning a world that bolsters the rich and powerful and scapegoats the poor, vulnerable, and foreigner. Radical discipleship and a prophetic witness invite us into a response that is both faithful to God and rooted in compassionate action on behalf of our suffering neighbor. The church's witness is in crisis because it is known more for apathy, hate, and power-hungry members than it is for embodying the good news in the public square.

The term "radical discipleship" can be misconstrued as extremist rather than grounded in the gospel. Most in the radical discipleship tradition may not mind being called extremists if that is understood as being extreme in following Jesus, loving our neighbors (everyone), embodying good news, and making visible the reign of God in our world. Rev. Dr. Martin Luther King Jr. was called an extremist in his day. "Though I was initially disappointed at being categorized as an extremist, as I continued to think about the matter, I gradually gained a measure of satisfaction from the label," he wrote from the Birmingham jail. "Was not Jesus an extremist for love: 'Love your enemies, bless them that curse you, pray for them that despitefully use you.' Was not Amos an extremist for justice: 'Let justice roll down like waters and righteousness like an ever-flowing stream.'" For King, the issue was whether we fully commit ourselves to faithfulness, not whether we appear extreme. The question "is not whether we will be extremists, but what kind of extremists we will be. Will we be extremists for hate or for love? Will we be extremists for the preservation of injustice or for the extension of justice?"[8] In that way, radical discipleship can be understood as extremist.

However, the word "radical" is actually about getting to *the root*. And the root of Christianity and discipleship is the story and person of Jesus Christ. What does it mean to return, again and again, to the story and person of Jesus Christ and take seriously his way? This is the meaning of "radical" for the radical discipleship tradition. Discipleship has drifted so far from its purpose that it rarely leads to cultivating authentic followers of Jesus who encounter, abide in, and make visible the Jesus story in their lives by accepting the socio-political consequences of following Jesus, renouncing and redistributing wealth, feeding the hungry, clothing the naked, making peace, and taking up our cross with genuine risk required for the sake of God's righteousness. Instead, we have been satisfied with devotional books that extract Bible verses from their context, spiritualize them, and make their application suitable for lives committed to pursuing comfort in the American dream. Ironically, we call "blessed" lives defined by the very wealth, overconsumption, and disregard of others' suffering that Jesus cursed. We need to discard our domesticated projections of Jesus and return to the root of our faith.

We cannot understand the meaning of the crucifixion without placing it within the broader context of Jesus' whole story. We must pay attention to what triggers his execution in the narrative: what most call "the cleansing of the temple" when Jesus overturns the tables of the temple money changers.[9] The temple leaders are not your everyday Jewish leaders in the village synagogues but rather the Jerusalem establishment who are also in cahoots with the Roman Empire. They are squeezing everyday worshipers with the temple tithe and adding to their poverty. Jesus disrupts and confronts business as usual by temporarily upsetting the flow of temple operations, exposing the injustice. Jesus told his disciples that they had to count the cost of discipleship and be willing to die—in fact, he had already told them that he would die when he went to Jerusalem. Jesus knowingly and voluntarily engaged in activity that would lead the powers of Rome and Jerusalem to kill him.

The way of the cross, then, is when we take up our cross and courageously bear witness to the reign of God while accepting the consequences and risks of faithfulness to the point of possible death. But the point of radical discipleship is not death, it is living as a gospel counter-witness to a sinful and violent society and manifesting the reign of God before a watching world. This is about truly embracing life. Whether things change is out of our control, but living faithfully and with integrity before God is up to us. Disciples of Jesus organize their lives in community with other disciples according to the principle of God's inbreaking reign right under the nose of the powers. Radical discipleship calls us to follow Jesus all the way through the storm of political violence because we anticipate sharing in the Messiah's resurrection.

As I named earlier, many use the word "prophetic" to talk about foretelling the future, having a special spiritual connection with God, or having spiritual authority to act and speak. These uses are more common in evangelical, apostolic, and Pentecostal traditions. In the prophetic stream of the Black Church, however, the word "prophetic" draws on the biblical example and wisdom of the Hebrew prophets, who became mouthpieces for God by forthtelling the people to repent from injustice and idolatry. "They sell the innocent for silver, and the needy for a pair of sandals," prophesied Amos. "They trample on the heads of the poor as on the dust of the ground and deny justice to the oppressed" (Amos 2:6b–7 NIV). They don't only unveil the evil; they also call you into righteous action. "Learn to do good; seek justice; rescue the oppressed; defend the orphan; plead for the widow" (Isaiah 1:17). More often than not, prophets suffer for their faithful enactment of God's call.

The prophetic tradition invites us, through divine imagination, to glimpse God's dream for us. That is, to conceive of the world otherwise, rather than remain stuck in the reasoning that the way things are will always be. And through deep hope in a God who is able to make a difference, prophets call us to join in the divine ushering of the world toward shalom.

While Anabaptists have typically leaned on the Gospels for developing Christian ethics and practices, the prophetic stream of the Black Church draws on biblical wisdom more broadly, with the exodus and the Prophets understood to be fulfilled in Jesus. Moses told Pharoah to let God's people go. God saw their suffering, was present to them, and liberated them from their enslavement. The prophets saw imperial idolatry and injustice and called the people into repentance. Matthew's gospel wants readers to understand that Jesus is more authoritative than Moses, and all three synoptic gospels describe how Jesus embodies, points to, and enacts the prophets for his time.

Through the Holy Spirit, we are indwelled with the Spirit of Christ, making us the body of Christ when we participate and embody the story of Jesus in our lives. As such, the church ought to be a prophethood. While some may have particular prophetic callings by God, the whole church is called to embody the way of the prophet in our communities and in the public square. As people drawn up in the way of Jesus, we have an irresistible message that is good news to the poor: Jesus is our liberator and judge, and he has begun a new reign in solidarity with the oppressed and vulnerable. Like weeping prophets, we bring an inconvenient announcement to the rich and powerful: Jesus is liberator and judge, and he calls us to repent by dropping everything, giving wealth to the poor, and living in shalom solidarity with the oppressed and vulnerable. When those who are last and those who are first in our present society accept Jesus' invitation into shalom-shaped solidarity, they will discover that his way brings greater humanity, life, and flourishing for everyone.

Anablacktivism invites a robust Christian way of life in the public square simultaneously influenced by a radical discipleship and a prophetic witness. It is not easy to live faithfully in a society built by white supremacy and Christian nationalism. We need disciples of Jesus who live as a radical counter-witness to the Messiah's story before a watching world, and who directly offer a prophetic witness of confrontation and truth-telling to the powers that be. Our faithful counter-witness is dependent on local worshiping communities that capably disciple people to encounter, follow, participate in, and make visible the way of Jesus. To be a holy prophethood called by God, we must be shaped by our sacred anti-imperial scriptures, provoked toward love and action by our communities, and inspired by the Holy Spirit into courageous and costly faith that accepts the risks of the call.

Prophetic discipleship is the kind of robust life in the public square needed—the antidote to white Christian nationalism as well as a range of other social concerns. White Christian nationalism entices Christians with the American Dream, whereas a radical prophethood taps into our sacred imagination so we can envision God's dream instead. Mainstream American Christians teach us to stamp Jesus' name onto the pursuit of plundered money, concentrated power, and the world's respect. Prophetic discipleship forms us in, with, and after the way of Jesus into abundant life where God is delighted because everyone belongs, everyone matters, and everyone can thrive.

Fugitives and martyrs

We must learn a new way of being, seeing, thinking, and engaging, and we often do not find it where and when we wish or desire. So where might we look? Where can we find new ways of living within a world organized by antiblackness and white Christian nationalism?

Fugitives and martyrs have loomed large in Black and Anabaptist imaginations, respectively. The fugitive and martyr each remind us of what faithfulness looks like while living within severe constraints under imperial domination bent toward one's destruction. And they uniquely unveil aspects of the Jesus story. However, we must be willing to reject nostalgia and self-justification of our present existence because of a romanticized past. When we do so, the memory of the fugitive and martyr invite us into new ways of living as the body of the Messiah under the powers.

At face value, the fugitive in Black history and imagination has been of one escaping the chains of antiblack oppression, gratuitous violence, and dehumanizing status as commodity. They are fleeing the master's plantation or leaving town before they become the next lynched victim. No one embodies this reality better than Harriet Tubman, our Black Moses. After escaping enslavement, she made over a dozen trips back down to the South to help plunder (liberate) Black people from their enslavers (original plunderers). Tubman became known for her stealthy and subversive capacity to evade capture and help others self-emancipate.

Still, when we consider fugitivity as a way of life, we can expand our imagination of how to live, move, and have our being beyond moments of escaping chattel slavery or Jim and Jane Crow violence. Our society is arranged through an antiblack lens reinforced by the state. Anti-BLM, anti-woke, anti-antiracism, anti–Black history, and anti-DEI forces are all antiblack efforts that are restructuring our society. To this day, Black people are overpoliced, brutalized, arrested, sentenced, and caged. Black neighborhoods already suffering from legacies of white flight are plundered through willful underfunding, predatory lending, subprime loans, rent exploitation, disinvestment, racist appraisal systems, and extortionary fees and fines designed for revenue generation. We must stay attentive to our relationship to the social order and how we move within it.

We live in a society where people not only are in denial that we live in the aftermath of slavery, but become offended when someone wants to consider how our past has made the present United States a sick and wounded nation. Politicians, judges, juries, policies, institutions, the history we teach, the stories we tell, and our media and cultural artifacts collectively uphold a white supremacist status quo. And that includes the mainstream white American church, which historically has been the most antiblack institution in the United States.

Anyone opposed to these forces must understand their witness and way of life within society. Many Black scholars use fugitivity to define Black ways of life that break from the social order. Fugitivity is comprehensive escape, stealth, and evasive practices that carve out a space to live, from below, that has rejected the logics of antiblackness. J. Kameron Carter calls fugitivity "an always already being-in-uncapturable-flight . . . from the terms of statism."[10] I think of fugitivity as "stealing away" as a way of life. It is the hush harbor of communal life. Always seeking opportunities to break with the patterns of this white supremacist and plundering world, one steals away outside the surveillance of the powers to cultivate genuine relationships, renouncing those who deny the image of God in others, to seek joy and mutual thriving, and to discover the meaning of shalom upon the land that we live on.

Tessie McGee, a secondary school history teacher in the 1930s, is one example of fugitivity. The twenty-eight-year-old McGee taught history at the only Black secondary school in her Louisiana parish. Since the state's all-white Department of Education and school boards restricted her lessons to its problematic curriculum—complete with the inevitable drop-in surveillance from visiting white officials—McGee unofficially adapted the curriculum through a fugitive practice. With the official curriculum laid openly on the desk, McGee would read aloud to her students from a textbook by Carter G. Woodson—an educator and historian often called the "father of Black history." As a student recalled much later in his life, "When the principal would come in, [McGee] would . . . simply lift her eyes to the outline that resided on the desk and teach us from the outline. When the principal disappeared, her eyes went back to the book in her lap."[11] McGee understood that Black education that subverted the dehumanization of Black people and challenged the justifications for antiblack violence and oppression in society were outlawed. She broke from the social order right there in that moment, without even leaving her desk, by carving out a flight toward freedom as a way of teaching Black students inside the classroom.

Fugitivity can be embodied and practiced in response to myriad ways that our policies and social norms counter God's dream for thriving. Scholar Jarvis Givens calls this "perpetual escape, always striving toward a world where what is known to be human is not premised on the subjection of black life."[12]

Martyrdom has also been perverted in ways that glorify death and miss the manner in which the martyr's actual life embodies something more substantial and truthful. The martyr has stood tall in the legacy and imagination of Anabaptism. However, white Anabaptists have frequently framed their tradition in ways that allowed for assimilation into the Doctrine of Discovery project of white supremacy and conquest while interpreting themselves through the lens of the persecuted. They justified themselves in the present because of their link to martyrs in the past.

Early Christians like Ignatius willingly joined in the suffering of Christ, seemingly glad to die at the hands of empire. Folks like Cyprian initially sought to avoid martyrdom, but when he was arrested and tried during the Valerian persecutions, he refused to renounce his faith and was beheaded. Despite a difference in motives, both Ignatius and Cyprian sought to live according to the reality of Jesus' life and teachings. They faithfully persisted with great personal consequences for doing so in the public square.

Within the Roman Empire, society was organized against the early church's way of life. Their whole way of life, not just their deaths, made them martyrs. The actual word "martyr" isn't defined by death—it translates as "witness." From that perspective, "martyrs" (including many sixteenth-century Anabaptists) are to be considered as such because they were credible living witnesses to Jesus. They persistently and truthfully made his story visible for their neighbors, even to the point of death in the public square.

Mennonite theologian Chris Huebner offers some helpful ways of understanding martyrdom and its relationship to truth. Truth, he suggests, isn't a proposition or final conclusion on a matter that we possess as Christians. Yet we can pursue and embody it. Huebner invites us to resist thinking about martyrdom as what happens when we hold on to a doctrinal belief in the face of death, or when someone has conquered their fear of death and persists courageously, or when someone's death is evidence that secures the truth (an apologetic proof) that they died for.[13] Those are instrumentalist ways of thinking about martyrdom and truth. That might be the prevailing approach, even in contemporary scholarship, but it misses a different way of life into which we are invited.

Huebner writes that knowledge is "an embodied social performance or practice."[14] We should seek to live truth. Martyrdom, for the church, is about "the truthful witness they embody."[15] Dying for one's beliefs doesn't automatically make one a martyr. Therefore the church must discern, through disciplined reflection on the birth, life, teachings, death, and resurrection of Jesus, who has lived truthfully. Martyrdom could be understood as one whose life embodies and makes visible the story of Jesus and unveils the reign of God in the public square, clashing with the powers. Martyrdom is a public practice for the living. Doing it fully and truthfully sometimes leads to death. This is especially meaningful as we grapple with how to live when the state is arresting your neighbors, is practicing neo-fascism that smothers difference and dissent, and is making Black life expendable.

Jesus' fugitivity and martyrdom

It could be easy to see fugitivity and martyrdom as opposing orientations—one seeks life, and the other embraces death. But prophetic, radical discipleship in the way of Jesus invites us to look in the mirror and see both the Black fugitive and Anabaptist martyr staring back. I think the gospel story told by Mark can help us see their paradoxical relationship through a lens of creative discernment and tension rather than as opposites.

The gospel of Mark is one of the most sociopolitically dangerous books in the Bible. In Mark's telling, Jesus transitions from concealing his identity from the imperial powers to declaring his messiahship publicly and for his followers. Biblical scholars call the stage of concealment the "messianic secret." One way of reading this is that we find Jesus practicing messianic fugitivity within the realm of the imperial powers and local authorities. He seems to want to evade surveillance and the watchful eye. He doesn't want his identity and the meaning of his presence to spread widely. So Jesus frequently commands people to not spread the news. When he exorcises demons or performs miracles, he says to tell no one (Mark 1:25, 34; 3:12; 5:43; 7:36). And though people do not listen and spread the word anyhow,

Jesus' behavior is subversive, as though he is trying to start an underground grassroots nonviolent revolution (God's kingdom). This is right under the nose of, and within the geography of, Caesar's rule. Jesus is stealing away as a way of life, breaking from the social order, escaping the watchful surveillance of Big Brother, carving out a hidden space from below where one can survive, and even thrive, under constraints. The first phase of Jesus' reign is executed through subversive fugitivity.

Midway through Mark's gospel, things shift dramatically. Jesus asks his disciples who people say that he is, and Peter answers that he is the Messiah (Mark 8:27–30). "Don't tell anyone," Jesus reminds the disciples. However, he then begins the first of several teachings that redefine his Messiahship with suffering, death, and resurrection (8:31). Not only does Jesus define his messianic reign through suffering rather than triumph and domination, but this reality shapes his teaching on what it means for his disciples to follow after him. For Jesus, there is no separation between his being the suffering anointed liberator of the people and the costly and dangerous life required to follow him that often and inevitably leads to state-sanctioned execution by the establishment. "If any wish to come after me, let them deny themselves and take up their cross and follow me," says Jesus. "For those who want to save their life will lose it, and those who lose their life for my sake, and for the sake of the gospel, will save it" (8:34–35). In chapters 8 to 10, Jesus moves into publicly announcing who he is, coupling this proclamation with the subversive and costly call to accept the existential consequences of following his way that lead to execution or that flip social status on its head (8:31–38; 9:30–37; 10:17–45). Brilliantly narrated, the fugitive disposition in Mark's gospel morphs into Jesus' public declaration not only of his identity but of the sociopolitical risks inherent to following Jesus in the public square.

Mark's gospel ends with Jesus going into Jerusalem and confronting and clashing with the ruling powers. The concentrated powers try to destroy Jesus' messianic movement by making him a public spectacle as just one more Jew hung on a tree. Rome, it seems, has the final word. His disciples are unwilling to participate in this costly and dangerous discipleship of the Messiah. They move underground as a suffering people, and thus abandon him.

Unlike the other three gospels, Mark's account ends ambiguously. Many Christian Bibles include two endings to the book of Mark, but the oldest manuscripts only have one, and it is the shorter version (16:1–8). The women leave the empty tomb in terror and amazement. We are not told what happens next.

This open-endedness invites us to live out the fragility of the Jesus way ourselves. *We* are the conclusion to the book. Everything the church does beyond Mark 16:8 is the rest of the story. Will we, like the disciples in Mark's account, continually misinterpret the meaning of Jesus, expecting the Jesus way to be about triumph, and getting our turn to dominate and have control? Or will we find a way to renounce domination and hierarchy, share in sufferings and joys, and begin to understand what it means to follow Jesus into our full humanity as beloved community? Will we learn to embody the story of Jesus truthfully in our communities and in the public square?

The Jesus way invites disciples to fugitivity and martyrdom. It embodies freedom and truthfulness. Fugitive discipleship invites us to steal away from the death-dealing social order, practicing escape as a way of life bent toward deepening and expanding freedom's insurrection whenever possible.

Sometimes public martyrdom—embodying the truthfulness of the Jesus story by directly clashing with and confronting evil—is our calling. This should only be done when we have accepted the risks and consequences of such a vulnerable way forward.

So we all must make a choice. Do we need to steal away and carve out a hush harbor space for our survival and communal joy, or do we need to go public and confront and clash with the powers that be? We need a community of trusted and Spirit-led siblings who are yielding to the Spirit and are ready to dance with God's movement to discern that decision. Both fugitivity and martyrdom are parts of the Jesus story. Ultimately, we do not get to tell others how to embody the Jesus story and when they ought to steal away or accept the risks of public faithfulness. I'll only caution that those who have already borne the brunt of oppression and violence are typically the ones embodying the truthfulness of Jesus in the public square, accepting the vulnerable possibility of death. And those who are already protected by the judicial system, police, military, and overall social arrangement are typically the ones unwilling to share in suffering. That contradicts God's social reversals, where the first are last and the last are first—it sounds like the status quo, which is neither fugitivity nor martyrdom.

Making the Way plain

In *Race: A Theological Account*, J. Kameron Carter explores how the West severed Christ from his Jewishness, conflated and collapsed Western civilization and Christianity, and constructed a white supremacist imagination. Western theology took on a scholarly posture of "objective" distance from those who suffer rather than from the posture of the crucified Christ.[16] At the end of Carter's book, an illuminating set of sentences orient us toward a new path:

> Christian theology must take its bearings from the Christian theological languages and practices that arise from the lived Christian worlds of dark peoples in modernity and how such peoples reclaimed (and in their own ways salvaged) the language of Christianity, and thus Christian theology, from being a discourse of death—their death. This is the language and practices by which dark people, insofar as many of them comported themselves as Christian subjects in the world, have imagined and performed a way of being in the world beyond the pseudotheological containment of whiteness.[17]

In other words, those racialized on the underside of white supremacist Christianity—those who endured chattel slavery, genocide, forcible displacement, and subsequent forms of racial oppression—have practiced a different kind of Christianity and God-talk. Mainstream Christianity in the West became an ideological tool of imperial plunder (stealing land, bodies, and labor) that required the death of racialized subjects, yet these "dark peoples" have embodied "a way of being in the world" that—in contrast to the Doctrine of Discovery—no longer leads to their death. In this way, they truly have "reclaimed" and "salvaged" Christian practice and discourse.

While I was raised in a particular Black church, my encounters with the broader Black Church and Anabaptist traditions together helped me salvage my faith from the currents of Western Christendom and the Doctrine of Discovery. I saw how both Black people and early Anabaptists have experienced the underside of Western European Christianity, though in different contexts. For

Anabaptists, Western Christendom was their death-dealing context, merging imperial domination and control bolstered through military violence with Christian rhetoric, doctrines, and symbols. For Black people, their context was late medieval Christendom and the modern "Christianized" West, which were deployed for enslavement, plunder, and supremacy over the earth. Both Black people and Anabaptists suffered at the hands of Christians. Both saw the Bible weaponized toward their destruction. Both found themselves within the crucible of suffering as their worlds were torn apart and destroyed in the name of Jesus. Once I understood the historical connections between Western Christendom and the Doctrine of Discovery, the power, promise, and paradox of these two traditions salvaged and nurtured my faith.

Of course, their sufferings are distinct. Anabaptists suffered because of their voluntary decision to try to take Jesus seriously by radically breaking with the ways of Christendom. Radical discipleship to Jesus resulted in Christian-on-Christian persecution. Black people suffered for existing beyond the European definitions of what white folk deemed to be human. And then their Christian faith independent of white people was also deemed dangerous, leading to horrific blowback. Society has morphed over the centuries, so now Anabaptism is considered a legitimate Christian expression, whether some disdain or celebrate it. In contrast, antiblackness has morphed over the years, revealing that even in varying circumstances, racist views and practices persist and are baked and embedded into our contemporary society and its habits and psyche.

Even with those differences, Black theology and Anabaptism together can help us navigate the sequel to Christianity's venture into empire-building, racialized slavery, and genocidal conquest, which is expressed through white Christian nationalism today.

Two different traditions have each participated in God's salvaging of Western Christianity from within. And maybe disciples of the Messiah who learn from their intergenerational wisdom might once again be able to perceive the Way that is liberating and peacemaking and resembles the life and teachings of Jesus. In the specificity of the Jesus way, we can embody something genuinely liberating and peacemaking. Through yieldedness and dancing with the Spirit, we join with our Creator. In the aftermath of so many centuries of plunder, death, and domination done by the hands of Christians, when we look in the mirror and see the Anabaptist martyr and the enslaved fugitive reflected back, we are then ready for radical discipleship and a prophetic witness in the way of Jesus.

NOTES

Introduction

1 This figure includes Christian as well as other religious service attendance. Jeffrey M. Jones, "Church Attendance Has Declined in Most U.S. Religious Groups," Gallup, March 25, 2024, https://news.gallup.com/poll/642548/church-attendance-declined-religious-groups.aspx.

2 Aaron Earls, "Public Trust of Pastors Hits New Record Low," Lifeway Research, January 24, 2024, https://research.lifeway.com/2024/01/24/public-trust-of-pastors-hits-new-record-low/.

3 Augustine of Hippo, "The Correction of the Donatists, Chapter 6.—21.," Catholic Library, accessed April 4, 2025, https://catholiclibrary.org/library/view?docId=Fathers-EN/Augustine.000079.

4 Penal substitutionary atonement theory has grown in prominence within Western Christianity since John Calvin began preaching it in the sixteenth century. It assumes that God requires retributive justice because God's wrath or divine law demands punishment; a wrathful Father has a loving Son take our place as a sacrifice. In brief, the theory emphasizes divine wrath and willingness to eternally torment people for finite sin. This theory distorts biblical understandings of salvation, misunderstands sacrificial offerings in the Levitical system, boxes God primarily into Western punitive reasoning, marginalizes the salvific meaning of the

resurrection, and rejects the ancient ways that the historic, global church have understood how Jesus saves.

5 Coined in 1947, the term "Jane Crow" emphasizes the distinct political, economic, and social discrimination faced by Black women.

6 Anthea Butler, *White Evangelical Racism: The Politics of Morality in America* (UNC Press Books, 2021), 2.

7 Robert P. Jones, *White Too Long: The Legacy of White Supremacy in American Christianity* (Simon & Schuster, 2021), 185. The Public Religion Research Institute (PRRI) collected self-reported data through surveys, data, and history, which Jones used to demonstrate that white Christians (evangelical, mainline, and Catholic) have sustained white supremacy through their faith.

8 Jones, 185.

9 Michael O. Emerson and Glenn E. Bracey II, *The Religion of Whiteness: How Racism Distorts Christian Faith* (Oxford University Press, 2024), 43.

10 Emerson and Bracey, 100–143.

11 Ja'han Jones, "Trump's 2023 Vow on Education Sounds a Lot Like Reparations—for White People," *The ReidOut* (blog), November 14, 2024, https://www.msnbc.com/the-reidout/reidout-blog/trump-department-education-dei-rcna180046.

12 See Matthew Thiessen, *A Jewish Paul: The Messiah's Herald to the Gentiles* (Baker Academic, 2023).

13 "Backs against the wall" is a famous quote from Howard Thurman's book *Jesus and the Disinherited*, which is shorthand for how Jesus has come for the "disinherited" of the world. The phrase "faces at the bottom of the well" comes from the title of Derrick Bell's influential book *Faces at the Bottom of the Well: The Permanence of Racism*, which illustrates Black people's social status at the bottom of the racial hierarchy.

Chapter 1

1 My grandfather had an honorary doctorate that recognized his significant impact in ministry.
2 I write about this experience in my first book, *Trouble I've Seen: Changing the Way the Church Views Racism* (Herald Press, 2016).
3 As we'll explore in subsequent chapters, the prophetic and liberationist streams of the Black Church emerged as a liberative and justice-oriented interpretation and expression of Christianity in response to slavery, Jim Crow, and subsequent forms of antiblack oppression.
4 John Howard Yoder was accused of sexual abuse by over fifty women over multiple decades. The specific nature of the abuses was wide-ranging. He accomplished the decades-long sexual violence by leveraging his power, influence, and trust as a world-famous ethicist, professor, and churchman. Historian Rachel Waltner Goossen wrote a comprehensive report on Yoder's history: "'Defanging the Beast': Mennonite Responses to John Howard Yoder's Sexual Abuse," *Mennonite Quarterly Review* 89, no. 1 (January 2015), https://www.goshen.edu/wp-content/uploads/sites/75/2016/06/MQRJanuary2015.pdf.
5 Goossen, "'Defanging the Beast.'"
6 There are valid critiques (made elsewhere) about some of the strategies of Occupy.
7 I write about some of my activism in *Who Will Be a Witness? Igniting Activism for God's Justice, Love, and Deliverance* (Herald Press, 2020).
8 Hubert L. Brown, *Black and Mennonite: A Search for Identity* (Herald Press, 1976).
9 See Tobin Miller Shearer, *Daily Demonstrators: The Civil Rights Movement in Mennonite Homes and Sanctuaries* (Johns Hopkins University Press, 2010).
10 J. Denny Weaver, "Theology in the Mirror of the Martyred and Oppressed: Reflections on the Intersections of Yoder and Cone," in *Wisdom of the Cross: Essays in Honor of John Howard Yoder*, ed. Stanley Hauerwas et al. (Eerdmans, 1999), 409–29.
11 J. Denny Weaver, *The Nonviolent Atonement*, 2nd ed. (Eerdmans, 2011).

12 Weaver eventually became an outside reader for my doctoral dissertation panel.
13 James Cone, *My Soul Looks Back* (Abingdon, 1982), 36.

Chapter 2

1 "The State of Church Attendance: Trends and Statistics [2024]," ChurchTrac, accessed January 9, 2025, https://www.churchtrac.com/articles/the-state-of-church-attendance-trends-and-statistics-2023.
2 "Signs of Decline & Hope Among Key Metrics of Faith," Barna Group, accessed January 9, 2025, https://www.barna.com/research/changing-state-of-the-church/.
3 "Church Closures: Insights to Save Your Ministry," ChurchTrac, accessed January 10, 2025, https://www.churchtrac.com/articles/church-closures-insights-to-save-your-ministry.
4 Alan Kreider, *The Patient Ferment of the Early Church: The Improbable Rise of Christianity in the Roman Empire* (Baker Academic, 2016).
5 Justo L. González, *The Story of Christianity: The Early Church to the Present Day* (Prince Press, 1999), 33–36.
6 R. Joseph Owles, *The Didache: The Teaching of the Twelve Apostles* (CreateSpace Independent Publishing Platform, 2014).
7 "Tertullian," accessed November 11, 2024, https://history.hanover.edu/courses/excerpts/344tert.html.
8 Tertullian, *The Apology* (Beloved Publishing LLC, 2015).
9 González, *Story of Christianity*, 82–90; David Bentley Hart, *The Story of Christianity: A History of 2,000 Years of the Christian Faith* (Quercus, 2015), 46–47.
10 González, *Story of Christianity*, 102–8; Hart, *Story of Christianity*, 62–64.
11 H. A. Drake, *Constantine and the Bishops: The Politics of Intolerance* (Johns Hopkins University Press, 2000).
12 González, *Story of Christianity*, 113–67; Hart, *Story of Christianity*, 62–65.
13 González, *Story of Christianity*, 234; Hart, *Story of Christianity*, 107.

14 Hart, *Story of Christianity*, 95–101; Gonzalez, *Story of Christianity*, 173–88.

15 González, *Story of Christianity*, 266–76; Hart, *Story of Christianity*, 149–55.

16 Hart, *Story of Christianity*, 175–90.

17 Hart, 191–210.

18 Peter Brown, *The Rise of Western Christendom: Triumph and Diversity, A.D. 200–1000*, 2nd ed. (Wiley-Blackwell, 2003), 24.

Chapter 3

1 Leland Harder, "Zwingli's Reaction to the Schleitheim Confession of Faith of the Anabaptists," *Sixteenth Century Journal* 11, no. 4 (1980): 51–66.

2 Stuart Murray, *Biblical Interpretation in the Anabaptist Tradition* (Pandora Press, 2000), 71–96.

3 Quoted in William Roscoe Estep, *The Anabaptist Story*, 3rd ed. (Wm. B. Eerdmans, 1960), 57.

4 See Gustav Bossert Jr., Harold S. Bender, and C. Arnold Snyder, "Sattler, Michael (d. 1527)," GAMEO, accessed November 27, 2024, https://gameo.org/index.php?title=Sattler,_Michael_(d._1527); C. Arnold Snyder, *The Life and Thought of Michael Sattler* (Herald Press, 1984); and John Howard Yoder, comp., *The Legacy of Michael Sattler* (Herald Press, 1973).

5 George Huntston Williams, *The Radical Reformation*, 3rd ed. (Penn State University Press, 1992).

6 C. Arnold Snyder, *Anabaptist History and Theology: Revised Student Edition* (Pandora Press, 1997), 78.

7 Snyder, *Anabaptist History and Theology*.

8 "Documents on the Peasants' War 1524–1526," accessed September 19, 2024, https://pages.uoregon.edu/dluebke/Reformations441/Bauernkrieg.html.

9 Some Anabaptist groups have developed ten essentials or seven shared convictions as well.

10 Stuart Murray and Sian Murray-Williams, *The Power of All: Building a Multivoiced Church* (Herald Press, 2012), 17.

11 Balthasar Hubmaier, a sixteenth-century Anabaptist leader, may seem like an outlier to my argument. He did believe there was an option for Anabaptists to govern society justly providing protection for the persecuted and vulnerable. His nuanced view demonstrates that there is no Anabaptist essence, but gravitational norms to engage while describing his own way forward.

12 Gustavo Gutiérrez, *A Theology of Liberation: History, Politics, and Salvation*, trans. Caridad Inda and John Eagleson, rev. ed. (Orbis Books, 1988).

13 See, e.g., Walter Wink, *Jesus and Nonviolence: A Third Way* (Augsburg Fortress, 2003).

Chapter 4

1 Tobin Miller Shearer, *Daily Demonstrators: The Civil Rights Movement in Mennonite Homes and Sanctuaries* (Johns Hopkins University Press, 2010), vii.

2 Martin Luther King Jr., *Strength to Love*, gift ed. (Fortress Press, 2010).

3 Ervin R. Stutzman, *From Nonresistance to Justice: The Transformation of Mennonite Church Peace Rhetoric, 1908–2008* (Herald Press, 2011); Leo Driedger and Donald B. Kraybill, *Mennonite Peacemaking: From Quietism to Activism* (Herald Press, 1994); and Miller Shearer, *Daily Demonstrators*.

4 David R. Swartz, "'Mista Mid-nights': Mennonites and Race in Mississippi," *Mennonite Quarterly Review* 78, no. 4 (October 2004), https://www.goshen.edu/mqr/2004/10/october-2004-swartz/.

5 Thieleman J. van Braght and Joseph F. Sohm, *Martyrs Mirror: The Story of Seventeen Centuries of Christian Martyrdom from the Time of Christ to A.D. 1660* (Herald Press, 1996); and David L. Weaver-Zercher, *Martyrs Mirror: A Social History* (Johns Hopkins University Press, 2016).

6 See, e.g., Barb Draper, "Facing History with Courage," *Canadian Mennonite*, February 25, 2015, https://www.canadianmennonite.org/stories/facing-history-courage.

7 Miller Shearer, *Daily Demonstrators*, 6.

8 Felipe Hinojosa, *Latino Mennonites: Civil Rights, Faith, and Evangelical Culture* (Johns Hopkins University Press, 2014), 220.

9 Darryl W. Stephens and Elizabeth Soto Albrecht, eds., *Liberating the Politics of Jesus: Renewing Peace Theology through the Wisdom of Women* (T&T Clark, 2020), 204.

Chapter 5

1 Gomes Eanes de Zurara, *The Chronicle of the Discovery and Conquest of Guinea*, 81.

2 Zurara, 81.

3 Willie James Jennings, *The Christian Imagination: Theology and the Origins of Race* (Yale University Press, 2010, 6.

4 "Papal Bull Dum Diversas 18 June, 1452," Doctrine of Discovery Project, July 23, 2018, https://doctrineofdiscovery.org/dum-diversas/.

5 Quoted in Jemar Tisby, "'They Should Be Good Servants': What Christopher Columbus Really Thought of Indigenous People," *Footnotes by Jemar Tisby* (Substack blog), October 9, 2023, https://jemartisby.substack.com/p/they-should-be-good-servants-what.

6 Robert P. Jones, *The Hidden Roots of White Supremacy: And the Path to a Shared American Future* (Simon & Schuster, 2023), 16–17.

7 "Patent Granted by Henry VII to John Cabot and His Sons, Mark 5, 1496," Doctrine of Discovery Project, July 23, 2018, https://doctrineofdiscovery.org/patent-cabot-henry-vii/.

8 Kathryn Gin Lum, *Heathen: Religion and Race in American History* (Harvard University Press, 2024).

9 Edward J. Blum and Paul Harvey, *The Color of Christ: The Son of God and the Saga of Race in America* (University of North Carolina Press, 2012), 43.

10 Paul Harvey, *Through the Storm, Through the Night: A History of African American Christianity* (Rowman & Littlefield, 2011), 9–27.

11 Harvey, 10.

12 See, e.g., Daniel Black, *The Coming* (St. Martin's Press, 2015).

13 Harvey, *Through the Storm*, 20–22; Jemar Tisby and Lecrae Moore, *The Color of Compromise: The Truth about the American Church's Complicity in Racism* (Zondervan, 2020), 37–39.

14 Edward E. Baptist, *The Half Has Never Been Told: Slavery and the Making of American Capitalism* (Basic Books, 2014), 126, 128.

15 Baptist, 118.

16 Baptist, 139.

17 Josiah H. G. Strong, *Our Country*, ed. Jurgen Herbst (Harvard University Press, 1963), 200, https://doi.org/10.4159/harvard.9780674335295.

18 Strong, 215, 216, 218.

19 Henry Goldschmidt and Elizabeth A. McAlister, *Race, Nation, and Religion in the Americas* (Oxford University Press, 2004), 35–54, https://www.loc.gov/catdir/toc/fy051/2003066225.html.

20 Jones, *Hidden Roots of White Supremacy*, 183–212.

21 See also Mark Charles and Soong-Chan Rah, *Unsettling Truths: The Ongoing, Dehumanizing Legacy of the Doctrine of Discovery* (IVP, 2019); Jones, *Hidden Roots of White Supremacy*; Sarah Travis, *Unsettling Worship: Reforming Liturgy for Right Relations with Indigenous Communities* (Cascade Books, 2023); and Sarah Augustine, *The Land Is Not Empty: Following Jesus in Dismantling the Doctrine of Discovery* (Herald Press, 2021).

22 Edward J. Blum, *Reforging the White Republic: Race, Religion, and American Nationalism, 1865–1898* (Louisiana State University Press, 2005), http://site.ebrary.com/id/10297300.

23 Douglas A. Blackmon, *Slavery by Another Name: The Re-Enslavement of Black Americans from the Civil War to World War II* (Doubleday, 2008).

24 Blackmon, 305.

25 "Reconstruction in America," Equal Justice Initiative, accessed September 28, 2024, https://eji.org/reports/reconstruction-in-america-overview/.

26 James Allen, *Without Sanctuary: Lynching Photography in America* (Twin Palms, 2000).

27 Jacqueline Royster, *Southern Horrors and Other Writings: The Anti-Lynching Campaign of Ida B. Wells, 1892–1900*, 2nd ed. (Bedford/St. Martin's, 2016).

28 Khalil Gibran Muhammad, *The Condemnation of Blackness: Race, Crime, and the Making of Modern Urban America* (Harvard University Press, 2010).

29 Richard Rothstein, *The Color of Law: A Forgotten History of How Our Government Segregated America*, 1st ed. (Liveright Publishing, 2017).

30 Mehrsa Baradaran, *The Color of Money: Black Banks and the Racial Wealth Gap* (The Belknap Press of Harvard University Press, 2017); and Meizhu Lui and United for a Fair Economy, *The Color of Wealth: The Story Behind the U.S. Racial Wealth Divide* (New Press, 2006).

31 David R. Roediger, *Working Toward Whiteness: How America's Immigrants Became White: The Strange Journey from Ellis Island to the Suburbs*, repr. (Basic Books, 2018).

32 Michelle Alexander, *The New Jim Crow: Mass Incarceration in the Age of Colorblindness* (New Press, 2012).

33 Jackie Wang, *Carceral Capitalism* (Semiotext, 2018), 151–92.

34 William A. Darity and A. Kirsten Mullen, *From Here to Equality: Reparations for Black Americans in the Twenty-First Century* (University of North Carolina Press, 2020), 28–47.

35 Robert P. Jones, *White Too Long: The Legacy of White Supremacy in American Christianity* (Simon & Schuster, 2021), 185.

Chapter 6

1 Vincent Harding, *There Is a River: The Black Struggle for Freedom in America* (Harcourt Brace Jovanovich, 1981).

2 Harding, xix.

3 Albert J. Raboteau, *Slave Religion: The "Invisible Institution" in the Antebellum South*, updated ed. (Oxford University Press, 2004).

4 Edward J. Blum and Paul Harvey, *The Color of Christ: The Son of God and the Saga of Race in America* (University of North Carolina Press, 2012), 94.

5 Korie Little Edwards, *The Elusive Dream: The Power of Race in Interracial Churches*, updated ed. (University Press, 2021).

6 W. E. B. Du Bois, *The Souls of Black Folk* (BoD – Books on Demand, 2023), 134.

7 Barbara Ann Holmes, *Joy Unspeakable: Contemplative Practices of the Black Church*, 2nd ed. (Fortress Press, 2017), 1–22.

8 Karen Baker-Fletcher, *Dancing with God: The Trinity from a Womanist Perspective* (Chalice Press, 2006), 163.

9 Baker-Fletcher, 168.

10 Dale P. Andrews, "Black Preaching Praxis," in *Black Church Studies: An Introduction*, by Stacey Floyd-Thomas et al. (Abingdon Press, 2007), 212.

11 Andrews, 212.

12 Scholars C. Eric Lincoln and Lawrence Mamiya helped formalize prophetic terminology when they described the priestly and prophetic sides of the Black Church:

> Priestly functions involve only those activities concerned with worship and maintaining the spiritual life of members; church maintenance activities are the major thrust. Prophetic functions refer to involvement in political concerns and activities in the wider community; classically prophetic activity has meant pronouncing a radical world of God's judgment. Some churches are closer to one end than to the other. Priestly churches are bastions of survival and prophetic churches are networks of liberation. But both types of churches also illustrate both functions, which means that liberation churches also perform the priestly functions and priestly churches contain liberation potential.

For more detail, see C. Eric Lincoln and Lawrence H. Mamiya, *The Black Church in the African American Experience* (Duke University Press, 1990), 12.

13 "Sojourner Truth's "Ain't I a Woman?," Nolo, accessed May 29, 2013, http://www.nolo.com/legal-encyclopedia/content/truth-woman-speech.html; Cheryl Townsend Gilkes, *If It Wasn't for the Women . . . : Black Women's Experience and Womanist Culture in Church and Community* (Orbis Books, 2000); James Cone, *God of the Oppressed* (Seabury Press, 1975).

14 Russell Contreras and Massey Delano, "The God Gap: How Church Attendance by Race Divides Voters," *Axios*, November 2, 2024, https://www.axios.com/2024/10/28/god-gap-church-religion-race-harris-trump.

Chapter 7

1 Eddie Glaude Jr., "The Black Church Is Dead," *Huffington Post*, April 26, 2010, https://www.huffpost.com/entry/the-black-church-is-dead_b_473815.
2 Glaude Jr., "The Black Church Is Dead."
3 James Cone, *Speaking the Truth: Ecumenism, Liberation, and Black Theology* (Wm. B. Eerdmans, 1986), 149.
4 The Romans Road method typically stitches together Romans 3:23 ("Since all have sinned and fall short of the glory of God"); 6:23 ("For the wages of sin is death, but the free gift of God is eternal life in Christ Jesus our Lord"); 5:8 ("But God proves his love for us in that while we were sinners Christ died for us"); 10:9–10 ("because if you confess with your mouth that Jesus is Lord and believe in your heart that God raised him from the dead, you will be saved. For one believes with the heart, leading to righteousness, and one confesses with the mouth, leading to salvation"); and 10:13 ("For 'everyone who calls on the name of the Lord shall be saved'"). Other "stops" on the road may be woven in, albeit broadly out of context of the full letter to the Romans.
5 Lisa Allen, *A Womanist Theology of Worship: Liturgy, Justice, and Communal Righteousness* (Orbis Books, 2021), 165.
6 Allen, 219–20.
7 Robert Beckford, *Decolonizing Contemporary Gospel Music through Praxis: Handsworth Revolutions* (Bloomsbury Academic, 2023), 6.
8 Beckford, 172–73.
9 Cone, *Speaking the Truth*, 150.
10 Marcia Y. Riggs, "*Plenty Good Room* Revisited: The Quest for a Radically Inclusive Twenty-First-Century Black Church," in *T&T Clark Handbook of African American Theology*, ed. Frederick L. Ware, Antonia Michelle Daymond, and Eric Lewis Williams (T&T Clark, 2019), 293.

11 James S. Logan, "The Ethics, Politics, and Civic Engagement of African American Theological Production," in *Handbook of African American Theology*, 244.

12 Besheer Mohamed, Kiana Cox, Jeff Diamant, and Claire Gecewicz, "Faith Among Black Americans," *Pew Research Center* (blog), February 16, 2021, https://www.pewresearch.org/religion/2021/02/16/faith-among-black-americans/.

13 See, e.g., Frank B. Wilderson III, *Red, White, and Black: Cinema and the Structure of U.S. Antagonisms*, illustrated ed. (Duke University Press, 2010); Frank B. Wilderson III, *Afropessimism* (Liveright, 2021); Christina Sharpe, *In the Wake: On Blackness and Being*, illustrated ed. (Duke University Press, 2016); and Saidiya Hartman et al., *Scenes of Subjection: Terror, Slavery, and Self-Making in Nineteenth-Century America*, ed. Cameron Rowland, updated ed. (W. W. Norton, 2022).

14 William R. Jones, *Is God a White Racist? A Preamble to Black Theology* (Beacon Press, 1997). First published 1973.

15 Kelly Brown Douglas, *Resurrection Hope: A Future Where Black Lives Matter* (Orbis Books, 2021), 184, 195.

Chapter 8

1 This and the following paragraphs draw on Euell A. Dixon, "Germantown Quaker Petition Against Slavery (1688)," January 14, 2022, https://www.blackpast.org/african-american-history/germantown-quaker-petition-against-slavery-1688/; "1688 Petition Against Slavery," The Historic 1770 Germantown Mennonite Meetinghouse, accessed October 14, 2024, http://www.meetinghouse.info/1688-petition-against-slavery.html; and Leonard Gross, Jan Gleysteen, and John L. Ruth, *Colonial Germantown Mennonites* (Cascadia Publishing House, 2007).

2 This section draws on Jeff Crocombe, "Weir, Samuel," 2008, 198, https://doi.org/10.1093/acref/9780195301731.013.38165; Spire Advertising Inc, "Samuel Weir Part 1," accessed October 15, 2024, https://www.maplegrovecob.org/blog/2017/10/16/samuel-weir-part-1; Landon West, *The Life of Elder Samuel Weir: (Colored)* (Covington, Ohio: Tribune Print Co., 1913); and Spire Advertising Inc., "You, Too, Can Be Set Free!," November

13, 2017, https://www.maplegrovecob.org/blog/2017/11/13/you-too-can-be-set-free.

3 Tobin Miller Shearer, "State of the Race: A Short History of Mennonite Racial Statements, 1940-1979," *Anabaptist Historians* (blog), October 3, 2019, https://anabaptisthistorians.org/2019/10/03/state-of-the-race-a-short-history-of-mennonite-racial-statements-1940-1979/.

4 Miller Shearer, "State of the Race."

5 Mennonite Church, "The Way of Christian Love in Race Relations (Mennonite Church, 1955)," Global Anabaptist Wiki, accessed October 15, 2024, https://anabaptistwiki.org/mediawiki/index.php/The_Way_of_Christian_Love_in_Race_Relations_(Mennonite_Church,_1955).

6 "1963 Racial Brokenness—Annual Conference," Church of the Brethren, accessed October 15, 2024, https://www.brethren.org/ac/statements/1963-racial-brokenness/; "2007 Separate No More – Annual Conference," Church of the Brethren, accessed October 15, 2024, https://www.brethren.org/ac/statements/2007-separate-no-more/.

7 Gordon Houser, "Group Seeks to Expand Work to Dismantle the Doctrine of Discovery," *Anabaptist World* (blog), February 3, 2017, https://anabaptistworld.org/group-seeks-expand-work-dismantle-doctrine-discovery/.

8 "With Actions and in Truth: A Lament of the Doctrine of Discovery—Annual Conference," accessed October 15, 2024, https://www.brethren.org/ac/statements/2023-doctrine-of-discovery/.

9 Of course, there are times when it is appropriate to focus on a particular group's suffering and oppression. But since the statements focus on the Doctrine of Discovery and its consequences, there ought to be more comprehensive understanding.

10 Hubert Brown, "Lark, James (1888-1978) and Rowena (1892-1970)," GAMEO, accessed October 17, 2024, https://gameo.org/index.php?title=Lark,_James_(1888-1978)_and_Rowena_(1892-1970).

11 Tobin Miller Shearer, *Daily Demonstrators: The Civil Rights Movement in Mennonite Homes and Sanctuaries* (Johns Hopkins University Press, 2010), 35–38.

12 Miller Shearer, 29–61.

13 Le Roy Bechler, *The Black Mennonite Church in North America, 1886–1986* (Herald Press, 1986), 47–54.

14 Miller Shearer, *Daily Demonstrators*, 100.

15 Henry Louis Gates Jr., *The Black Church: This Is Our Story, This Is Our Song* (Penguin Press, 2021), 109–10.

16 From Harding's 1965 resignation letter, quoted in Miller Shearer, *Daily Demonstrators*, 126.

17 Hubert Brown, *Black and Mennonite: A Search for Identity* (Herald Press, 1976), 47.

18 Brown, 48.

19 Brown, 79.

20 Brown, 81, 86, 91.

21 Brown, 94, 95.

22 Brown, 107–16.

23 Nekeisha Alexis-Baker, "Freedom of the Cross: John Howard Yoder and Womanist Theologies in Conversation," in *Power and Practices: Engaging the Work of John Howard Yoder*, ed. Jeremy Bergen and Anthony G. Siegrist (Herald Press, 2009), 88.

24 Alexis-Baker, 89–91.

25 Alexis-Baker, 93.

26 Mziwandile Nkutha with Andrew Suderman, "From Missionwary to Missionary: The Complexity of a South African Christianity," *MissionWary?* (podcast); 1:32:32, https://youtu.be/hzfXEGgHuRo.

Chapter 9

1 Quoted in Mark Galli and Ted Olsen, *131 Christians Everyone Should Know* (Broadman & Holman, 2000), 289.

2 James Cone, *God of the Oppressed* (Seabury Press, 1975), 109–10.

3 J. Denny Weaver, *God without Violence: A Theology of the God Revealed in Jesus*, 2nd ed. (Cascade Books, 2020), 32.

4   Matthew Thiessen, *A Jewish Paul: The Messiah's Herald to the Gentiles* (Baker Academic, 2023).
5   Karen Baker-Fletcher, *Dancing with God: The Trinity from a Womanist Perspective* (Chalice Press, 2006), 10.
6   Baker-Fletcher, 44–45.
7   Baker-Fletcher, 168–69.
8   "Letter from a Birmingham Jail [King, Jr.]," accessed October 31, 2024, https://www.africa.upenn.edu/Articles_Gen/Letter_Birmingham.html.
9   See Matthew 21:12–17; Mark 11:15–18; Luke 19:45–47; John 2:14–16.
10 J. Kameron Carter, *The Anarchy of Black Religion: A Mystic Song* (Duke University Press, 2023), 76.
11 Quoted in Jarvis R. Givens, *Fugitive Pedagogy: Carter G. Woodson and the Art of Black Teaching* (Harvard University Press, 2021), 2.
12 Givens, 25.
13 Chris K. Huebner, *A Precarious Peace: Yoderian Explorations on Theology, Knowledge, and Identity* (Herald Press, 2006), 135.
14 Huebner, 137.
15 Huebner, 144.
16 J. Kameron Carter, *Race: A Theological Account* (Oxford University Press, 2008).
17 Carter, 378.

THE AUTHOR

REV. DR. DREW G. I. HART is an author, speaker, and professor of theology at Messiah University, where he has directed the Thriving Together: Congregations for Racial Justice program since 2021. With a decade of pastoral experience, Hart is a leading voice in Christian ethics, Black theology, and Anabaptism. He is the author of *Trouble I've Seen* and *Who Will Be A Witness?*, and a coeditor of and contributor to *Reparations and the Theological Disciplines*. Hart has received several community awards for his activism and scholarship. He lives with his family in Harrisburg, Pennsylvania.